Medical Chinese
Internship Volume 1
(Version 2.0)

医学汉语
实习篇 1　第 2 版

主编 ◎ 邓淑兰（中山大学）
　　　莫秀英（中山大学）

参编学校（以汉语拼音为序）

东南大学	赣南医学院
广西医科大学	江苏大学
南方医科大学	南京医科大学
四川大学	苏州大学
泰山医学院	天津医科大学
温州医学院	西安交通大学
新乡医学院	中国传媒大学
中山大学	

北京大学出版社
PEKING UNIVERSITY PRESS

图书在版编目(CIP)数据

医学汉语. 实习篇. 1 / 邓淑兰，莫秀英主编. —2版. —北京：北京大学出版社，2020.10
ISBN 978-7-301-31645-0

Ⅰ.①医… Ⅱ.①邓…②莫… Ⅲ.①医学–汉语–对外汉语教学–教材 Ⅳ.①H195.4

中国版本图书馆CIP数据核字(2020) 第178368号

书 名	医学汉语 实习篇Ⅰ（第2版） YIXUE HANYU SHIXIPIAN Ⅰ (DI-ER BAN)
著作责任者	邓淑兰 莫秀英 主编
责任编辑	任 蕾
标准书号	ISBN 978-7-301-31645-0
出版发行	北京大学出版社
地 址	北京市海淀区成府路205号 100871
网 址	http://www.pup.cn 新浪微博：@北京大学出版社
电子信箱	zpup@pup.cn
电 话	邮购部 010-62752015 发行部 010-62750672 编辑部 010-62753334
印 刷 者	北京市科星印刷有限责任公司
经 销 者	新华书店
	787毫米×1092毫米 16开本 21印张 333千字 2007年12月第1版 2020年10月第2版 2020年10月第1次印刷
定 价	78.00元

未经许可，不得以任何方式复制或抄袭本书之部分或全部内容。
版权所有，侵权必究
举报电话：010-62752024 电子信箱：fd@pup.pku.edu.cn
图书如有印装质量问题，请与出版部联系，电话：010-62756370

本教材获得中山大学 2020 年重点教材项目资助

主　编　邓淑兰（中山大学）
　　　　莫秀英（中山大学）
副主编　乐　琦（中国传媒大学）
　　　　林华生（中山大学）
　　　　张　曦（南京医科大学）
　　　　熊　芳（南方医科大学）

编写者

东南大学	陶　咏　佟　迅
赣南医学院	钟富有
广西医科大学	周红霞　王　晨
江苏大学	江永华　吴卫疆
南方医科大学	熊　芳　张阿娜　唐　蓓
南京医科大学	张　曦　李　娜
四川大学	谢　红
苏州大学	何立荣　林齐倩
泰山医学院	李　楠　王松梅　肖　强　王　倩
天津医科大学	石再俭
温州医学院	胡　臻
西安交通大学	李馨郁
新乡医学院	郗万富
中国传媒大学	乐　琦
中山大学	邓淑兰　莫秀英　林华生

英文翻译　唐永煌　邓晋松　张　冔　莫　伟　梁　铭
英文审订　张海青　廖海青　倪晓宏

修订说明

自 2007 年北京大学出版社出版《医学汉语——实习篇Ⅰ》之后，2009 年、2012 年相继出版了Ⅱ册、Ⅲ册，并已多次印刷，得到了各高校医学汉语教师和医科留学生的认可。不过，《医学汉语——实习篇Ⅰ》出版使用已逾十年，随着新媒体和新技术的不断出现，为了更好地满足一线教师和学习者的需求，主编团队和北京大学出版社商讨了教材修订方案。本次修订主要由中山大学和南方医科大学的医学汉语教学团队负责。

鉴于该教材广受使用者的欢迎，教材修订遵循原版的编写原则，强调实用性、针对性。修订内容具体如下：

一、体例

教材体例方面，在目录前增加了"实习生介绍""医护人员主要职别介绍"和"医院主要科室名称"。其中"实习生介绍"列出了教材课文中出现的三名外国留学生的名字、性别、国籍和一名中国医学生的名字、性别。"医护人员主要职别介绍"列出了主任医生、副主任医生、主治医生、医师、住院医师、护士长、护士等常用的职别。"医院主要科室名称"为医院住院部的常见科室名称，并且大多出现在本套教材的课文中。如：内科、外科、妇产科、儿科、传染病科、五官科、精神科等，其中内科和外科还列出了常见的细分科室，内科有呼吸内科、消化内科、心血管内科、血液科、肾内科等；外科有普通外科、肝胆外科、神经外科、骨科、泌尿外科等。

课文体例方面有两个变化：

第一，每篇课文的题目后增加了科室名和病名。如"第一课　今天你感觉怎么样？（呼吸内科—肺炎）"，增加的"呼吸内科—肺炎"说明本课中的病人得了肺炎，在呼吸内科住院治疗。这一简单的提示便于学生整体了解课文的主题内容。

第二，在生词前增加了"学习目标和重难点"，以便学生了解本课的学习要点和难点。如：《第三课 他是典型的支气管扩张的病例》学习目标和重难点：

1. 区分"病历"和"病例"，掌握与支气管扩张相关的词语
2. 掌握支气管扩张病人的主要症状
3. 向病人家属交待支气管病人要注意的事项

每课的学习目标和重难点基本包括：生词语、病例的相关信息（病史、病因、症状、检查、治疗）以及医嘱等。这一提示便于学生整体把握课文的主要内容。

二、课文内容

对原课文的内容进行了完善和修订，有些课文的内容修改较多，有些课文改动较少。生词因课文的修改而稍有调整。修改主要有以下几种情况：

（一）删减人物数量

如第一课"今天你感觉怎么样？"第一版课文第一篇对话共设计了5个人物：一位指导医生、两个病人和两个实习生，对话内容主要是这5个人物第一次见面的寒暄。为了简化人物关系，第二版删减了实习生阿卜杜拉和病人王京，另一名实习生白瑞蒂修改为莎娜。

（二）增、删课文内容

如第一课"今天你感觉怎么样？"第一篇会话删减了王京和阿卜杜拉的寒暄，并把第二篇会话中实习生询问病人病情的部分内容调整到第一篇对话中；第二篇会话的内容再进行相应的增补调整。修订后的课文与医学相关的内容体现得更为集中。

（三）完善语言表达

这类修订主要针对原版课文语言不规范、不简洁的部分进行完善。如第十四课"甲亢病人发病时会有哪些典型症状？"第二篇会话中关于甲亢病人发病时典型症状的描述，原版为"心悸、胸闷……食欲旺盛、体重下降、乏力、腹泻、甲状腺肿大，**并有血管杂音和震颤**、眼球突出等"，修改为"心悸、胸闷……食欲旺盛、体重下降、乏力、腹泻、甲状腺肿大、**血管有杂音和震颤**、眼球突出等"。原版关于甲亢典型症状的描述主要是主谓式结构，"并有血管杂音和震颤"这个句子和前面的短语结构不一致，且"和"连接的是一个名词和动词，不符合语法规范。修订后的结构和前面描述症状的主谓式一致。

三、注释

对原有的注释进行了增删，并对其中一些注释增加了图释，图释的内容均为专业术语，以便学生更好地理解掌握。注释的例句把原版中表现普通生活的句子换成了和医学相关的例句。

四、练习

本次修订对练习进行了较大的修改。结合一线教师的反馈意见和学生的需求，我们把每课的练习分为课堂练习和课外练习。

课堂练习包括三种题型：听与读；替换与扩展；口语练习。口语练习有的是看图对话，有的是有信息差的交际活动。

课外练习主要包括：看汉字，写拼音；看拼音，根据生词表写汉字；词语搭配；选择合适的词语填空；根据问句写出合适的应答句；根据病人的情况写出合适的问句；完成对话；根据课文内容判断正误；根据课文的内容回答问题；口语练习；节奏汉语；写作练习。口语练习提供了复述思路的提示，帮助学生顺利快捷地记忆课文内容。节奏汉语是以唱歌学汉语的形式记忆课文的主要内容，歌词的内容包括每课疾病的名称、症状、检查、治疗或者医嘱，乐曲由医学留学生编写表演。

五、教材辅助

充分利用新媒介，大幅增加与课文内容和练习相关的资料，特别是医学留学生模拟的医院实习视频、师生之间进行课外交流的网络平台等。我们希望在这个融媒体的时代，能够借助新媒介，更好地突出学生的主体性，给予学生更大的自主学习空间，促进医学汉语教学的改革。

本次修订，中山大学的邓淑兰和莫秀英负责全部课文、生词、注释和部分练习的修订工作。南方医科大学的熊芳、张阿娜、唐蓓等负责线上学习平台和节奏汉语的编写。节奏汉语的表演者为南方医科大学MBBS专业的留学生，他们是Abinash Panda、Cliff Syndor、Wajahat Ali Raza、Dan Jouma Amadou Maman Lawali Niger、Sonjoy Sutradhar Monilal、Pherbak Kharmawphlang Nohwir、Kiruba Gideon、Evan Noel Dympep、Virginio Bibang Ndong。中山大学汉语国际教育硕士梁铭负责修订部分的英文翻译。修订工作基于第一版，参与第一版编写的十四所高等院校的作者均为第二版作者。在此对为本教材修订提供帮助的所有同人表示感谢。

本教材的修订，得到了北京大学出版社任蕾、邓晓霞两位编辑的大力支持和帮助，在此表示由衷的感谢。

书中错漏之处在所难免，敬请同行和读者批评指正。（dengshl@mail.sysu.edu.cn　zhuzimxy@163.com）

编者
2019年5月于广州康乐园

第一版序

《医学汉语——实习篇》是一套 special purpose Chinese 教材。Special purpose Chinese，有人翻译成"特殊用途汉语"，有人翻译成"专用汉语"。前者是直译，后者是意译。我更倾向于使用后者。

专用汉语跟通用汉语有很大的区别。后者是一般学习者学习用的，前者是为了某种专门需要而学习用的。这两种汉语反映在教学实施和教材编写上，也有许多不同。如词汇选择，专用汉语跟通用汉语就明显不同。"感冒""嗓子""不舒服"等是通用词汇，"呼吸道""感染""支气管""扩张"等是医科专用词汇。除了词汇，专用汉语教材的课文、注释、练习等项目都跟通用汉语不同。

一般来说，专用汉语可以大致分为两个方面：专业汉语、职业汉语。专业汉语是为了使学习者能用汉语学习某个专业而设置的，如医科汉语、商科汉语。专业汉语有时涉及面比较广：如科技汉语，是为了用汉语学习理工科专业而设置的；社科汉语，是为了用汉语学习社会科学专业而设置的。职业汉语是为了让学习者从事某项职业而设置的，如商务汉语、法律汉语。学习者可能已经掌握了相关专业，但不懂汉语，必须通过这种学习，使自己能在某种程度上用汉语从事相关职业。

不难看出，专用汉语不但跟通用汉语有别，而且难度比较大。一种语言作为外语学习和使用，往往先从通用语言开始，发展到一定程度，才会需要专用语言。近几年，对专用汉语，如医科汉语、商科汉语的需求迅速增加，说明汉语在国际上的影响越来越大，地位越来越高。

一般的教材编写有几个阶段：准备阶段、实施阶段、修订阶段。《医学汉语——实习篇》的编者，在这几个阶段都做足了功课。比如说，准备工作：首先，编写者大多教过医科留学生基础阶段的通用汉语课程，不少还上过医学汉语课，有较为丰富的经验。其次，主编莫秀英和副主编林华生专门对进入见习实习阶段的留学生做了问卷调查和询问调查，了解使用者的需求。编写大纲的初稿，就建立在事实调查的基础之上。最后，主编召集大部分编写者（十几所高校的老师）在中山大学开过一个专门的研讨会，仔细讨论了教材编写大纲和具体的编写分工、程序等。

实施阶段的工作也做得相当好。前面讲过，专用汉语不同于通用汉语的最大特点在于二者的词汇选择不同。如何选择词汇，是医科实习汉语教材的第一关。这部教材以学习医科的本科生实习的实际需求为依据，合理选择在住院部实习时经常要使用的词汇，作为词汇教学的主要内容。此外，该教材在句式选用、课文及练习的设计方面也有不少特点。如课文设计，考虑到实习的基本需要，有对话也有成段表达。而这些对话或成段表达都可能在实习医生和病人之间或者实习医生和指导医生之间产生。练习的设计，既考虑到实习汉语的要求，也考虑到学习者的实际水平和学习兴趣，形式灵活多样。此外，这部教材在词汇量控制、课文长度、课时容量等方面都有仔细的斟酌、认真的考量。

目前，在中国大陆学习医科的外国留学生有一万多人，而且人数还会持续增长，需求还会不断增加。跟其他专用汉语教材一样，医科汉语教材的编写才刚刚开始。我们相信，随着时间的推移，随着教学实践的发展，医科汉语跟其他专用汉语教材一样，会不断积累经验，越编越好。

周小兵

2007 年 11 月 12 日

第一版编写说明

《医学汉语——实习篇Ⅰ》是一本针对临床医学专业全英语教学的外国留学生到中国医院见习、实习而编写的教材。使用对象一般已学过基础汉语，掌握《汉语水平词汇与汉字等级大纲》中的甲、乙级词汇或《高等学校外国留学生汉语教学大纲》（长期进修）中的初级阶段词汇1300～1500个，掌握基本的汉语语法和常用句式，HSK成绩达到三级左右。同时也适合具有一定汉语水平、对医学汉语感兴趣的外国人使用。

编写之前，我们以座谈和问卷两种形式对正在实习或已经完成实习的外国留学生进行调查，调查内容是见习和实习阶段使用汉语的情况。根据调查结果及各院校老师的教学经验，我们确定了本教材的内容和生词范围。

本丛书的内容主要是医院住院部各科室常用的汉语，也涉及一些门诊常用的汉语，以说和听为主，兼顾写。具体来说，包括医院各科室的中文名称、常用药物的中文名称、人体各种结构的中文名称、常见病的中文名称、各种常见病主要症状及体征的汉语表达、实验室检验报告及病历的书写、住院部里医生与病人的日常用语、实习生与指导医生的日常用语等。

虽然使用本教材的学生的汉语水平只达到了初级，但根据课程设置的目的和使用对象对教材实用性的要求，本教材选用生词不以《汉语水平词汇与汉字等级大纲》中的甲、乙级词汇或《高等学校外国留学生汉语教学大纲》（长期进修）中的初级词汇为标准，而以医院住院部和门诊部常用的词汇为标准。因此，生词中大部分是超纲词，这是本教材不同于普通汉语教材之处，也是本教材以实用性为主的特色。我们认为，这些词对一般人来说是超纲的，因为使用频率非常低，但对到医院见习和实习的留学生来说并不算超纲，因为使用频率非常高，所以掌握这些词汇对他们的见习和实习都非常有用。

整套教材分Ⅰ、Ⅱ、Ⅲ三册，每册17课，共51课。每课容量约为4课时。各课内容根据我国三甲医院住院部各科室纵向排列，比较重要的科室（如内、外、妇、儿等）课数较多，个别科室只用1课。每课由生词、课文、注释、练习、附录组成。

生词每课约18～25个，每个词条均配有拼音、词性、英文翻译。

课文由1～2个对话和1个成段表达构成。课文的角色主要由2～4位留学生充当，贯穿整套教材；每课另有不固定的指导医生、病人等。课文内容是医院里实习生之间以及实习生与指导医生、病人、病人家属、护士的对话或成段表述。

注释包括课文中出现的语法难点和常用语、常用格式、常用句式以及专业词语的解释。针对使用对象的特点，每项注释都配有英文翻译。

练习部分注重说、听、写三方面的训练，每课有8～10道练习题。题型有听与读、替换与扩展、看汉字写拼音、看拼音写汉字、选词填空、根据问句写出答句、根据答句写出问句、完成对话、看图对话、根据话题成段表述、把短文改成对话、把对话改成短文、有信息差的模拟交际练习、词语搭配、组词、根据情景问问题、根据情景回答问题等。

附录部分是一些常用专业词语或与课文内容相关的常用词语，均配有拼音和英文翻译。这部分词语不要求课堂内讲授，只作为学生扩充词汇量的一个参考。

生词、课文及部分练习配有MP3，以方便进行听说教学。

本丛书在中山大学国际交流学院周小兵教授的组织指导下，由十四所高等院校合作编写而成。参加Ⅰ册编写的院校有中山大学、南京医科大学、南方医科大学、东南大学、西安交通大学、四川大学、天津医科大学、广西医科大学、江苏大学、苏州大学、泰山医学院、温州医学院、新乡医学院、赣南医学院。中山大学国际交流学院莫秀英任主编，负责总体设计、统稿、审稿及部分稿件的修改。林华生（中山大学）、张曦（南京医科大学）、乐琦（南方医科大学）任副主编，负责部分稿件的审阅、修改。莫秀英、乐琦负责校对。课文编写、生词确定由莫秀英、林华生、张曦、乐琦完成。注释、练习和附录由各院校参编教师完成，莫秀英、乐琦、张曦、林华生修改。生词、课文、注释和附录的英文翻译由暨南大学第一附属医院唐永煌教授、南方医科大学留学生管理部邓晋松先生（留英MBA）和广东省第二中医院张羿医师、莫伟医师负责。英文审订由中山大学外语学院张海青副教授、廖海青副教授及中山大学北校区外语中心倪晓宏副教授负责。全书由周小兵教授审订。

在编写过程中，我们参阅了大量网上资料，在此特对在网上提供相关资料的作者表示感谢。

本教材的顺利完成，得到了北京大学出版社吕幼筠、贾鸿杰两位编辑的大力支持和帮助，在此表示由衷的感谢。我们还要感谢中山大学国际交流学院副院长刘传华先生，他为组织联系各院校编写本教材做了大量的工作。还要感谢中山大学国际交流学院的吴门吉博士，她在教材的设想阶段为我们设计了调查问卷，对整个教材的总体设计帮助甚大。还要感谢中山大学留学生办公室的陈佩中先生和陈宇英女士，他们热心地为我们组织留学生进行座谈和问卷调查。最后我们要感谢中山大学中山医学院的外国留学生，他们不仅热情地配合我们做调查，还主动给我们提供对临床见习、实习有帮助的书目，甚至无偿赠送一些非常实用的图书。本书在编写过程中，也得到各相关院校领导的大力支持，在此一并表示衷心感谢。

本书是医学专业实习汉语教材的一个新尝试，错漏之处在所难免，敬请同行和读者批评指正。

编者　zhuzimxy@163.com

2007 年 8 月于广州康乐园

✤ 实习生介绍 ✤

莎娜 女，巴基斯坦留学生

白瑞蒂 女，印度留学生

李力 男，中国医学生

卡奇 男，斯里兰卡留学生

✤ 医护人员主要职别介绍 ✤

主任医师	主任护师
副主任医师	副主任护师
主治医师	主管护师
医师	护师
医士	护士

医院主要科室名称

内科	呼吸内科	hūxī nèikē	respiratory medicine
	消化内科	xiāohuà nèikē	gastroenterology
	心血管内科	xīnxuèguǎn nèikē	cardiology
	血液科	xuèyèkē	hematology
	肾内科	shèn nèikē	nephrology
	（代谢与）内分泌科	(dàixiè yǔ) nèifēnmìkē	metabolism and endocrinology
外科	普通外科	pǔtōng wàikē	general surgery
	肝胆外科	gāndǎn wàikē	hepatobiliary surgery
	神经外科	shénjīng wàikē	neurosurgery
	骨科	gǔkē	orthopedics
	泌尿外科	mìniào wàikē	urology
	（心）胸外科	(xīn) xiōng wàikē	thoracic surgery
妇产科	妇科	fùkē	gynecology
	产科	chǎnkē	obstetrics
儿科	新生儿科	xīnshēng'érkē	neonatal department
传染科		chuánrǎnkē	infectious disease department
五官科	耳鼻喉科	ěrbíhóukē	ENT
	眼科	yǎnkē	ophthalmology
	口腔科	kǒuqiāngkē	stomatology

（续表）

皮肤科		pífūkē	dermatology
精神科		jīngshénkē	psychiatrics
中医科		zhōngyīkē	traditional Chinese medicine
急诊科		jízhěnkē	emergency room
病理科		bìnglǐkē	pathology
放射科		fàngshèkē	radiology
检验科		jiǎnyànkē	laboratory
治疗室 （注射室）		zhìliáoshì (zhùshèshì)	therapeutic room (injection room)
挂号处		guàhàochù	registration office
住院处		zhùyuànchù	admission office
取药处 （药房）		qǔyàochù (yàofáng)	pharmacy
收费处		shōufèichù	cashier
病案室		bìng'ànshì	medical records department

目　录

第 一 课	今天你感觉怎么样？（呼吸内科—肺炎）	1
第 二 课	哮喘病是不能着凉的（呼吸内科—哮喘）	14
第 三 课	他是典型的支气管扩张的病例（呼吸内科—支气管扩张）	27
第 四 课	昨天不是已经好多了吗？（消化内科—急性肠胃炎）	43
第 五 课	他怎么会得这种病？（消化内科—急性胰腺炎）	58
第 六 课	你以前有过这样的腹痛吗？（消化内科—胆囊结石和胆囊炎）	74
第 七 课	要马上转到外科做手术（消化内科—胃溃疡）	88
第 八 课	不能太激动（心血管内科—冠心病）	103
第 九 课	快把病人转到心血管内科吧（心血管内科—心肌梗死）	118
第 十 课	她是不是可以出院了？（神经内科—脑中风）	132
第十一课	检查结果出来了（血液科—急性白血病）	146
第十二课	她不是胖，是浮肿（肾内科—肾炎）	160
第十三课	这是不是肾病综合征？（肾内科—肾病综合征）	176
第十四课	甲亢病人发病时会有哪些典型症状？（内分泌科—甲亢）	191
第十五课	他怎么又来了？（内分泌科—糖尿病）	207
第十六课	我们现在有了新疗法（普外科—胆石症）	224
第十七课	饭后运动不会直接诱发阑尾炎（普外科—阑尾炎）	240

附录一	交际活动 A	256
附录二	交际活动 B	258
附录三	英文翻译	260
附录四	课外练习部分参考答案	294
附录五	生词总表	300

第一课　今天你感觉怎么样？

（呼吸内科—肺炎）

扫码听

学习目标和重难点：
1. 与肺炎相关的词语
2. 向肺炎病人了解情况
3. 向指导医生汇报肺炎病人的情况

一　生词

1.	负责	fùzé	动	to be responsible for
2.	床位	chuángwèi	名	bed
3.	病历	bìnglì	名	case history
4.	诊断	zhěnduàn	动	to diagnose
5.	肺炎	fèiyán	名	pneumonia
6.	感觉	gǎnjué	动	to feel
7.	胸口	xiōngkǒu	名	chest
8.	痰	tán	名	sputum
9.	厉害	lìhai	形	serious
10.	干咳	gānké	动	to have a dry cough
11.	肺	fèi	名	lung
12.	湿啰音	shīluóyīn	名	moist rale
13.	炎症	yánzhèng	名	inflammation
14.	呼吸	hūxī	动	to respire, to breathe

15.	继续	jìxù	动	to continue
16.	拍	pāi	动	to have (an x-ray film)
17.	X光片	X-guāngpiàn	名	X-ray film
18.	片状	piànzhuàng	名	patch
19.	模糊	móhu	形	dim, unclear
20.	阴影	yīnyǐng	名	shadow, opacity
21.	症状	zhèngzhuàng	名	symptom

二 课文

人物： 指导医生——马文
rénwù: zhǐdǎo yīshēng Mǎ Wén

实习生——莎娜
shíxíshēng Shānà

呼吸 内科 住院 病人——江海山
hūxī nèikē zhù yuàn bìngrén Jiāng Hǎishān

1. 会话

马　文： 早上　好！
　　　　 Zǎoshang hǎo!

江海山： 马　医生，早上　好！
　　　　 Mǎ yīshēng, zǎoshang hǎo!

马　文： 我　给　你们 介绍 一下儿，这　是　实习生　莎娜，这
　　　　 Wǒ gěi nǐmen jièshào yíxiàr, zhè shì shíxíshēng Shānà, zhè

是 5 床 的 江 海 山。
shì wǔ chuáng de Jiāng Hǎishān.

莎　娜： 您 好！
Nín hǎo!

江海山： 你 好！
Nǐ hǎo!

马　文： 江 海山，莎娜 负责
Jiāng Hǎishān, Shānà fùzé

你 的 床位，有 什么 事 可以 跟 她 说。
nǐ de chuángwèi, yǒu shénme shì kěyǐ gēn tā shuō.

江海山： 哦，好 的。莎娜，你 是 哪 国 人？
Ò, hǎo de. Shānà, nǐ shì nǎ guó rén?

莎　娜： 我 是 巴基斯坦人，我 的 汉语 不 太 好，请 你 跟 我
Wǒ shì Bājīsītǎnrén, wǒ de Hànyǔ bú tài hǎo, qǐng nǐ gēn wǒ

说 话 慢 一点儿，好 吗？
shuō huà màn yìdiǎnr, hǎo ma?

江海山： 你 的 汉语 说 得 非常 好，我 都 听懂 了。
Nǐ de Hànyǔ shuō de fēicháng hǎo, wǒ dōu tīngdǒng le.

莎　娜： 谢谢！我 看了 您 的 病历，昨天 入 院 时 的 诊断
Xièxie! Wǒ kànle nín de bìnglì, zuótiān rù yuàn shí de zhěnduàn

是 肺炎。今天 您 感觉 怎么样？
shì fèiyán. Jīntiān nín gǎnjué zěnmeyàng?

江海山： 打 针、吃 药 后，我 感觉 好 点儿 了。
Dǎ zhēn, chī yào hòu, wǒ gǎnjué hǎo diǎnr le.

2. 会话

莎　娜： 江　先生，今天您 胸口 还疼吗？有 没有 痰？
Jiāng xiānsheng, jīntiān nín xiōngkǒu hái téng ma? Yǒu méiyǒu tán?

江海山： 咳嗽 厉害 时 胸口 还是 疼。主要 是 干咳，痰
Késou lìhai shí xiōngkǒu háishi téng. Zhǔyào shì gānké, tán

不 多。
bù duō.

莎　娜： 我再给您 听听 肺。嗯，还是 有 湿啰音。
Wǒ zài gěi nín tīngting fèi. Ǹg, háishi yǒu shīluóyīn.

江海山： 有 湿啰音 说明 什么 问题 呢？
Yǒu shīluóyīn shuōmíng shénme wèntí ne?

莎　娜： 说明 您的肺部 还 有 炎症。来，再 量量
Shuōmíng nín de fèibù hái yǒu yánzhèng. Lái, zài liángliang

体温。
tǐwēn.

（10 分钟 后）
(shí fēnzhōng hòu)

江海山： 哦，医生，我 还是 发 烧， 38.9度。
Ò, yīshēng, wǒ háishi fā shāo, sānshíbā diǎn jiǔ dù.

莎　娜： 体温还 挺 高 的，这也 说明 还 有 炎症。
Tǐwēn hái tǐng gāo de, zhè yě shuōmíng hái yǒu yánzhèng.

您头 疼 不 疼？
Nín tóu téng bu téng?

江海山： 头 有点儿 疼。
Tóu yǒu diǎnr téng.

莎 娜： 您 觉得 呼吸 怎么样？
Nín juéde hūxī zěnmeyàng?

江海山： 还是 比较 急，咳嗽 还是 很 厉害。
Háishi bǐjiào jí, késou háishi hěn lìhai.

莎 娜： 您 先 休息 一下儿，继续 打针 吃药。我 去 把
Nín xiān xiūxi yíxiàr, jìxù dǎ zhēn chī yào. Wǒ qù bǎ

你的 情况 告诉 马 医生。
nǐ de qíngkuàng gàosu Mǎ yīshēng.

3. 成段表达 （莎娜对马医生说）

马老师，我看了5 床 的 病历，还问了问他今天的
Mǎ lǎoshī, wǒ kànle wǔ chuáng de bìnglì, hái wènle wèn tā jīntiān de

情况。 他昨天入院 时体温40度，呼吸比较急，咳嗽很
qíngkuàng. Tā zuótiān rù yuàn shí tǐwēn sìshí dù, hūxī bǐjiào jí, késou hěn

厉害，咳嗽时 胸口 疼，但主要是干咳，痰不多。肺部有
lìhai, késou shí xiōngkǒu téng, dàn zhǔyào shì gānké, tán bù duō. Fèibù yǒu

湿啰音，昨天 拍 的 X光片 上 能 看到肺部有 小 片
shīluóyīn, zuótiān pāi de X-guāngpiàn shang néng kàndào fèibù yǒu xiǎo piàn

状 模糊阴影，诊断 是肺炎。刚才我问他今天的 情况
zhuàng móhu yīnyǐng, zhěnduàn shì fèiyán. Gāngcái wǒ wèn tā jīntiān de qíngkuàng

时，他说打针 用药 后感觉好一点儿了，但还是有头
shí, tā shuō dǎ zhēn yòng yào hòu gǎnjué hǎo yìdiǎnr le, dàn háishi yǒu tóu

疼、干咳、呼吸比较急、胸口 疼 等 症状。 我给他听了
téng, gānké, hūxī bǐjiào jí, xiōngkǒu téng děng zhèngzhuàng. Wǒ gěi tā tīngle

肺，还是有 湿啰音。体温 38.9度。 我叫他先 好好儿
fèi, háishi yǒu shīluóyīn. Tǐwēn sānshíbā diǎn jiǔ dù. Wǒ jiào tā xiān hǎohāor

休息，继续 打针 吃药。
xiūxi, jìxù dǎ zhēn chī yào.

注释

1. 住院病人（inpatient）

通常将入住医院的病人称为住院病人，将到医院看门诊的病人称为门诊病人（outpatient），将送入急诊室的病人称为急诊病人（emergent patient）。

Normally we call patients admitted to hospital as "住院病人". Patients who go to a hospital to have out-patient services are called "门诊病人". Patients sent to the emergency department are referred to as "急诊病人".

2. 这是5床的江海山（先生）。

医院住院部的病床习惯上都用数字编上号，方便工作和管理。有些不知道病人姓名的工作人员，会用床号来称呼病人。比如说"5床吃完药没有"等。

In the inpatient department, the beds are usually numbered for convenience of administration. When the patients' names are unknown, their bed numbers are called instead of their names. For example "5床吃完药没有" and so on.

介绍人时如果要表示客气，可以在姓名后加上"先生／小姐／女士／爷

爷／奶奶"等称呼。但在实际的对话中，医生介绍病人时一般只说姓名。

For introduction if we want to express the politeness, we can add the calls before patients' names: "先生/小姐/女士/爷爷/奶奶" and so on. In the practical dialogue, when doctors introduce patients, doctors only call their names usually.

3. 今天你感觉怎么样？

住院部医生、护士、实习生每天例行检查病房时的习惯用语，目的是了解病人的病情跟昨天比有没有好转、好转的程度以及有什么新的变化等。回答常常是"（我觉得）好点儿了／跟昨天差不多"等。

In inpatient department when the doctors, nurses and interns make routine ward-round, they often use this phrase in order to know if the patients' conditions are better than yesterday or the degree of the improvement and any new changes. The answer is usually "(我觉得) 好点儿了/跟昨天差不多" and so on.

4. 湿啰音

这是人体吸气时气体通过呼吸道内的稀薄分泌物形成水泡破裂所产生的声音，又叫水泡音。

This is a bubbling sound heard on auscultation, caused by the pressure of a fluid secretion in the bronchial tubes or in a cavity.It is also called "水泡音".

5. 发烧

口语里一般把发烧时体温在39度以上叫作"发高烧"或"高烧"，37.3度～38度叫作"发低烧"或"低烧"。临床上分别称为"高热"和"低热"。

In spoken Chinese if the temperature is over 39℃, it is called "发高烧" or "高烧"; if the temperature is between 37.3～37.5℃, it is called "发低烧" or "低烧". Clinically the names are "高热" and "低热" respectively.

四 练习

(一) 课堂练习

1. 听与读

量体温
拍 X 光片
肺部有湿啰音
肺部有小片状模糊阴影

再给你听听
再给你量量
再给你看看

有胸口疼的症状
有头疼的症状
有发高烧的症状
有咳嗽的症状
有肺炎的症状

感觉怎么样
感觉呼吸怎么样
感觉好点儿了
感觉头有点儿疼
感觉呼吸比较急
感觉咳嗽很厉害

2. 替换与扩展

(1) A：今天感觉怎么样？
　　B：今天感觉身体好点儿了。

咳嗽	不厉害
头	不太疼
胸口	不疼

(2) 我感觉头还有点儿疼。

胸口
肚子
腿
手

(3) 有什么事可以跟他说。

有什么情况
有什么症状
哪里不舒服

第一课　今天你感觉怎么样？

（4）昨天入院时病人发烧到40度。

> 咳嗽很厉害
> 主要是干咳
> 胸口非常疼
> 肺部有湿啰音
> 肺部X光片上有小片状模糊阴影

3. **口语练习：参考使用下列词语看图对话**

　　场景提示：实习生和病人的对话。病人咳嗽，说胸口很疼，实习生根据所给词语问病人情况，并给病人量体温，体温是38.9度。

呼吸　干咳　肺炎　炎症　痰　胸口

（二）课外练习

1. 看汉字，写拼音

床位_____　　症状_____　　肺炎_____　　炎症_____

阴影_____　　痰_____　　湿啰音_____　　诊断_____

2. 看拼音，根据生词表写汉字

gānké_____　　hūxī_____　　bìnglì_____　　pāi_____

móhu_____　　xiōngkǒu_____　　piànzhuàng_____

3. 选择合适的词语填空（每个词语只能用一次）

> 干咳　症状　量　继续　胸口　呼吸　湿啰音　诊断　感觉　拍　炎症

（1）3床的X光片有模糊阴影，_____是肺炎。

（2）肺炎有哪些_____？

（3）你的病还没好，要_____吃药。

（4）病人的_____不太急。

（5）你先给他_____体温吧。

（6）他还发高烧，肺部听到_____，说明还有_____。

（7）你今天_____好点儿了吗？

（8）我咳嗽没有痰，是_____。

（9）你马上去_____个X光片吧。

（10）_____还疼吗？

4. 根据问句写出合适的应答句

（1）指导医生：5床还头疼吗？

　　实习生：_____。

（2）指导医生：5床的体温是多少？

　　实习生：_____。

（3）指导医生：5床的肺部X光片有阴影吗？

　　实习生：_____。

（4）指导医生：对5床的诊断，病历上写的是什么？

　　实习生：_____。

（5）指导医生：5床今天好点儿了吗？

实 习 生：_____。

5. 完成下列对话

（1）医生：今天你感觉_____？

病人：还有点儿_____。

医生：咳嗽厉害吗？

病人：不太_____。

医生：_____多不多？

病人：痰不太多。

（2）马文：莎娜，你负责的病人怎么样？

莎娜：我让护士给他量了_____，还是38.9度。

马文：哦，还在发_____。

莎娜：是啊，他的病比较厉害。

马文：拍了_____没有？

莎娜：拍了。肺部有_____。

马文：诊断是什么？

莎娜：是_____。

6. 口语练习：复述成段表达的内容

 向指导医生汇报病人情况

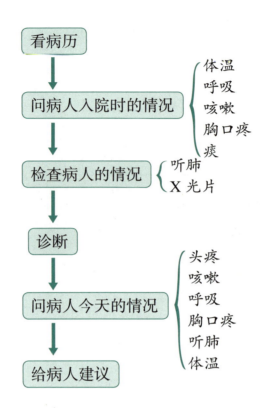

7. 节奏汉语

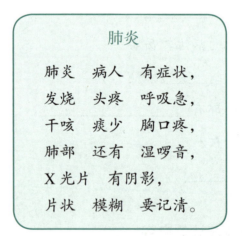

8. 写作练习：把练习5的第二个对话改成对病人情况的叙述

常用专业词语

非典型性肺炎	fēidiǎnxíngxìng fèiyán	atypical pneumonia
细菌性肺炎	xìjūnxìng fèiyán	bacterial pneumonia
病毒性肺炎	bìngdúxìng fèiyán	viral pneumonia
真菌性肺炎	zhēnjūnxìng fèiyán	mycotic pneumonia
支原体肺炎	zhīyuántǐ fèiyán	mycoplasma pneumonia
大叶性肺炎	dàyèxìng fèiyán	lobar pneumonia
支气管肺炎	zhīqìguǎn fèiyán	broncho pneumonia
间质性肺炎	jiānzhìxìng fèiyán	interstitial pneumonia

第二课　哮喘病是不能着凉的

（呼吸内科—哮喘）

扫码听

学习目标和重难点：
1. 与哮喘病相关的词语
2. 向病人了解哮喘发作时的情况
3. 向另一位实习生讲述哮喘病人的情况

一　生词

1. 值班	zhí bān		to be on duty
2. 着凉	zháo liáng		to have a cold
3. 哮喘	xiàochuǎn	名	asthma
4. 发作	fāzuò	动	to be attacked with, to attack
5. 急促	jícù	形	rapid (breathing)
6. 额部	ébù	名	forehead
7. 冒（汗）	mào（hàn）		to perspire, to sweat
8. 冷汗	lěnghàn	名	cold sweat
9. 唇	chún	名	lip
10. 指	zhǐ	名	finger
11. 发绀	fāgàn	动	cyanosis
12. 平卧	píngwò	动	to be supine
13. 听诊	tīngzhěn	动	to auscultate

第二课　哮喘病是不能着凉的

14. 呼气	hū qì		to breath out, to exhale
15. 哮鸣音	xiàomíngyīn	名	wheezing, stridor
16. 吸气	xī qì		to inhale air, to draw in breath
17. 难受	nánshòu	形	uncomfortable
18. 恢复	huīfù	动	to recover
19. 正常	zhèngcháng	形	normal
20. 治疗	zhìliáo	动	to cure, to treat
21. 及时	jíshí	形	in time, timely

二 课文

人物： 指导医生——陈东
rénwù： zhǐdǎo yīshēng　Chén Dōng

实习生——卡奇、李力
shíxíshēng　Kǎqí、Lǐ Lì

呼吸内科 住院 病人——张英梅（女，54岁）
hūxī nèikē zhù yuàn bìngrén　Zhāng Yīngméi (nǚ, wǔshísì suì)

1. 会话

陈　东： 卡奇，今天你得特别注意 23 床 的病人。
　　　　 Kǎqí, jīntiān nǐ děi tèbié zhùyì èrshísān chuáng de bìngrén.

卡　奇： 她怎么了？
　　　　 Tā zěnme le?

陈 东： 值班 医生 说 昨晚 她 洗 澡 的 时候 着 凉，半夜
Zhíbān yīshēng shuō zuówǎn tā xǐ zǎo de shíhou zháo liáng, bànyè

哮喘 又 发作 了。
xiàochuǎn yòu fāzuò le.

卡 奇： 她 有 什么 症状？
Tā yǒu shénme zhèngzhuàng?

陈 东： 呼吸 急促、额部 冒 冷汗、
Hūxī jícù、 ébù mào lěnghàn、

唇 指 发绀、不 能
chún zhǐ fāgàn、 bù néng

平卧。
píngwò.

卡 奇： 那 我 现在 去 给 她 看看，做 个 肺部 听诊 吧。
Nà wǒ xiànzài qù gěi tā kànkan, zuò ge fèibù tīngzhěn ba.

陈 东： 哦，好 的。
Ò, hǎo de.

卡 奇： 陈 老师，听诊 时 我 要 注意 什么 呢？
Chén lǎoshī, tīngzhěn shí wǒ yào zhùyì shénme ne?

陈 东： 你 注意 一下儿 呼气 时 有 没有 哮鸣音。
Nǐ zhùyì yíxiàr hū qì shí yǒu méiyǒu xiàomíngyīn.

2. 会话

卡　奇：　张　阿姨，您 好！现在 感觉 怎么样？
　　　　　Zhāng āyí, nín hǎo! Xiànzài gǎnjué zěnmeyàng?

张阿姨：　好 多 了。
　　　　　Hǎo duō le.

卡　奇：　我 来 给 您 听听 肺 吧。
　　　　　Wǒ lái gěi nín tīngting fèi ba.

张阿姨：　好。谢谢！
　　　　　Hǎo. Xièxie!

卡　奇：　来，吸气——，呼气——。很 好，现在 已经 没有
　　　　　Lái, xī qì——, hū qì——. Hěn hǎo, xiànzài yǐjīng méiyǒu

　　　　　哮鸣音 了。
　　　　　xiàomíngyīn le.

张阿姨：　昨天 半夜 的 时候 我 可 难受 了。
　　　　　Zuótiān bànyè de shíhou wǒ kě nánshòu le.

卡　奇：　您 当时 有 什么 感觉？
　　　　　Nín dāngshí yǒu shénme gǎnjué?

张阿姨：　我 不 能 躺着 睡觉，呼吸 急促，头 上 都 是
　　　　　Wǒ bù néng tǎngzhe shuì jiào, hūxī jícù, tóu shang dōu shì

　　　　　冷汗，坐着 的 时候 才 感觉 舒服 一点儿。
　　　　　lěnghàn, zuòzhe de shíhou cái gǎnjué shūfu yìdiǎnr.

卡　奇：　哮喘病 是 不 能 着 凉 的，以后 您 一定 要
　　　　　Xiàochuǎnbìng shì bù néng zháo liáng de, yǐhòu nín yídìng yào

特别 注意。
tèbié zhùyì.

张阿姨：好 的，我 一定 会 注意 的，哮喘 发作 起来 太
Hǎo de, wǒ yídìng huì zhùyì de, xiàochuǎn fāzuò qǐlái tài

难受 了。
nánshòu le.

卡 奇：还 好，您 这次 是 住院 的 时候 发作 的，如果 在家
Hái hǎo, nín zhè cì shì zhù yuàn de shíhou fāzuò de, rúguǒ zài jiā

发作 就 更 麻烦 了。
fāzuò jiù gèng máfan le.

3. 成段表达（卡奇对李力说）

李力，今天 我们 呼吸内科 有 一 位 哮喘 病人，昨天
Lǐ Lì, jīntiān wǒmen hūxī nèikē yǒu yí wèi xiàochuǎn bìngrén, zuótiān

晚上 洗澡 的 时候 着 凉 了，哮喘病 又 发作 了。听说
wǎnshang xǐ zǎo de shíhou zháo liáng le, xiàochuǎnbìng yòu fāzuò le. Tīngshuō

当时 她 呼吸 急促、额部 冒 冷汗、唇 指 发绀、不 能 平卧，
dāngshí tā hūxī jícù, ébù mào lěnghàn, chún zhǐ fāgàn, bù néng píngwò,

呼气时 有 哮鸣音。发作 得 可 厉害 了。今天 陈 老师 让我
hū qì shí yǒu xiàomíngyīn. Fāzuò de kě lìhai le. Jīntiān Chén lǎoshī ràng wǒ

特别 注意她的 情况。我 去 给 她 做了 肺部 听诊。她 呼气时
tèbié zhùyì tā de qíngkuàng. Wǒ qù gěi tā zuòle fèibù tīngzhěn. Tā hū qì shí

已经 没有 哮鸣音 了，嘴唇 和 手指 的 颜色 也 恢复 正常
yǐjing méiyǒu xiàomíngyīn le, zuǐchún hé shǒuzhǐ de yánsè yě huīfù zhèngcháng

了，躺着 也 不 觉得 难受，感觉 好 多 了。我 告诉 她 以后
le, tǎngzhe yě bù juéde nánshòu, gǎnjué hǎo duō le. Wǒ gàosu tā yǐhòu

注意 不要 着 凉，如果 在家 的 时候 哮喘病 发作，治疗
zhùyì búyào zháo liáng, rúguǒ zài jiā de shíhou xiàochuǎnbìng fāzuò, zhìliáo

不 及时 就 麻烦 了。
bù jíshí jiù máfan le.

注释

1. 她怎么了？

"××怎么了"是医生询问病人情况的习惯用语。目的是初步了解病人的情况，以便做出正确的诊断。如：

"××怎么了" is a common question asked by doctors at the preliminary stage when trying to find out a patient's condition. e.g.

（1）你怎么了？

（2）5床的唇部怎么了？

2. 平卧

脸朝上躺着。

It means that a person lies on his back (or takes a supine).

3. 那我现在去给她看看，做个肺部听诊吧。

"那"在这里是连词，表示顺着前面话语的意思，引出应有的结果或做出判断、决定等（前面的话语可以是对方说的，也可以是自己提出的问题或假设）。这里的"那"也可以用"那么"。这个句子是卡奇顺着前面陈医生说的症状而做出该去给病人做肺部听诊的判断、决定。如：

"那" in this case is a conjunction which connects the meaning of the previous words/sentences with those that follow. It usually indicates result, judgment or decision, as a response to what others say, or question/presumption raised by the speaker himself. "那" can also be replaced by "那么". In this particular sentence, Kaqi makes a decision to listen to the patient's lungs after Dr. Chen told him about the patient's symptoms. Here are more examples:

（1）你肺炎还没完全好呢，那就继续打针、吃药吧。

（2）你觉得很不舒服？那就去医院看看吧。

4. 哮鸣音

干啰音的一种。它是在肺部听诊时听到的正常呼吸音以外的一种附加声音，是由于气管、支气管狭窄或部分阻塞，呼吸时发生湍流所产生的高调的音响。多发生于支气管炎、细支气管炎及支气管炎哮喘时。

Wheezing is manifested as high-pitched, musical, variable sounds with breathing, most prominently during expiration. The sound is generated by gas flowing through narrowed or irregular airways. In some instances it is immediately audible, but in most cases, it is heard only by auscultation of the chest. Generally, wheezing is due to asthma, although a variety of conditions may be associated with this finding.

5. 好多了（adj. + 多了）

"多了"用在形容词的后面，表示程度高，一般用在有比较意义的句子中。这里的"好多了"是指"现在感觉比昨天好多了"。如：

"多了" is used after adjectives, means high degree. Generally it is used in comparative sentences. "好多了" here means "现在感觉比昨天好多了". e.g.

（1）现在体温比昨天低多了。

（2）这个病房比那个病房干净多了。

6. 昨天半夜的时候我可难受了。（可 + adj. / v.）

这里的"可"是一个副词，后面常跟形容词或动词，表示强调。如：

"可" is an adverb here, usually followed by verbs or adjectives. It can be used to emphasize the expression. e.g.

（1）她昨天咳嗽得可厉害了。

（2）他胸口疼得可难受了。

（3）他哮喘又发作了，医生您可来了！

四 练习

（一）课堂练习

1. 听与读

哮喘发作	恢复正常	可厉害了
呼吸急促	恢复治疗	可麻烦了
唇指发绀	恢复健康	可难受了
肺部听诊	及时检查	可疼了
冒冷汗	及时治疗	可冷了
哮鸣音	治疗及时	可不舒服了

怎么了	要注意什么
有什么感觉	要注意他的呼吸
感觉怎么样	要注意他的情况
有什么不舒服	注意不要着凉
哪儿不舒服	注意平卧
有什么症状	注意听有没有哮鸣音
感觉好点儿了吗	注意有没有湿啰音

2. 替换与扩展

（1）<u>她</u>怎么了？

> 你的脸
> 你的嘴唇
> 他的眼睛
> 那位病人的额部
> 3床的腿

（2）<u>发作</u>得可<u>厉害</u>了。

> 病　　　难受
> 咳嗽　　厉害
> 恢复　　快
> 治疗　　及时

（3）<u>陈老师</u>让我<u>特别注意她的情况</u>。

> 马　　给23床的病人做肺部听诊
> 江　　给9床的病人量一下儿体温
> 王　　看一下儿10床的病历
> 白　　看一下儿8床的X光片

（4）A：23 床感觉很难受。
　　　B：那我现在 <u>去看看她</u> 吧。

> 给她做肺部听诊
> 给她拍个 X 光片
> 给她治疗
> 叫她平卧
> 量量她的体温

3. 口语练习：交际活动

全班分为 A、B 两组，A 组看附录一，B 组看附录二，准备好后每次各组随机抽取一人进行有信息差的对话。

（二）课外练习

1. 看汉字，写拼音

哮喘_____　　哮鸣音_____　　呼气_____　　唇_____

听诊_____　　发绀_____　　吸气_____　　指_____

平卧_____　　额部_____　　值班_____　　治疗_____

2. 看拼音，根据生词表写汉字

zháo liáng_____　　jíshí_____　　mào lěnghàn_____

jícù_____　　huīfù_____　　fāzuò_____

nánshòu_____

3. 词语搭配（每个词语只能用一次）

拍　冒　量　打　听　写　吃

针　病历　X光片　药　冷汗　肺　体温

4. 根据病人的情况写出合适的问句

（1）病　人：我昨晚洗澡的时候着凉了，哮喘病又发作了。

实习生：_____？

（2）病　人：昨天半夜的时候我可难受了。

实习生：_____？

（3）病　人：我感觉呼吸很快，头上直冒冷汗。

实习生：_____？

5. 完成下列对话

（1）李力：卡奇，听说你负责的那位哮喘病人昨天晚上又_____了。

卡奇：是啊，昨天晚上她_____的时候_____了，所以哮喘病又发作了。

李力：当时有什么_____？

卡奇：呼吸_____，额部冒_____，唇指_____，不能_____。

李力：呼气时有_____吗？

卡奇：_____医生说当时有，但是我今天去给她做了_____，现在已经没有了。

（2）陈医生：23床的那个病人今天感觉_____？

实习生：比昨天_____。昨天晚上她哮喘病发作得_____。

陈医生：你今天去给她做_____了吗？

实习生：做了，呼气时已经没有_____了。

陈医生：其他情况_____？

实习生：嘴唇和手指的颜色_____正常了，_____也不觉得难受了。我还告诉她以后要特别_____，不能再_____了。

6. 口语练习：复述成段表达的内容

向另一位实习生讲述病人的情况

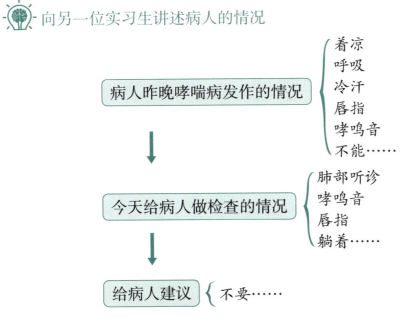

7. 节奏汉语

> 哮喘病
>
> 哮喘　发作　很厉害，
> 呼吸急促　冒冷汗，
> 唇指发绀　难　平卧，
> 呼气时　有　哮鸣音。
> 注意千万　别着凉，
> 治疗　及时　没麻烦。

8. 写作练习：把课文的第二个对话改成对病人情况的叙述

常用专业词语

支气管痉挛	zhīqìguǎn jìngluán	bronchospasm
气促	qìcù	to breathe hard; panting
过敏反应	guòmǐn fǎnyìng	anaphylaxis
支气管哮喘	zhīqìguǎn xiàochuǎn	bronchial asthma
外源性支气管哮喘	wàiyuánxìng zhīqìguǎn xiàochuǎn	extrinsic bronchial asthma
内源性支气管哮喘	nèiyuánxìng zhīqìguǎn xiàochuǎn	intrinsic bronchial asthma
心源性哮喘	xīnyuánxìng xiàochuǎn	cardiac asthma

第三课　他是典型的支气管扩张的病例

（呼吸内科—支气管扩张）

扫码听

学习目标和重难点：

1. 区分"病历"和"病例"，掌握与支气管扩张相关的词语
2. 掌握支气管扩张病人的主要症状
3. 向病人家属交代支气管扩张病人要注意的事项

一　生词

1.	家属	jiāshǔ	名	family members
2.	支气管	zhīqìguǎn	名	bronchus, bronchial tube
3.	扩张	kuòzhāng	动	to dilate
4.	病例	bìnglì	名	case
5.	记录	jìlù	动	to record, to write down
6.	反复	fǎnfù	副	repeatedly, again and again
7.	急性	jíxìng	形	acute
8.	呼吸道	hūxīdào	名	windpipe
9.	感染	gǎnrǎn	动	to infect
10.	病史	bìngshǐ	名	medical history, case history
11.	大量	dàliàng	形	mass, a great deal of
12.	咯血	kǎ xiě		hemoptysis
13.	典型	diǎnxíng	形	representative, typical

14.	排	pái	动	to exclude, to eject, to discharge
15.	暂时	zànshí	形	temporary
16.	消失	xiāoshī	动	to disappear
17.	指头	zhǐtou	名	finger
18.	杵状指	chǔzhuàngzhǐ	名	clubbed finger
19.	造影	zàoyǐng	动	to visualize
20.	确诊	quèzhěn	动	to diagnose
21.	患	huàn	动	to contract (an illness), to suffer from
21.	过敏	guòmǐn	动	to be allergic to

二 课文

人物： 指导 医生——刘 川花
rénwù: zhǐdǎo yīshēng　　Liú Chuānhuā

实习 生——白瑞蒂
shíxíshēng　　Báiruìdì

呼吸内科 病房 2 床 病人——苏军（男，39 岁）
hūxī nèikē bìngfáng 2 chuáng bìngrén　　Sū Jūn (nán, sānshíjiǔ suì)

病人 家属——何桃（苏军的妻子）
bìngrén jiāshǔ　　Hé Táo (Sū Jūn de qīzi)

1. 会话

刘川花： 白瑞蒂，你 见过 支气管 扩张 的 病例 吗？
　　　　 Báiruìdì, nǐ jiànguo zhīqìguǎn kuòzhāng de bìnglì ma?

白瑞蒂： 见过，就在那张桌子上，我给您拿过来。
Jiànguo, jiù zài nà zhāng zhuōzi shang, wǒ gěi nín ná guolai.

（把2床的病历拿给刘医生）
（bǎ èr chuáng de bìnglì ná gěi Liú yīshēng）

刘川花： 啊？不对，不对。我说的是支气管扩张这
Á? Bú duì, bú duì. Wǒ shuō de shì zhīqìguǎn kuòzhāng zhè

种病的例子，不是记录病人情况的病历。
zhǒng bìng de lìzi, bú shì jìlù bìngrén qíngkuàng de bìnglì.

白瑞蒂： 哦，对不起！我还以为您要看这个病历呢。
Ò, duìbuqǐ! Wǒ hái yǐwéi nín yào kàn zhège bìnglì ne.

唉！"病例"和"病历"听起来都一样，汉语
Ài! "Bìnglì" hé "bìnglì" tīng qilai dōu yíyàng, Hànyǔ

真麻烦。
zhēn máfan.

刘川花： 是啊，所以你要努力学好汉语啊！哦，你已经
Shì a, suǒyǐ nǐ yào nǔlì xué hǎo Hànyǔ a! Ò, nǐ yǐjīng

把2床的病历拿来了，那就先看看病人
bǎ èr chuáng de bìnglì nálai le, nà jiù xiān kànkan bìngrén

的情况吧。
de qíngkuàng ba.

白瑞蒂： 好。（边看病历边念）入院前有反复发作的
Hǎo. (biān kàn bìnglì biān niàn) Rù yuàn qián yǒu fǎnfù fāzuò de

急性呼吸道感染的病史；入院前一天病人大量
jíxìng hūxīdào gǎnrǎn de bìngshǐ; Rù yuàn qián yì tiān bìngrén dàliàng

咯血……
kǎ xiě……

刘川花: 他是典型的支气管扩张的病例。我带你去
Tā shì diǎnxíng de zhīqìguǎn kuòzhāng de bìnglì. Wǒ dài nǐ qù

看看他吧。
kànkan tā ba.

白瑞蒂: 好啊。
Hǎo a.

2. 会话

何 桃: 刘医生好！
Liú yīshēng hǎo!

刘川花: 你们好！这是实习生
Nǐmen hǎo! Zhè shì shíxíshēng

白瑞蒂。
Báiruìdì.

白瑞蒂: 你们好！啊！这些花儿
Nǐmen hǎo! Ā! Zhèxiē huār

真漂亮！真香啊！
zhēn piàoliang! Zhēn xiāng a!

何 桃: 这是苏军的同事送来的。
Zhè shì Sū Jūn de tóngshì sònglai de.

刘川花: 不要把花儿放在病房里，有支气管疾病的
Búyào bǎ huār fàngzài bìngfáng li, yǒu zhīqìguǎn jíbìng de

人 容易 对 花粉 过敏。
rén róngyì duì huāfěn guòmǐn.

何 桃： 哦，原来 这样 啊。那 我 马上 拿走。
Ò, yuánlái zhèyàng a. Nà wǒ mǎshàng názǒu.

刘川花： 白瑞蒂，你 先 给2 床 做 听诊 吧。
Báiruìdì, nǐ xiān gěi èr chuáng zuò tīngzhěn ba.

白瑞蒂： 好。刘老师，我 听 不 到 湿啰音。
Hǎo. Liú lǎoshī, wǒ tīng bú dào shīluóyīn.

刘川花： （对何） 刚才 他 排过 痰 吗？
(duì Hé) Gāngcái tā páiguo tán ma?

何 桃： 刚才 他 咳嗽 很 厉害，吐了 很 多 痰。
Gāngcái tā késou hěn lìhai, tǔle hěn duō tán.

刘川花： （对白） 病人 在 排痰 后 湿啰音 可以 暂时 消失，
(duì Bái) Bìngrén zài pái tán hòu shīluóyīn kěyǐ zànshí xiāoshī,

你 过 一会儿 再 听 就 能 听到 了。
nǐ guò yíhuìr zài tīng jiù néng tīngdào le.

白瑞蒂： 您 看，他 的 指头 好像 特别 大、特别 胖。
Nín kàn, tā de zhǐtou hǎoxiàng tèbié dà, tèbié pàng.

刘川花： 这 叫 杵状指，支气管 扩张 病人 如果 患 病
Zhè jiào chǔzhuàngzhǐ, zhīqìguǎn kuòzhāng bìngrén rúguǒ huàn bìng

时间 长，有 三 分之 一 会 出现 这 种 症状。
shíjiān cháng, yǒu sān fēnzhī yī huì chūxiàn zhè zhǒng zhèngzhuàng.

白瑞蒂： 哦，我 明白 了。
Ò, wǒ míngbai le.

3. 成段表达 （白瑞蒂对何桃说）

您 丈夫 前天 做了 支气管 造影，已经 确诊 患了
Nín zhàngfu qiántiān zuòle zhīqìguǎn zàoyǐng, yǐjīng quèzhěn huànle

支气管 扩张。患 支气管 疾病的人容易对花粉、烟雾
zhīqìguǎn kuòzhāng. Huàn zhīqìguǎn jíbìng de rén róngyì duì huāfěn、yānwù

等 过敏，所以您 不要把 朋友 送来的花儿放在 病房
děng guòmǐn, suǒyǐ nín búyào bǎ péngyou sònglai de huār fàngzài bìngfáng

里，也不能 让亲戚朋友在 病房里抽 烟，要保持 病房
li, yě bù néng ràng qīnqi péngyou zài bìngfáng li chōu yān, yào bǎochí bìngfáng

空气的 新鲜。如果他出汗很多，要给他多喝点儿水。
kōngqì de xīnxiān. Rúguǒ tā chū hàn hěn duō, yào gěi tā duō hē diǎnr shuǐ.

注意 不要 着 凉。还要 常 看看他有 没有发高烧 和
Zhùyì búyào zháo liáng. Hái yào cháng kànkan tā yǒu méiyǒu fā gāoshāo hé

咯 血，如果发现 这些 症状，要及时 告诉我们。您可以
kǎ xiě, rúguǒ fāxiàn zhèxiē zhèngzhuàng, yào jíshí gàosu wǒmen. Nǐ kěyǐ

让 他多吃些 鸡蛋、肉、鱼、豆腐和新鲜的水果 蔬菜，
ràng tā duō chī xiē jīdàn、ròu、yú、dòufu hé xīnxiān de shuǐguǒ shūcài,

每次 不要吃太多，每天 多吃几次。
měi cì búyào chī tài duō, měi tiān duō chī jǐ cì.

注释

1. 病例 / 病历

"病例"和"病历"都是名词,读音也一样,但意思和用法不一样。

"病例" and "病历" are homophones. They have the same pronunciation but are different in meaning and usage.

"病例"的意思是某种疾病的实际例子。医生之间交谈时常用这个词。如:

"病例" are medical cases. It is a commonly used in conversations between doctors. e.g.

(1) 这种病例很常见。

(2) 你见过支气管扩张的病例吗?

(3) 这是个典型的肺炎病例。

"病历"是医生对病人病情的诊断和治疗方法的记录。医生看过病以后,要给病人写病历;病人去医院看病,要带上写着自己病历的本子,叫作病历本。如:

"病历" is a patient's medical record, or case history kept by doctors. It includes the diagnosis as well as the treatment for the patient. When patients go to see doctors, they need to bring along their book of medical record, which is called "病历本". e.g.

(4) 哎呀,我忘了带病历本了。

(5) 这是医生给我写的病历。

2. 急性

发作急剧的、变化快的(病)。如:急性呼吸道感染、急性支气管炎。

A disease or disorder that lasts a short time, comes on rapidly, and is accompanied by distinct symptoms. e.g. "急性呼吸道感染" "急性支气管炎".

临床上通常根据病人发病的缓急情况不同分为急性、亚急性和慢性三种类型。

According to the difference in symptoms, clinical patients are usually divided into three types: acute, subacute and chronic.

3. 病史

病人曾经患过的疾病及治疗情况叫作病史，病史在诊断时有较大参考价值，因此医生问诊时会详细询问病人的病史。

The medical history is an account of all medical events and problems a person has experienced, which is especially helpful when a diagnosis is needed. Therefore, the doctor will ask the patient to provide detailed medical history during the interrogation.

4. 咯血

喉部或喉以下呼吸道出血经口腔排出。咯出的血液呈鲜红色，常带有泡沫。常见于肺结核、肺炎、支气管扩张、肺癌等病或胸部外伤。也说咳血。

Hemoptysis refers to the expectoration of blood from some part of the respiratory tract like the throat or lungs. The blood expectorated is generally bright red, with frothy masses. It is frequently seen in pulmonary tuberculosis, pneumonia, bronchiectasis and lung cancer or injuries of the chest. It can also be called the spitting of the blood.

5. 排

"排"有动词、名词、量词等多种用法，本课是动词，意思是放出，指生物把体内的废物放出体外。临床上常用的有：排痰、排汗、排尿（niào）、排便等。

"排" can be a verb, a noun, a measure word and others. In this lesson, it is used as a verb, meaning "to discharge, to eject wastes to vitro". In clinical situation, "排痰" "排汗" "排尿" "排便" etc. are often used.

6. 杵状指

"杵状指"是名词短语，意思是像粗大的木棒样子的手指。杵，是一头粗一头细的圆木棒；状，是形状、样子；指，就是手指、指头。

"杵状指" is a noun phrase, which means clubbed finger. "杵" is a pestle, a wooden club with one thick end and one thin end. "状" is the shape, pattern. "指" is the finger.

"状"常常跟在名词性词语后面，构成表示物体形状的名词性词语。如片状、块状、柱状、圆柱状、粉末状等。

"状" is often used after noun phrases, to refer to object shapes. e.g. "片状" "块状" "柱状" "圆柱状" "粉末状" etc.

7. 造影

通过口服或注射某些X射线不能透过的药物，使某些器官在X射线下显示出来，以便检查疾病。

By oral administration or injection of some drugs that can not be transmitted by X-rays, some organs can be shown in X-rays in order to detect disease.

四 练习

（一）课堂练习

1. 听与读

支气管	咯血	造影	病历
支气管扩张	大量咯血	做造影	2床的病历
呼吸道	过敏	支气管造影	记录病人情况的病历
呼吸道感染	花粉过敏	做支气管造影	那位病人的病历
肺炎	杵状指		

出现……症状	病例	有……病史
出现杵状指的症状	肺炎病例	有肺炎的病史
出现大量咯血的症状	支气管扩张病例	有支气管扩张的病史
出现呼吸道感染的症状	呼吸道感染病例	有呼吸道感染的病史
出现花粉过敏的症状	花粉过敏病例	有花粉过敏的病史

2. 替换与扩展

（1）你见过<u>支气管扩张</u>的病例吗？

> 肺炎
> 哮喘
> 呼吸道感染
> 花粉过敏

（2）入院前一天病人<u>大量咯血</u>。

> 咳嗽得很厉害
> 一直头疼
> 发高烧
> 胸口很疼
> 呼吸非常急促

（3）我还以为你<u>要看这个病历</u>呢。

花粉过敏
患了呼吸道感染
做了支气管造影
有支气管扩张的病史

3. 口语练习：参考使用下列词语看图对话

场景提示：（1）实习生给病人做肺部听诊，并询问病人病情；（2）实习生查看病人的手指，发现手指又肥又大，和病人问答；（3）实习生向指导医生汇报情况，与指导医生对话。

听诊　湿啰音　排过痰　暂时消失　指头又肥又大　杵状指　确诊
典型　支气管扩张　病例

（二）课外练习

1. 看汉字，写拼音

咯血_____　　病例_____　　杵状指_____

呼吸道_____　支气管_____　造影_____

确诊_____　　过敏_____　　暂时_____

感染_____　　典型_____　　患_____

2. 看拼音，根据生词表写汉字

bìngshǐ _____   kuòzhāng _____   jìlù _____

dàliàng _____   fǎnfù _____   pái _____

zhǐtou _____   xiāoshī _____   jíxìng _____

3. 选择合适的词语填空（每个词语只能用一次）

> 反复 杵状指 过敏 排 患 病例 咯血 确诊 感染 暂时 病历

（1）你见过支气管扩张的_____吗？

（2）我把2床的_____拿来了。

（3）病人入院前有急性呼吸道_____的病史。

（4）他的支气管扩张病_____发作了好几次。

（5）入院前一天病人_____了。

（6）这个孩子_____了急性呼吸道感染，住院了。

（7）医生_____他患了支气管扩张。

（8）这种病人对花粉、烟雾等_____。

（9）病人在_____痰后湿啰音可以_____消失。

（10）患支气管扩张时间长的病人可能会出现_____的症状。

4. 根据问句写出合适的应答句

（1）指导医生：2床有什么病史？

实习生：_____。

（2）指导医生：2床听诊有湿啰音吗？

实习生：_____。

（3）指导医生：2床刚才排过痰吗？

　　　实 习 生：＿＿＿＿＿＿＿＿＿＿＿＿＿＿＿＿＿。

（4）指导医生：怎样确诊2床患了支气管扩张？

　　　实 习 生：＿＿＿＿＿＿＿＿＿＿＿＿＿＿＿＿＿。

（5）指导医生：支气管扩张病例都有杵状指吗？

　　　实 习 生：＿＿＿＿＿＿＿＿＿＿＿＿＿＿＿＿＿。

5. 完成下列对话

（1）指导医生：2床入院前的情况＿＿＿＿＿＿＿＿＿＿＿＿？

　　　实 习 生：（念病历）他有＿＿＿＿＿＿＿＿＿＿＿＿的病史，入院

　　　　　　　　前一天＿＿＿＿＿＿＿＿＿＿＿＿。

　　　指导医生：这是典型的＿＿＿＿＿＿＿＿＿＿＿＿。

　　　实 习 生：哦。这种病例还有＿＿＿＿＿＿＿＿＿＿＿＿？

　　　指导医生：支气管扩张病人如果患病时间长，三分之一会出现＿＿＿＿

　　　　　　　　＿＿＿＿＿＿症状。

　　　实 习 生：什么叫＿＿＿＿＿＿＿＿＿＿＿＿？

　　　指导医生：就是手指头＿＿＿＿＿＿＿＿＿＿＿＿。

（2）医　　生：病人现在的情况＿＿＿＿＿＿＿＿＿＿＿＿？

　　　病人家属：他睡着了。刚才他＿＿＿＿＿＿＿＿＿＿＿＿，吐了很多痰。

　　　　　　　　请问医生，我丈夫患的是＿＿＿＿＿＿＿＿＿＿＿＿？

　　　医　　生：前天我们给他做了＿＿＿＿＿＿＿＿＿＿＿＿，已经确诊他

　　　　　　　　患的是支气管扩张。

　　　病人家属：他爱抽烟，＿＿＿＿＿＿＿＿＿＿＿＿？

医　　生：不行！抽烟对他的_____，支气管病人

　　　　　容易对花粉、烟雾_____。

病人家属：哦。还要注意_____？

医　　生：注意多给他_____，不要_____。

　　　　　如果发现他出现_____的症状，马上告

　　　　　诉我们。另外，让他多吃些_____，

　　　　　每次不要吃太多，可以多吃几次。

病人家属：知道了，_____！

医　　生：_____。

6. 口语练习：复述成段表达的内容

告诉病人家属检查结果及病人要注意的事项

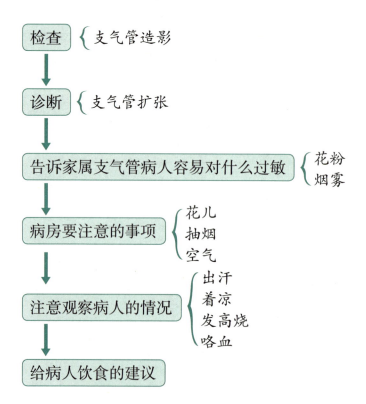

7. 节奏汉语

支气管扩张

支气管扩张 很 典型,
呼吸道 反复 遇 感染,
咳嗽 厉害 痰很多,
杵状指,大又肥,
支气管 造影 来确诊。
烟雾 花粉 致 过敏,
病人 前面 别抽烟,
空气 新鲜 最重要。
多喝水,别着凉,
发烧 咯血 速就医。
蛋、肉、水果要多吃,
豆腐 蔬菜 也 别少。

8. 写作练习：把练习 5 的第二个对话改成对病人情况的叙述

几种常见的支气管疾病名称

急性气管支气管炎	jíxìng qìguǎn zhīqìguǎnyán	acute tracheo bronchitis
急性细支气管炎	jíxìng xìzhīqìguǎnyán	acute bronchiolitis
慢性支气管炎（简称慢支）	mànxìng zhīqìguǎnyán	chronic bronchitis
支气管哮喘（简称哮喘）	zhīqìguǎn xiàochuǎn	bronchial asthma
支气管扩张	zhīqìguǎn kuòzhāng	bronchiectasis
支气管腺瘤	zhīqìguǎn xiànliú	bronchial adenoma

第四课　昨天不是已经好多了吗？

（消化内科—急性肠胃炎）

扫码听

学习目标和重难点：

1. 与急性肠胃炎相关的词语
2. 向病人了解急性肠胃炎发作时的情况
3. 向指导医生汇报病人的情况

一　生词

1.	消化	xiāohuà	动	to digest
2.	肠胃炎	chángwèiyán	名	enterogastritis
3.	全身	quánshēn	名	the whole body, all over (the body)
4.	无力	wúlì	动	to feel weak
5.	拉	lā	动	to empty the bowels
6.	呕吐	ǒutù	动	to vomit
7.	按	àn	动	to press
8.	腹部	fùbù	名	belly, abdomen
9.	哎哟	āiyō	叹	ouch
10.	大便	dàbiàn	名	stool, feces, excrement
11.	常规	chángguī	名	routine
12.	（化）验	(huà) yàn	动	to examine, to check

13. 化验单	huàyàndān	名	test form
14. 汇报	huìbào	动	to report, to give an account of
15. 输液	shū yè		to transfuse
16. 好转	hǎozhuǎn	动	to make a turn for the better
17. 恶心	ěxin	形	feel sick
18. 严重	yánzhòng	形	serious, critical
19. 腹泻	fùxiè	动	to diarrhea
20. 水样便	shuǐyàngbiàn	名	watery diarrhea
21. 压痛	yātòng	名	tenderness
22. 异样	yìyàng	形	different, unusual

二 课文

人物： 指导 医生——周 大明
rénwù: zhǐdǎo yīshēng　Zhōu Dàmíng

　　　实习生——莎娜
　　　shíxíshēng　Shānà

　　　消化 内科 住院 病人——李刚（男，44 岁，老板）
　　　xiāohuà nèikē zhù yuàn bìngrén　Lǐ Gāng (nán, sìshísì suì, lǎobǎn)

第四课　昨天不是已经好多了吗？

1. 会话

李　刚：医生　早上　好！
　　　　Yīshēng zǎoshang hǎo!

莎　娜：您好！李　先生，您是急性　肠胃炎　刚　住进来
　　　　Nín hǎo! Lǐ xiānsheng, nín shì jíxìng chángwèiyán gāng zhù jinlai

　　　　的 吧？现在 感觉 怎么样？
　　　　de ba? Xiànzài gǎnjué zěnmeyàng?

李　刚：我 肚子 还是 很 疼，全身
　　　　Wǒ dùzi háishi hěn téng, quánshēn

　　　　无力，今天 已经 拉了 10
　　　　wúlì, jīntiān yǐjīng lāle shí

　　　　多 次 了。
　　　　duō cì le.

莎　娜：（看病历）还有 呕吐 吗？
　　　　(kàn bìnglì) Hái yǒu ǒutù ma?

李　刚：不 吐 了。
　　　　Bú tù le.

莎　娜：您 躺下 吧，我 先 按按 您 的 腹部。这儿，疼
　　　　Nín tǎngxià ba, wǒ xiān àn'an nín de fùbù. Zhèr, téng

　　　　不 疼？
　　　　bu téng?

李　刚：哎哟，疼死 了！哎哟！不 行 了，不 行 了……
　　　　Āiyō, téngsǐ le! Āiyō! Bù xíng le, bù xíng le……

莎　娜：怎么了？
　　　　Zěnme le?

李　刚：对不起！我又要上洗手间了！
　　　　Duìbuqǐ! Wǒ yòu yào shàng xǐshǒujiān le!

（李刚从洗手间回来）
（Lǐ Gāng cóng xǐshǒujiān huílái）

莎　娜：又拉肚子了吧？肚子还疼吗？
　　　　Yòu lā dùzi le ba? Dùzi hái téng ma?

李　刚：嗯，现在没那么疼了，不过肚子还是不太舒服。
　　　　Ńg, xiànzài méi nàme téng le, búguò dùzi háishi bú tài shūfu.

莎　娜：那请您再躺下来，我再给您检查一下儿。
　　　　Nà qǐng nín zài tǎng xialai, wǒ zài gěi nín jiǎnchá yíxiàr.

李　刚：好的。……哎呀，不行了，不行了，我又要
　　　　Hǎo de. … Āiyā, bù xíng le, bù xíng le, wǒ yòu yào

　　　　上洗手间了！
　　　　shàng xǐshǒujiān le!

2. 会话 （3天后）

莎　娜：李老板，听值班医生说您昨晚又拉了
　　　　Lǐ lǎobǎn, tīng zhí bān yīshēng shuō nín zuówǎn yòu lāle

　　　　七八次。
　　　　qī-bā cì.

李　刚：是啊。大便 就像 水 一样，拉得 我 都 没 力气
　　　　Shì a. Dàbiàn jiù xiàng shuǐ yíyàng, lā de wǒ dōu méi lìqi

　　　　站 起来 了。
　　　　zhàn qǐlai le.

莎　娜：怎么 回事 啊？昨天 不是 已经 好 多 了 吗？
　　　　Zěnme huíshì a? Zuótiān bú shì yǐjīng hǎo duō le ma?

李　刚：昨天 下午 朋友 来看 我，听 我 说 病 好 多 了，
　　　　Zuótiān xiàwǔ péngyou lái kàn wǒ, tīng wǒ shuō bìng hǎo duō le,

　　　　就叫 我 一起 出去 吃 海鲜。
　　　　jiù jiào wǒ yìqǐ chūqu chī hǎixiān.

莎　娜：啊？您 还 去 吃 海鲜 啊？
　　　　Á? Nín hái qù chī hǎixiān a?

李　刚：（脸 红）我 最 喜欢 吃 海鲜 了，所以 忍不住 吃了
　　　　(liǎn hóng) Wǒ zuì xǐhuan chī hǎixiān le, suǒyǐ rěn bú zhù chīle

　　　　一点儿。
　　　　yìdiǎnr.

莎　娜：唉！您 呀！先 做 个 大便 常规 检查，再 验验
　　　　Ài! Nín ya! Xiān zuò ge dàbiàn chángguī jiǎnchá, zài yànyan

　　　　血 吧。我 给 您 开 化验单。
　　　　xiě ba. Wǒ gěi nín kāi huàyàndān.

李　刚：医生，真 不 好意思。
　　　　Yīshēng, zhēn bù hǎoyìsi.

莎　娜：您 呀，以后 可 不要 乱 吃 东西 了，特别是 生 病
　　　　Nín ya, yǐhòu kě bú yào luàn chī dōngxi le, tèbié shì shēng bìng

的 时候。
de shíhou.

李 刚: 知道了。这次病得这么厉害，我以后再也不
Zhīdao le. Zhè cì bìng de zhème lìhai, wǒ yǐhòu zài yě bù

敢 乱 吃 了。
gǎn luàn chī le.

3. 成段表达 （莎娜对周医生说）

周 老师，我向 您 汇报一下儿 8 床 的 情况。病人
Zhōu lǎoshī, wǒ xiàng nín huìbào yíxiàr bā chuáng de qíngkuàng. Bìngrén

三 天 前因急性 肠胃炎 住院。经过 输液 治疗后，病情
sān tiān qián yīn jíxìng chángwèiyán zhù yuàn. Jīngguò shū yè zhìliáo hòu, bìngqíng

很 快 好 转。本来 想 让 他 明天 出 院 的，可是 昨晚
hěn kuài hǎo zhuǎn. Běnlái xiǎng ràng tā míngtiān chū yuàn de, kěshì zuówǎn

他 跟 朋友去外面 吃了海鲜，回来后 肠胃炎 又 急性
tā gēn péngyou qù wàimiàn chīle hǎixiān, huílái hòu chángwèiyán yòu jíxìng

发作了。先 是 恶心，接着就 呕吐，腹部 疼痛，又 出现了
fāzuò le. Xiān shì ěxin, jiēzhe jiù ǒutù, fùbù téngtòng, yòu chūxiànle

严重 的腹泻，昨晚腹泻七八次，病人 说 都是 水样便，
yánzhòng de fùxiè, zuówǎn fùxiè qī-bā cì, bìngrén shuō dōu shì shuǐyàngbiàn,

腹部 检查有 明显 的压痛感。刚才我查房时给他开了
fùbù jiǎnchá yǒu míngxiǎn de yātònggǎn. Gāngcái wǒ chá fáng shí gěi tā kāile

大便 常规 检查 和 血常规 检查 的 化验单，了解 一下儿
dàbiàn chángguī jiǎnchá hé xuèchángguī jiǎnchá de huàyàndān, liǎojiě yíxiàr

大便 和 血常规 有 什么 异样。结果 出来 后 我 再 向 您
dàbiàn hé xuèchángguī yǒu shénme yìyàng. Jiéguǒ chūlai hòu wǒ zài xiàng nín

报告。
bàogào.

注释

1. 疼死了。（adj. + 死了）

"死"在这里表示程度达到极点，跟"adj. + 极了"意思差不多，与"生死"的"死"意义无关。句子的主语也可放在"死"的后面。如：

"死" is used to refer to the high degree of some feelings. Used this way, it means the same as "adj. + 极了", but has nothing to do with the "死" in the phrase like "生死". The subject of the sentence can also be placed after the word "死". e.g.

（1）我热死了。

（2）累死我了！

2. 我又要上洗手间了！

"S + 又要 + v.+ 了"在汉语口语中，表示动作已经多次发生，并即将再次发生。如：

In oral Chinese, "S + 又要 + v. + 了" means that the action has occurred many times, and is about to happen again. e.g.

（1）迈克又要迟到了。

（2）山本又要生气了。

（3）老师又要批评他了。

3. 听值班医生说您昨晚又拉了七八次。

"听 + sb. + 说"表示说话人把自己听到某人说的事告诉听话人。如：

"听 + sb. + 说" means the speaker says he hears something from somebody else. e.g.

（1）（卡奇对白瑞蒂说）听张医生说8床病人病得很厉害。

（2）（莎娜对指导医生说）听李老板说他的肚子还是很疼。

4. 我给您开化验单。

"开"，在这里是动词，意思是"写""填写"。"开化验单"的意思是填写化验单，如开处方、开介绍信、开证明。

"开", here is a verb. It means to write, to fill out. "开化验单" means to fill out laboratory form. e.g. "开处方" (to prescribe; to write out a prescription) "开介绍信" "开证明".

5. 再也

副词"再"表示动作的重复，副词"也"表示动作或状态相同。这两个副词连用为"再也"时，后面一般要求有否定副词"不""没（有）"呼应，表示相同的动作不会或没有重复出现。如：

As an adverb, "再" means the repetition of an action, "也" means that some actions or some conditions are the same. When these two adverbs are used together as "再也", a negative adverb such as "不" "没（有）" is required to be used after "再也", which means the same action will not or do not happen again.e.g.

（1）这次病得这么厉害，我以后再也不敢乱吃了。
（2）这次哮喘发作这么严重，我以后再也不敢洗冷水澡了。

6. 水样便

临床上一般把稀得像水一样的大便称为水样便。

In general clinic human excrement that looks like liquid is called watery diarrhea.

四 练习

（一）课堂练习

1. 听与读

全身无力	又要上洗手间了	听值班医生说
急性发作	又要呕吐了	听实习医生说
腹部疼痛	又要拉肚子了	听指导老师说
恶心呕吐	又要做检查了	听病人家属说
水样便	再也不敢乱吃东西了	大便常规检查
压痛感	再也不敢乱服药了	血常规检查
开化验单	再也不能太晚休息了	尿常规检查
输液治疗	再也不能喝酒了	身体常规检查

2. 替换与扩展

（1）<u>大便检查</u>不是已经好多了吗？

腹泻
腹痛
感冒
过敏的症状

（2）<u>肠胃炎</u>又急性发作了。

胃炎
肠炎
肺炎
支气管炎

（3）先<u>做个大便常规检查</u>，再<u>验验血</u>吧。

挂号	看病
问问医生	吃药
拍X光片	确定下一步治疗方法
做个血常规检查	看看要不要住院
做身体常规检查	决定能不能做手术

（4）这次<u>病</u>得这么厉害，我以后再也不敢了。

咳
头疼
肚子拉
呕吐
发作

3. 口语练习：交际活动

全班分为 A、B 两组，A 组看附录一，B 组看附录二，准备好后每次各组随机抽取一人进行有信息差的对话。

（二）课外练习

1. 看汉字，写拼音

消化_____　　水样便_____　　呕吐_____　　腹泻_____

腹部_____　　肠胃炎_____　　大便_____　　输液_____

化验单_____　　异样_____　　常规_____

2. 看拼音，根据生词表写汉字

wúlì_____　　quánshēn_____　　lā_____

yánzhòng_____　　àn_____　　yātòng_____

ěxin_____　　hǎozhuǎn_____　　huìbào_____

3. 词语搭配（每个词语只能用一次）

开	血
吃	腹泻
做	洗手间
验	肚子
出现	化验单
上	海鲜
拉	常规检查

4. 选择合适的词语填空（每个词语只能用一次）

> 全身　无力　腹泻　严重　肠胃炎　拉　常规　好转　呕吐　大便

（1）您是急性_____刚住进来的吧？

（2）马老师，8床_____得很厉害啊，怎么办？

（3）从早上到现在，2床已经_____七八次了。

（4）医生，我的病_____吗？

（5）_____就像水一样。

（6）拉得我都_____站起来了。

（7）昨天下午开始我_____过敏。

（8）注意别着凉，着凉了容易_____肚子。

（9）先做个大便_____检查。

（10）吃药后肠胃炎_____了吗？

5. 根据病人的情况写出合适的问句

（1）病　人：哎哟，疼死了！疼死了！

　　　实习生：_____？

（2）病　人：医生，我昨晚又拉了七八次。

　　　实习生：_____？

（3）病　人：医生，我现在全身无力。

　　　实习生：_____？

6. 完成下列对话

（1）李刚：医生早上好！

莎娜：您好！李先生，您是_____刚住进来的吧？现在感觉怎么样？

李刚：我_____还是很疼，全身_____，今天已经拉了10多次了。

莎娜：（看病历）还有_____吗？

李刚：不吐了。

莎娜：您_____吧，我先按按您的_____。这儿，_____？

李刚：哎哟，_____了！哎哟！不行了，不行了……。

（2）莎娜：李老板，听值班医生说您昨晚_____。

李刚：是啊。_____就像水一样，拉得我都_____站起来了。

莎娜：_____啊？昨天不是已经好多了吗？

李刚：昨天下午朋友来看我，听我说病好多了，就_____。

莎娜：啊？您还去吃海鲜啊？

李刚：（脸红）我最喜欢吃海鲜了，所以_____吃了一点儿。

莎娜：唉！您呀！先做个_____，再验验血吧。我给您开_____。

李刚：医生，真_____。

7. 口语练习：复述成段表达的内容

 向指导医生汇报病人的情况

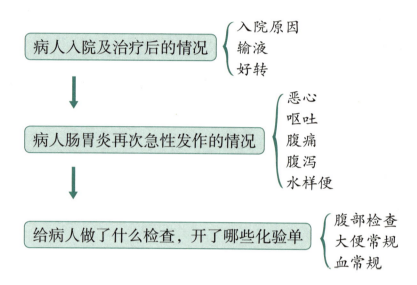

8. 节奏汉语

急性肠胃炎

肠胃炎发作有症状，
恶心、呕吐、腹部疼，
严重腹泻水样便；
腹部检查有压痛，
大便验血来化验，
千万不要吃海鲜。

9. 写作练习：把课文的第二个对话改成对病人情况的叙述

第四课　昨天不是已经好多了吗？

常用专业词语

胃黏膜	wèiniánmó	gastric mucosa
肠黏膜	chángniánmó	intestinal mucosa
腹部痉挛	fùbù jìngluán	ventral convulsion
腹部绞痛	fùbù jiǎotòng	ventral angina
脱水	tuō shuǐ	dehydration
葡萄球菌	pútaoqiújūn	staphylococcus
大肠杆菌	dàchánggǎnjūn	coliform
沙门杆菌	shāméngǎnjūn	salmonella
病毒感染	bìngdú gǎnrǎn	virus infection

第五课　他怎么会得这种病？

（消化内科—急性胰腺炎）

扫码听

学习目标和重难点：
1. 与急性胰腺炎相关的词语
2. 向病人了解平时的饮食习惯
3. 向另一位实习生讲述急性胰腺炎病人的情况及发病原因

一　生词

1.	血清	xuèqīng	名	blood serum
2.	淀粉酶	diànfěnméi	名	amylase
3.	胰腺	yíxiàn	名	pancreas
4.	肿大	zhǒngdà	形	swelling, swollen
5.	边缘	biānyuán	名	edge, margin
6.	体征	tǐzhēng	名	physical sign
7.	皮肤	pífū	名	skin, cutis
8.	斑	bān	名	spot, macula
9.	主诉	zhǔsù	动	chief complaint
10.	持续	chíxù	动	to last, to continue
11.	放射	fàngshè	动	to radiate
12.	为	wéi	动	to be
13.	茅台	Máotái	名	the name of a famous white spirit of China

14. 命	mìng	名	life
15. 长期	chángqī	名	a long period of time
16. 引起	yǐnqǐ	动	to give rise to, to lead to, to cause
17. 蛋白	dànbái	名	protein
18. 脂肪	zhīfáng	名	fat
19. 暴饮暴食	bàoyǐn-bàoshí		to eat and drink too much
20. 疾病	jíbìng	名	disease, sickness, illness

二 课文

人物： 指导 医生——邓 洁
rénwù: zhǐdǎo yīshēng　Dèng Jié

实习生——莎娜、李 力
shíxíshēng　Shānà、Lǐ Lì

消化 内科 11 床 病人——朱治齐（男， 55 岁，经理）
xiāohuà nèikē shíyī chuáng bìngrén　Zhū Zhìqí (nán, wǔshíwǔ suì, jīnglǐ)

1. 会话

邓 洁： 莎娜， 你 去 看看 11 床
　　　　Shānà,　nǐ qù kànkan shíyī chuáng

的 血清 和 CT 检查 结果
de xuèqīng hé CT jiǎnchá jiéguǒ

出来 没有。
chūlai méiyǒu.

急性胰腺炎！

莎 娜：出来了。您 看看。
　　　　Chūlai le. Nín kànkan.

邓 洁：哦。血清 淀粉酶 升高，CT 检查 胰腺 肿大，
　　　　Ò. Xuèqīng diànfěnméi shēnggāo, CT jiǎnchá yíxiàn zhǒngdà,

　　　　胰腺 周围 边缘 模糊。
　　　　yíxiàn zhōuwéi biānyuán móhu.

莎 娜：根据 这些 我们 能 确诊 他 得了 急性 胰腺炎 吗？
　　　　Gēnjù zhèxiē wǒmen néng quèzhěn tā déle jíxìng yíxiànyán ma?

邓 洁：他的腹部 体征 是 什么？
　　　　Tā de fùbù tǐzhēng shì shénme?

莎 娜：腹部 检查 左 上 腹 有 压痛，腰部 皮肤 有
　　　　Fùbù jiǎnchá zuǒ shàng fù yǒu yātòng, yāobù pífū yǒu

　　　　灰紫色 斑。
　　　　huīzǐsè bān.

邓 洁：病人 的 主诉 呢？
　　　　Bìngrén de zhǔsù ne?

莎 娜：他跟 朋友 去饭店吃 饭，吃了很多肉和海鲜，
　　　　Tā gēn péngyou qù fàndiàn chī fàn, chīle hěn duō ròu hé hǎixiān,

　　　　还喝了很多酒。回家以后 上 腹部 突然 持续
　　　　hái hēle hěn duō jiǔ. Huí jiā yǐhòu shàng fùbù tūrán chíxù

　　　　疼痛， 很 快 就 向 左 腰背 放射， 接着 就
　　　　téngtòng, hěn kuài jiù xiàng zuǒ yāobèi fàngshè, jiēzhe jiù

　　　　呕吐、发 烧。
　　　　ǒutù, fā shāo.

邓 洁： 根据 病人 的 主诉、体征 和 检查 结果，我 看 可以
Gēnjù bìngrén de zhǔsù, tǐzhēng hé jiǎnchá jiéguǒ, wǒ kàn kěyǐ

诊断 为 急性 胰腺炎 了。
zhěnduàn wéi jíxìng yíxiànyán le.

2. 会话

朱治齐： 大夫，我 得 的 是 什么 病？
Dàifu, wǒ dé de shì shénme bìng?

莎 娜： 急性 胰腺炎。
Jíxìng yíxiànyán.

朱治齐： 怎么 会 得 这 种 病？
Zěnme huì dé zhè zhǒng bìng?

莎 娜： 您呀，您 这个 病 是 吃 出来、喝 出来 的。
Nín ya, nín zhège bìng shì chī chulai、hē chulai de.

朱治齐： 是 不 是 因为 这些 东西 不 干净？
Shì bu shì yīnwèi zhèxiē dōngxi bù gānjìng?

莎 娜： 不 是 因为 不 干净，是 因为 吃了 太 多 的 肉 和
Bú shì yīnwèi bù gānjìng, shì yīnwèi chīle tài duō de ròu hé

海鲜，同时 还 喝了 很 多 酒。您 到底 喝了 多少
hǎixiān, tóngshí hái hēle hěn duō jiǔ. Nín dàodǐ hēle duōshao

酒 啊？
jiǔ a?

朱治齐： 差不多 一斤 茅台 吧。
Chàduō yì jīn Máotái ba.

莎 娜： 啊？一斤茅台！真 是 不要 命 了！您 平时 也
Á? Yì jīn Máotái! Zhēn shì búyào mìng le! Nín píngshí yě

常常 喝 酒 吧？
chángcháng hē jiǔ ba?

朱治齐： 是啊。
Shì a.

莎 娜： 就是因为您 长期 喝酒，这次也喝了很多酒，
Jiù shì yīnwèi nín chángqī hē jiǔ, zhè cì yě hēle hěn duō jiǔ,

同时 又 吃了 很多 肉和海鲜，所以就 引起
tóngshí yòu chīle hěn duō ròu hé hǎixiān, suǒyǐ jiù yǐnqǐ

急性 胰腺炎 了。
jíxìng yíxiànyán le.

朱治齐： 哦，吃喝 多了也 这么 危险 啊。
Ò, chīhē duōle yě zhème wēixiǎn a.

莎 娜： 是啊，以后您可别一次吃太多的肉了，最好
Shì a, yǐhòu nín kě bié yí cì chī tài duō de ròu le, zuìhǎo

也别喝酒了。
yě bié hē jiǔ le.

3. 成段表达 （莎娜对李力说）

李力，你知道吗？我们消化内科有位病人，入院的时候肚子疼得脸都青了，腰也直不起来，还吐个不停，病得可厉害了！主诉上腹部持续疼痛，向左腰背放射。腹部检查发现左上腹有压痛，腰部皮肤有灰紫色斑。血清检查淀粉酶升高，CT检查胰腺肿大。邓老师告诉我他患的是急性胰腺炎。他自己还不知道他的病是怎么引起的呢！唉！现在的人生活好了，常去饭店吃吃喝喝，喝起来还真不要命，一喝就是一两斤白酒，还要吃那么多高蛋白、高脂肪的东西。现在因为暴饮暴食得各种疾病的人越来越多了。

注释

1. 主诉

主诉（chief complaint，即 CC），是指病人在看病时对自己病情的描述。病人的主诉可为医生提供对其疾病的诊断线索，应同时包括主要症状（或体征）及其持续的时间。

Chief complaint is the description of health condition given by patients when seeing doctors. Patients' chief complaint can help doctors to diagnose diseases. Chief complaints should include main symptoms (or body signs) as well as duration.

2. 怎么会得这种病？

病人及病人家属在得知病情以后常用"怎么会得……"表示惊奇和疑问。也可以在"怎么"前加上主语。医生常常会对此做出病理解释。如：

To express surprise and doubt, a patient and his family often ask "怎么会得……" after the patient has been diagnosed. Before "怎么" you may add a subject. When this happens, doctors usually give pathological explanations. e.g.

（1）怎么会得支气管扩张？

（2）怎么会得肺炎？

（3）我怎么会得这种病？

3. 您这个病是吃出来、喝出来的。（v./adj. + 出来）

这句话的意思是指病人因不注意饮食习惯和饮食卫生而引起了疾病。"您这个病是……出来的"是医护人员与病人交谈时的习惯用语（非正式），用于推测病人的病因。

The meaning of this sentence is that the disease develops due to bad habits and poor hygiene condition of drinking and eating. "您这个病是……出来的" is an informal expression used in dialogues between medical workers and patients, to speculate the causes of certain disease.

"出来"在这里用的是引申的意义，跟在动词或形容词后面，表示动作或状态使事物从无到有。如"吃出来"的意思是"吃"的动作使疾病从无到有了，"出来"中间还可插入一些词语，构成"v./adj. + 出病来""v./adj. + 出毛病来""v./adj. + 出肺炎来"等。

Here the extending meaning of "出来" is used. "出来" follows a verb or an adjective to refer to an action or state which develops gradually. For example, "吃出来" means the action "吃" causes the disease. Between "出" and "来", we may insert some words to form the following patterns: "v./adj. + 出病来" "v./adj. + 出毛病来" "v./adj. + 出肺炎来" etc.

4. 真是不要命了！

这是一个感叹句。"真是"在这里是副词，表示语气的强调。如：

This is an exclamatory sentence. Here "真是" is an adverb which shows emphasis. e.g.

（1）真是太难受了！
（2）她的病真是太严重了！

"不要命了"通常是指人们在做某些事情时不考虑后果的严重性而盲目或冲动地采取行动。如：

"不要命了" usually indicates someone acts on impulse or blindness without considering the severe consequence. For example:

（3）这么危险的事都去做，你不要命了吗？

5. 您可别一次吃太多的肉了。

"可别"表示一种劝阻，医生常用这个词劝阻病人某种有害健康的行为。如：

"可别" is an expression of dissuading sb. from doing sth. Doctors often use this word to dissuade patients from acting or behaving in ways that are harmful to their health. e.g.

（1）你可别吸太多烟了。

（2）你可别喝太多酒了。

"可别" 也可以用于日常生活中，是长辈对晚辈、上级对下级的劝阻。如：

"可别" can be used in everyday life for the dissuasion of the elder to the younger, or the higher position to the lower position. e.g.

（3）小明，你可别太晚睡觉了！（爸爸对孩子说）

（4）你下次上课可别迟到了！（老师对学生说）

6. 吐个不停（v.+个＋不停）

量词"个"用在某些单音节动词和补语之间，不表示具体的量，作用是使语气显得轻松、随便。"v.＋个＋不停"表示动作持续进行或表示动作持续的时间太长，引起别人的注意或不满。如：

Here, inserted between a mono-syllabic verb and a complement, measure word "个" does not show quantity. Its function is to make the manner of speech become relaxed and informal. "v.＋个＋不停" refers to actions that last or persist for so long that they cause dissatisfaction. e.g.

（1）他一洗完澡就咳个不停。

（2）昨晚她吃完饭就拉个不停。

第五课　他怎么会得这种病？

四 练习

（一）课堂练习

1. 听与读

胰腺炎	腹部检查	血清淀粉酶升高
急性胰腺炎	血清检查	胰腺肿大
引起急性胰腺炎	CT 检查	左上腹有压痛
得了急性胰腺炎	B 超检查	腰部皮肤有灰紫色斑

高蛋白	吐个不停
高脂肪	拉个不停
腹部体征	咳个不停
暴饮暴食	吃个不停

2. 替换与扩展

（1）病人的<u>血清</u>检查结果出来了。

　　CT
　　大便
　　腹部
　　血常规

（2）您可别<u>一次吃太多肉</u>了。

　　再喝酒
　　再吃海鲜
　　着凉
　　把花放在房间里

（3）您这个病是<u>吃</u>出来的。

喝
急
气
饿

（4）我看可以确诊为<u>胰腺炎</u>了。

肺炎
哮喘病
支气管扩张
急性肠胃炎

3. 口语练习：参考使用下列词语看图对话

场景提示：病人腹部疼痛、呕吐、发烧，实习生根据所给词语询问病情和发病原因，并给病人量体温，做腹部检查，告诉病人血清和CT检查结果及诊断。

持续疼痛　放射　呕吐　发烧　血清
淀粉酶　胰腺肿大　边缘　急性胰腺炎

（二）课外练习

1. 看汉字，写拼音

胰腺_____   边缘_____   放射_____   血清_____

淀粉酶_____   斑_____   蛋白_____   脂肪_____

2. 看拼音，根据生词表写汉字

tǐzhēng_____   pífū_____   yǐnqǐ_____

jíbìng_____   chángqī_____   zhǔsù_____

mìng_____   chíxù_____   zhǒngdà_____

3. 选择合适的词语填空（每个词语只能用一次）

> 高蛋白　暴饮暴食　主诉　引起　检查　淀粉酶
> 急性　放射　持续　肿大　长期

（1）我们要把病人的　　　　　写在病历上。

（2）11 床说他昨天中午喝完一瓶茅台后就出现　　　　　的头痛症状。

（3）吃了不干净的海鲜，容易　　　　　腹泻。

（4）腹部　　　　　发现左上腹有压痛。

（5）血清检查　　　　　升高，CT 检查胰腺　　　　　。

（6）医生告诉我他患的是　　　　　胰腺炎。

（7）得了这种病要　　　　　吃药。

（8）病人上腹部突然持续疼痛，很快就向左腰背　　　　　。

（9）吃太多＿＿＿＿＿＿高脂肪的东西很难消化。

（10）因为＿＿＿＿＿＿得各种疾病的人越来越多了。

4. 根据问句写出合适的应答句

（1）指导医生：11床的血清检查结果是什么？

　　　实习生：_____。

（2）指导医生：CT检查有什么异常吗？

　　　实习生：_____。

（3）指导医生：他的腹部体征是什么？

　　　实习生：_____。

（4）指导医生：病人的主诉呢？

　　　实习生：_____。

（5）指导医生：根据什么可以确诊？

　　　实习生：_____。

5. 完成下列对话

（1）医　　生：_____检查结果出来没有？

　　　实习生：出来了，病人的血清_____升高，能不能确诊他患的是_____？

　　　医　　生：我觉得还应该做CT检查，看看胰腺_____。

　　　实习生：还有什么检查能诊断_____？

　　　医　　生：还可以检查_____。他的腹部_____是什么？

　　　实习生：腹部检查_____有压痛。

（2）朱治齐：大夫，我得的是什么病？

莎　娜：是_____。

朱治齐：怎么会得_____？

莎　娜：您这个病是_____、喝出来的。

朱治齐：是不是因为吃的东西不干净？

莎　娜：不是因为不干净，是因为吃了太多的肉和海鲜，加上长期_____，所以就引起_____了。

6. 口语练习：复述成段表达的内容

向另一位实习生讲述急性胰腺炎病人的情况

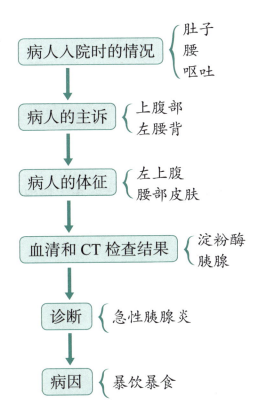

7. 节奏汉语

> **急性胰腺炎**
>
> 主诉、体征和检查,
> 帮助确诊胰腺炎。
> 吃肉、海鲜,还喝酒,
> 上腹疼痛放射左腰背,
> 呕吐、发烧、太难受,
> 腰部皮肤灰紫斑,
> 血清检查淀粉酶,
> 检查结果会升高,
> CT检查胰腺肿大,
> 胰腺周围边缘模糊。
> 高蛋白,高脂肪,
> 暴饮暴食还喝酒,
> 容易引发胰腺炎。

8. 写作练习:把练习5的两个对话分别改成对病人情况的叙述

第五课　他怎么会得这种病？

常用专业词语

急性胰腺炎	jíxìng yíxiànyán	acute pancreatitis
急性出血性胰腺炎	jíxìng chūxuèxìng yíxiànyán	acute hemorrhagic pancreatitis
胰脂酶	yízhīméi	pancreatic lipase
胰腺瘤	yíxiànliú	pancreatoncus
胰管梗阻	yíguǎn gěngzǔ	pancreatemphaxis
胰腺囊肿	yíxiàn nángzhǒng	pancreatic cyst
胰周脓肿	yí zhōu nóngzhǒng	subpancreatic abscess

第六课　你以前有过这样的腹痛吗？

（消化内科—胆囊结石和胆囊炎）

扫码听

学习目标和重难点：
1. 与胆囊结石和胆囊炎相关的词语
2. 向病人了解胆囊结石发作时的情况
3. 向指导医生汇报胆囊结石和胆囊炎病人的情况

一　生词

1.	一直	yìzhí	副	all the time
2.	侧	cè	名	side
3.	剧痛	jùtòng	名	megalgia, sharp pain
4.	割	gē	动	to cut or slice (with a knife)
5.	发冷	fā lěng		to be algid, to feel chilly
6.	小便	xiǎobiàn	名	urine
7.	油腻	yóunì	形	pinguid, greasy, oily
8.	发病	fā bìng		(of a disease) occur, (of a person) fall ill
9.	再次	zàicì	副	once again
10.	B超	B chāo	名	B-mode ultrasonic
11.	胆囊	dǎnnáng	名	gallbladder, cholecyst
12.	结石	jiéshí	名	calculus, lithiasis
13.	抗生素	kàngshēngsù	名	antibiotic

第六课　你以前有过这样的腹痛吗?

14. 解痉药	jiějìngyào	名	spasmolytic
15. 体格	tǐgé	名	physique
16. 墨菲征	mòfēizhēng	名	Murphy's Sign
17. 呈	chéng	动	to be, to assume
18. 阳性	yángxìng	名	positive
19. 初步	chūbù	形	primary
20. 建议	jiànyì	动	to suggest
21. 进一步	jìnyíbù	副	more, further

二 课文

人物： 指导 医生——汪 广平
rénwù:　zhǐdǎo yīshēng　Wāng Guǎngpíng

实习生——卡奇
shíxíshēng　Kǎqí

消化 内科 15 床 病人——陈言（男，27 岁）
xiāohuà nèikē shíwǔ chuáng bìngrén　Chén Yán (nán, èrshíqī suì)

1. 会话

卡　奇： 15 床，现在 您 哪儿 不 舒服？
　　　　 Shíwǔ chuáng, xiànzài nín nǎr bù shūfu?

陈　言： 我 肚子 疼。
　　　　 Wǒ dùzi téng.

卡　奇：是　上　腹部 吗？
　　　　Shì shàng fùbù ma?

陈　言：对。
　　　　Duì.

卡　奇：疼了 多　长　时间 了？
　　　　Téngle duō cháng shíjiān le?

陈　言：从　　前天　晚上　10 点
　　　　Cóng qiántiān wǎnshang shí diǎn

　　　　开始 肚子 一直 在 疼。
　　　　kāishǐ dùzi yìzhí zài téng.

卡　奇：您 指指 看，是 哪儿 疼？
　　　　Nín zhǐzhi kàn, shì nǎr téng?

陈　言：开始 时，是 上　腹部 疼，后来 是 右侧 腹部 剧痛，
　　　　Kāishǐ shí, shì shàng fùbù téng, hòulái shì yòucè fùbù jùtòng,

　　　　就是 这儿。
　　　　jiùshì zhèr.

卡　奇：您 觉得 是 什么　样 的 疼？
　　　　Nín juéde shì shénme yàng de téng?

陈　言：持续地 疼，越来越 疼，像 刀 割 一样。坐着 疼，
　　　　Chíxù de téng, yuèláiyuè téng, xiàng dāo gē yíyàng. Zuòzhe téng,

　　　　躺着 也 疼，疼死 我 了。
　　　　tǎngzhe yě téng, téngsǐ wǒ le.

卡　奇：其他 地方 也 跟着 疼 吗？
　　　　Qítā dìfang yě gēnzhe téng ma?

陈 言： 背部右侧也跟着疼，腰的右侧也感到不舒服。
Bèibù yòucè yě gēnzhe téng, yāo de yòucè yě gǎndào bù shūfu.

卡 奇： 剧痛之后发冷吗？有没有发烧？
Jùtòng zhīhòu fā lěng ma? Yǒu méiyǒu fā shāo?

陈 言： 没发冷，但有点儿低烧。
Méi fā lěng, dàn yǒudiǎnr dīshāo.

卡 奇： 小便是什么颜色？
Xiǎobiàn shì shénme yánsè?

陈 言： 深黄色。
Shēn huángsè.

卡 奇： 您还记得前天晚上吃什么了吗？
Nín hái jìde qiántiān wǎnshang chī shénme le ma?

陈 言： 记得。前天晚上，我们单位有个宴会，我
Jìde. Qiántiān wǎnshang, wǒmen dānwèi yǒu ge yànhuì, wǒ

吃了很多牛排、鸡肉和煎蛋。回家后就觉得
chīle hěn duō niúpái, jīròu hé jiāndàn. Huí jiā hòu jiù juéde

不舒服，恶心，还吐了。
bù shūfu, ěxin, hái tù le.

卡 奇： 一共吐了几次？
Yígòng tùle jǐ cì?

陈 言： 四五次吧。
Sì-wǔ cì ba.

卡 奇： 吐的是什么东西？有没有血或绿色的东西？
Tù de shì shénme dōngxi? Yǒu méiyǒu xiě huò lǜsè de dōngxi?

陈　言：吐的 主要 是 喝 的 和 吃 的 东西，没有 血 和 绿色
　　　　Tù de zhǔyào shì hē de hé chī de dōngxi, méiyǒu xiě hé lǜsè

　　　　的 东西。
　　　　de dōngxi.

卡　奇：您 以前 有过 这样 的 腹痛 吗？
　　　　Nín yǐqián yǒuguo zhèyàng de fùtòng ma?

陈　言：有过。这样 的 疼 已经 有 8 年 多 了，每年 都
　　　　Yǒuguo. Zhèyàng de téng yǐjīng yǒu bā nián duō le, měi nián dōu

　　　　发作 一两 次。
　　　　fāzuò yì-liǎng cì.

卡　奇：请 您 想 一 想，每次 发作 都 是 在 吃了 太多
　　　　Qǐng nín xiǎng yi xiǎng, měi cì fāzuò dōu shì zài chīle tài duō

　　　　油腻 的 东西 以后 吗？
　　　　yóunì de dōngxi yǐhòu ma?

陈　言：多数 是 这样。有 时候 工作 太累 或者 玩儿
　　　　Duōshù shì zhèyàng. Yǒu shíhou gōngzuò tài lèi huòzhě wánr

　　　　得 太累 也 会 发病。
　　　　de tài lèi yě huì fā bìng.

2. 成段表达 （卡奇对汪医生说）

15 床 病人 右 上腹 疼痛 已经 有 8 年，一般 是
Shíwǔ chuáng bìngrén yòu shàng fù téngtòng yǐjīng yǒu bā nián, yìbān shì

在吃了太多油腻东西或者太累后发作。前天在宴会上吃了牛排、鸡肉和煎蛋又再次发作。开始时是上腹部疼，后来是右侧腹部剧痛，疼痛是持续性的。发病时不发冷，但有点儿低烧。以前做过B超和腹部CT检查，诊断为胆囊结石和胆囊炎。曾经用过抗生素和解痉药治疗。我刚才给他做了体格检查，他的主要体征是上腹疼痛，胆囊肿大，墨菲征呈阳性。我的初步诊断是胆结石和胆囊炎，建议他做进一步检查。

三 注释

1. 您指指看，是哪儿疼？

这是医生检查病人身体、询问病情时的常用语。当病人说不清楚疼痛的具体部位时，就可以用这个句子询问。病人听到这个问句，通常会伸出手指指示疼痛的具体部位，这样医生就可以根据病人所指的部位进行检查。

This is a commonly asked question when doctors examine patients' body and ask about their condition. You can ask this question if the patient cannot identify exactly which part of the body hurts. When asked this question, patients usually point to the aching spot, doctors can then examine that part of the body.

2. 发冷

在高热病人的体温上升期，常伴有畏寒、寒战等症状，俗称"发冷"。

Hyperpyrexia patient often fears cold and has chillness in temperature rising period. The popular name is "发冷".

3. 您以前有过这样的腹痛吗？（有/得/患/用 + 过 + O.）

这是医生了解病人过去的病史时常用的句型，常在"有"前加上"以前"。如：

This is a usual question asked when a doctor wants to find out about the medical history of a patient. "以前" is usually added before "有". e.g.

（1）您丈夫以前有过皮肤过敏吗？
（2）您得过哮喘病吗？
（3）您曾经用过什么药？

4. 胆囊结石

临床常见的外科疾病，生活中通常简称为"胆结石"。严格说来，"胆结石"不仅包括胆囊结石,还包括胆管结石。

Gallbladder calculus is the common surgical disease in clinical. It is often called "胆结石" in daily life. Strictly speaking, "胆结石" includes not only gallbladder calculus but also bile-duct calculus.

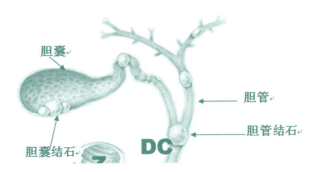

5. 体格检查

体格检查是医生运用眼、手、耳、鼻等感官或借助简单器械对患者进行身体检查的基本方法,包括视诊、触诊、叩诊、听诊和嗅诊。

A physical examination is an evaluation of the body and its functions using inspection, palpation (feeling with the hands), percussion (tapping with the fingers), and auscultation (listening) and olfaction (smelling). A complete health assessment also includes gathering information about a person's medical history and lifestyle, doing laboratory tests, and screening for disease.

6. 墨菲征呈阳性

"阳性"是诊断疾病时对某种试验或化验所得结果的表示方法。如果体内有某种病原体存在或对某种药物有过敏反应,则结果呈阳性,常用"+"表示。如,乙型肝炎表面抗原(HbsAg)检查结果为阳性(+),说明这是一位乙型肝炎病人或是乙型肝炎病毒携带者。

In medicine, Murphy's sign refers to a physical examination maneuver that is part of the abdominal examination and a finding elicited in ultrasonography.

It is useful for differentiating right upper quadrant abdominal pain. Typically, it is positive in cholecystitis, but negative in choledocholithiasis and ascending cholangitis. Getting a test result of "阳性" (meaning "positive", normally represented by a "+" sign) indicates the presence of a particular disease, condition, or organism.

医生左手掌平放在病人右肋下部，以拇指指腹在胆囊点处用力按压腹壁，然后让病人缓慢深吸气，如果吸气过程中因疼痛而引起吸气终止，称墨菲征呈阳性，见于急性胆囊炎。

To find out whether a patient has acquired Murphy's Sign, a doctor places his palm horizontally with ribs on the lower right side of the patient. While pressing hard with his fingers on the belly where the gallbladder lines beneath, he asks the patient to breathe in slowly. If in the process the patient stops breathing in due to pain, it means Murphy's Sign is positive. It often occurs in acute cholecystitis.

四 练习

（一）课堂练习

1. 听与读

腹痛	胆囊	每年都发作一两次
肚子疼	胆囊炎	玩儿得太累也会发病
腰背痛	胆囊结石	
压痛		指指看，是哪儿疼
剧痛	墨菲征	是什么样的疼
	墨菲征呈阳性	其他地方也跟着疼吗
抗生素		小便是什么颜色
解痉药	建议做进一步检查	

2. 替换与扩展

（1）A：现在你哪儿不舒服？
　　　B：我肚子疼。

上腹部疼
右侧腹部剧痛
肚子像刀割一样疼
肚子疼死了
全身发冷
全身冒冷汗

（2）曾经用过抗生素。

用	解痉药
做	CT 检查
拍	X 光片
做	体格检查
输	液

（3）你指指看，是哪儿疼？

不舒服
有压痛
有持续性的疼痛
疼得像刀割一样

（4）你以前有过这样的腹痛吗？

有	这样的咳嗽
有	这样的腹泻
有	这样的症状
得	肺炎
患	胆囊炎
用	解痉药

3. 口语练习：交际活动

全班分为 A、B 两组，A 组看附录一，B 组看附录二，准备好后每次各组随机抽取一人进行有信息差的对话。

（二）课外练习

1. 看汉字，写拼音

剧痛_____　　墨菲征_____　　胆囊_____

阳性_____　　右侧_____　　抗生素_____

解痉药_____　　体格_____　　胆结石_____

2. 看拼音，根据生词表写汉字

chéng_____　　jìnyíbù_____　　zàicì_____　　chūbù_____

fā lěng_____　　xiǎobiàn_____　　jiànyì_____　　fā bìng_____

yóunì_____　　yìzhí_____　　gē_____　　B chāo_____

3. 选择合适的词语填空（每个词语只能用一次）

> 肿大　侧　胆囊炎　再次　抗生素　B 超　呈　初步　油腻　一直

（1）病人说从前天晚上开始_____腹痛。

（2）我以前用过_____治疗。

（3）吃太多_____的东西容易引起_____发作。

（4）15 床说开始是上腹痛，后来是右_____腹部剧痛。

（5）那位病人前天宴会上吃了煎蛋、牛排后胆囊炎又_____发作。

（6）你去给他做_____检查吧。

（7）我给15床做了体格检查，发现他的胆囊_____，墨菲征_____阳性。

（8）我的_____诊断是胆囊炎和胆囊结石。

4. 根据病人情况写出合适的问句

（1）病　人：我从前天晚上10点开始肚子一直在疼。

　　　实习生：_____。

（2）病　人：我右侧腹部剧痛。

　　　实习生：_____。

（3）病　人：我回家以后就觉得不舒服，恶心，还吐了。

　　　实习生：_____。

（4）病　人：我已经疼了8年多了，每年都发作一两次。

　　　实习生：_____。

5. 完成下列对话

汪医生：卡奇，你有没有问过15床病人的情况？

卡　奇：问过了，我初步诊断是_____和_____。

汪医生：他最近是不是吃了太多_____的东西或者太累了？

卡　奇：他是前天参加宴会时吃了太多牛排、鸡肉和煎蛋后发病的。

汪医生：以前有过_____？

卡　奇：有。15床_____疼痛已经有8年了。

汪医生：病人以前用过什么药？

卡　奇：曾经用过_____和_____。

汪医生：病人的_____是什么颜色？

卡　奇：深黄色。

汪医生：给他做过＿＿＿＿＿＿检查了吗？

卡　奇：做过了，病人＿＿＿＿＿肿大，＿＿＿＿＿征呈＿＿＿＿性。

汪医生：还要做进一步检查后才可以确诊。

卡　奇：好的。

6. 口语练习：复述成段表达的内容

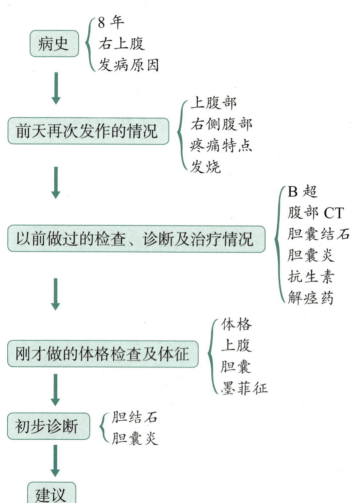

7. 节奏汉语

> **胆囊结石胆囊炎**
>
> 病人主诉上腹痛，
> 接着右腹有剧痛，
> 持续疼痛像刀割，
> 剧痛之后没发冷，
> 恶心呕吐发低烧。
> 小便颜色深黄色，
> 油腻东西吃太多，
> 或者劳累后发作。
> 胆囊肿大上腹痛，
> 墨菲征呈阳性，
> 腹部CT和B超，
> 胆囊结石胆囊炎。
> 抗生素、解痉药，
> 药物治疗效果好。

8. 写作练习：把练习5的对话改成对病人情况的叙述

常用专业词语

胆囊癌	dǎnnáng'ái	carcinoma of gallbladder
胆石症	dǎnshízhèng	cholelithiasis
胆红素尿	dǎnhóngsù niào	bilirubinuria
胆囊积水	dǎnnáng jīshuǐ	hydrops of gallbladder
胆囊切除术	dǎnnáng qiēchúshù	cholecystectomy

第七课　要马上转到外科做手术
（消化内科—胃溃疡）

扫码听

学习目标和重难点：

1. 与胃溃疡相关的词语
2. 和指导医生、其他实习生讨论胃溃疡病人的情况
3. 如何建议病人家属接受手术治疗
4. 向指导医生汇报胃溃疡病人的情况

一　生词

1.	胃溃疡	wèikuìyáng	名	gastric ulcer
2.	并	bìng	连	and, also
3.	胃出血	wèichūxiě	名	gastric hemorrhage
4.	潜血	qiánxuè	名	occult blood
5.	遇	yù	动	to meet, to be caught
6.	止	zhǐ	动	to stop, to halt
7.	门诊	ménzhěn	名	clinic
8.	胃穿孔	wèichuānkǒng	名	gastric perforation
9.	手术	shǒushù	名	surgery, operation
10.	失去	shīqù	动	to lose
11.	危险	wēixiǎn	形	dangerous, risky
12.	接受	jiēshòu	动	to accept, to receive

13.	既然	jìrán	连	so long as, since
14.	办	bàn	动	to do, to transact
15.	转科	zhuǎn kē		to transfer to another department
16.	手续	shǒuxù	名	formality, procedure
17.	吩咐	fēnfù	动	to give instructions
18.	面色	miànsè	名	complexion, colour (of the facial skin)
19.	苍白	cāngbái	形	pale
20.	四肢	sìzhī	名	(four) limbs

二 课文

人物：　　指导 医生——汪　广平
rénwù:　　zhǐdǎo yīshēng　　Wāng Guǎngpíng

　　　　　实习生——白瑞蒂、莎娜、卡奇、李力
　　　　　shíxíshēng　Báiruìdì、Shānà、Kǎqí、Lǐ Lì

　　　　　消化 内科 9 床 病人——李强（男，38 岁）
　　　　　xiāohuà nèikē jiǔ chuáng bìngrén　Lǐ Qiáng (nán、sānshíbā suì)

　　　　　病人 家属——王花（李强的妻子）
　　　　　bìngrén jiāshǔ　Wáng Huā (Lǐ Qiáng de qīzi)

1. 会话

汪广平： 今天我们一起来讨论一下儿9床的病情。
Jīntiān wǒmen yìqǐ lái tǎolùn yíxiàr jiǔ chuáng de bìngqíng.

你们先说说9床的病史吧。
Nǐmen xiān shuōshuo jiǔ chuáng de bìngshǐ ba.

卡 奇：（读病历）李强，男，38岁。以前患过胃溃疡，
(dú bìnglì) Lǐ Qiáng, nán, sānshíbā suì. Yǐqián huànguo wèikuìyáng,

并有胃出血病史。
bìng yǒu wèichūxiě bìngshǐ.

白瑞蒂： 二十天前，大便检查潜血阳性。
Èrshí tiān qián, dàbiàn jiǎnchá qiánxuè yángxìng.

莎 娜： 最近他工作很忙，常常出差。三天前
Zuìjìn tā gōngzuò hěn máng, chángcháng chū chāi. Sān tiān qián

外出遇上大雨着了凉，喝了一杯酒后，突然
wàichū yùshang dàyǔ zháole liáng, hēle yì bēi jiǔ hòu, tūrán

吐血不止。
tù xiě bù zhǐ.

李 力： 他的妻子急忙把他送到我们医院，门诊检查
Tā de qīzi jímáng bǎ tā sòngdào wǒmen yīyuàn, ménzhěn jiǎnchá

为胃出血，马上把他转到住院部。
wéi wèichūxiě, mǎshàng bǎ tā zhuǎndào zhùyuànbù.

白瑞蒂： 经过两天的住院治疗，大口吐血的情况
Jīngguò liǎng tiān de zhù yuàn zhìliáo, dà kǒu tù xiě de qíngkuàng

第七课　要马上转到外科做手术

还没 好转。
hái méi hǎozhuǎn.

汪广平：这样 的 情况 可能
Zhèyàng de qíngkuàng kěnéng

会 引起 胃穿孔。
huì yǐnqǐ wèichuānkǒng.

卡　奇：那 要 不要 转到 外科 做 手术？
Nà yào buyào zhuǎndào wàikē zuò shǒushù?

汪广平：立即 转到 外科，要是 太 迟 就 会 失去 手术
Lìjí zhuǎndào wàikē, yàoshì tài chí jiù huì shīqù shǒushù

的 机会。你们 先 去 跟 他 和 家属 说 清楚
de jīhuì. Nǐmen xiān qù gēn tā hé jiāshǔ shuō qīngchu

情况 吧。
qíngkuàng ba.

白瑞蒂、卡奇、莎娜、李力：好，我们 马上 去。
Hǎo, wǒmen mǎshàng qù.

2. 会话

卡　奇：您 是 9 床 的 家属 吗？
Nín shì jiǔ chuáng de jiāshǔ ma?

王　花：我 是 他 的 妻子。他 刚才 又 吐 血 了。
Wǒ shì tā de qīzi. Tā gāngcái yòu tù xiě le.

李　强：医生，我 的 肚子 很 疼 啊！
Yīshēng, wǒ de dùzi hěn téng a!

李　力：您的 情况 是胃溃疡引起的 胃出血。
　　　　Nín de qíngkuàng shì wèikuìyáng yǐnqǐ de wèichūxiě.

王　花：啊！严重 吗？怎么 办？
　　　　Á! Yánzhòng ma? Zěnme bàn?

莎　娜：汪 医生 说要马上 转到 外科做 手术。
　　　　Wāng yīshēng shuō yào mǎshàng zhuǎndào wàikē zuò shǒushù.

王　花：做 手术？那会不会有 危险？不 做 手术
　　　　Zuò shǒushù? Nà huì bu huì yǒu wēixiǎn? Bú zuò shǒushù

　　　　不 行 吗？
　　　　bù xíng ma?

白瑞蒂：李 先生 住院 这 两 天 我们 用了 内科 的
　　　　Lǐ xiānsheng zhù yuàn zhè liǎng tiān wǒmen yòngle nèikē de

　　　　治疗 方法，可是吐血的 情况 没有 好转。
　　　　zhìliáo fāngfǎ, kěshì tù xiě de qíngkuàng méiyǒu hǎozhuǎn.

　　　　现在 最好 马上 转到 外科 进行 手术 治疗。
　　　　Xiànzài zuìhǎo mǎshàng zhuǎndào wàikē jìnxíng shǒushù zhìliáo.

卡　奇：对，如果 不 快 点儿 进行 手术，可能 会 有 危险
　　　　Duì, rúguǒ bú kuài diǎnr jìnxíng shǒushù, kěnéng huì yǒu wēixiǎn

　　　　啊。希望 你们 能 接受 医生 的 意见。
　　　　a. Xīwàng nǐmen néng jiēshòu yīshēng de yìjiàn.

王　花：哦。既然 医生 这样 说，我 同意，我 同意。
　　　　Ò. Jìrán yīshēng zhèyàng shuō, wǒ tóngyì, wǒ tóngyì.

白瑞蒂：来，我 带 你 去 办 转 科 手续。
　　　　Lái, wǒ dài nǐ qù bàn zhuǎn kē shǒuxù.

卡　奇：我们 跟 护士 说 一下儿，准备 把 李 先生 转到
　　　　Wǒmen gēn hùshi shuō yíxiàr, zhǔnbèi bǎ Lǐ xiānsheng zhuǎndào

外科。
wàikē.

3. 成段表达 （卡奇对汪医生说）

汪 老师，按照 您的 吩咐，我们 去看 9 床 了。刚才
Wāng lǎoshī, ànzhào nín de fēnfu, wǒmen qù kàn jiǔ chuáng le. Gāngcái

他又吐血 了，肚子 很 疼，面色 苍白，四肢 发冷，全身
tā yòu tù xiě le, dùzi hěn téng, miànsè cāngbái, sìzhī fā lěng, quánshēn

出 冷汗。家属 很 紧张，很 着急。我们 说 李强 的 出血
chū lěnghàn. Jiāshǔ hěn jǐnzhāng, hěn zháojí. Wǒmen shuō Lǐ Qiáng de chū xiě

很 严重，可能 会 引起 胃穿孔，必须 马上 转到 外科
hěn yánzhòng, kěnéng huì yǐnqǐ wèichuānkǒng, bìxū mǎshàng zhuǎndào wàikē

做 手术。开始 的 时候 家属 担心 做 手术 有 危险，不
zuò shǒushù. Kāishǐ de shíhou jiāshǔ dānxīn zuò shǒushù yǒu wēixiǎn, bú

太 想 做 手术。经过 我们 的 解释，最后 她 同意 给 丈夫
tài xiǎng zuò shǒushù. Jīngguò wǒmen de jiěshì, zuìhòu tā tóngyì gěi zhàngfu

做 手术 了。白瑞蒂 现在 带 家属 去 办 转 科 手续，我们
zuò shǒushù le. Báiruìdì xiànzài dài jiāshǔ qù bàn zhuǎn kē shǒuxù, wǒmen

通知了 护士，并 和 她们 一起 做了 转 科 的 准备 工作。
tōngzhīle hùshi, bìng hé tāmen yìqǐ zuòle zhuǎn kē de zhǔnbèi gōngzuò.

您 看看 我们 还 需要 做 什么？
Nín kànkan wǒmen hái xūyào zuò shénme?

注释

1. 胃溃疡

胃黏膜发生溃烂的疾病，症状是饭前、饭后上腹部疼痛、恶心、呕吐，有时有嗳气、吐酸水。

Gastric ulcer is the ulceration developed in gastric mucosa. The symptoms include pain in the upper abdomen, nausea and vomiting before and/or after meals, as well as occasional belching and throwing up sour liquid.

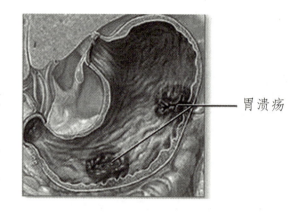

胃溃疡

2. 潜血

又称隐（yǐn）血，是指肉眼看不到、显微镜也无法观察到，只有用化学方法才可能测出来的出血。大便潜血阳性说明消化道内有出血情况。

The other name for "潜血" is "隐血". It refers to bleeding that cannot be seen by naked eyes, nor even under microscope. The bleeding can only be detected by chemical tests. If blood is positive in stool, it indicates hemorrhage of internal digestive tract.

3. 要马上转到外科做手术。

临床上某科室收治病人后，由于病情变化或治疗方案改变，需要转到其他科室做相应的检查和治疗。本课中患者因胃溃疡合并胃出血来到消化内科住院，由于出血严重且有穿孔的危险，危及生命，急需转到外科进行手术治疗。

Clinically, after a patient is admitted to one department, he sometimes needs to be transferred to other departments to receive treatment due to the change of his condition or original plan of treatment. In this lesson, the patient was originally admitted to the internal digestive department due to gastric ulcer with hemorrhage. But due to his severe bleeding and the danger of perforation, which would threaten his life, it is urgent for him to be transferred to the surgery department for operation.

4. 不做手术不行吗？［不 v. (+ O.) + 不行吗？］

这是口语中常用的双重否定式疑问句，意思跟"一定要做手术吗"差不多。当说话人不太想做句子中"v. (O.)"的动作或事情，但又不知道不做行不行时，常用这种问句。如：

This is an interrogation with a double negative form, commonly used in spoken Chinese, which means almost the same as "一定要做手术吗". When the speaker is not willing to do the action ("v. (O.)"), but is not sure if it is alright not to do it, he asks this question. e.g.

（1）不转到外科不行吗？

（2）不做 CT 检查不行吗？

5. 内科的治疗方法

指不做手术、用药物进行治疗的方法。又称"保守治疗"，是相对于外科手术治疗来说的。

The theraphy of internal medicine is also called "保守治疗" (conservative treatment), this therapy treats patients with no surgical operation, but with medicines only.

四 练习

（一）课堂练习

1. 听与读

胃痛	潜血	手续
胃穿孔	潜血阳性	办手续
胃出血	潜血呈阳性	办转科手续
胃溃疡	大便检查潜血阳性	办转院手续

吐血不止	手术
大口吐血	做手术
面色苍白	进行外科的手术治疗
四肢发冷	接受内科的治疗方法

2. 替换与扩展

（1）以前患过<u>胃溃疡</u>。

　　肺炎
　　哮喘
　　胆囊炎
　　胃出血

（2）马上把他转到<u>住院部</u>。

　　呼吸内科
　　消化内科
　　外科
　　皮肤科

第七课　要马上转到外科做手术

（3）我带你去办转科手续。

出院
住院
转院

（4）他面色苍白。

唇指发绀
呼吸急促
额部冒冷汗
吐血不止

（5）他大口吐血的情况还没好转。

皮肤过敏　　已经好转
呼吸困难　　有些好转
上腹疼痛　　没有那么严重了
肺部感染　　还是很严重

（6）不做手术不行吗？

拍X光片
用抗生素
做支气管造影
输液

97

3. 口语练习：参考使用下列词语看图对话

场景提示：实习生和病人家属的对话。一个患胃溃疡的病人再次吐血，腹部剧痛。根据指导医生的吩咐，实习生说服病人家属同意马上把病人转到外科做手术。

胃溃疡　吐血　胃出血　胃穿孔　危险　接受　手术　办转科手续

（二）课外练习

1. 看汉字，写拼音

胃溃疡_____　　潜血_____　　苍白_____

胃出血_____　　手续_____　　吩咐_____

胃穿孔_____　　转科_____　　既然_____

2. 看拼音，根据生词表写汉字

shǒushù_____　　shīqù_____　　wēixiǎn_____　　bàn_____

ménzhěn_____　　sìzhī_____　　miànsè_____　　zhǐ_____

3. 词语搭配（每个词语只能用一次）

做	门诊
止	家属
办	手术
失去	胃溃疡
吩咐	治疗
看	手续
患	血
接受	机会

4. 选择合适的词语填空（每个词语只能用一次）

门诊　危险　接受　止　潜血　四肢　手术　办　吩咐　失去

（1）5床昨天着凉后突然咳嗽不_____。

（2）我妈妈是昨天下午从_____转到住院部的。

（3）6床现在的情况比较危险，马上转到外科做_____吧。

（4）卡奇，快去通知病人马上转科，太迟会_____手术的机会。

（5）他面色苍白，_____发冷，全身出冷汗。

（6）按照汪医生的_____，我们把病人转到内科了。

（7）我带你去_____转科手续。

（8）家属同意_____手术治疗了。

（9）大便检查结果出来了，_____阳性。

（10）做手术会不会有_____？

5. 根据问句写出合适的应答句

（1）指导医生：9床住院前的大便检查结果怎么样？

　　　实 习 生：_____。

（2）指导医生：9床的门诊诊断是什么？

　　　实 习 生：_____。

（3）指导医生：那位胃出血病人现在面色怎么样？

　　　实 习 生：_____。

（4）指导医生：胃溃疡可能会引起哪些危险的情况？

　　　实 习 生：_____。

（5）指导医生：胃出血情况很严重的时候，应该怎么办？

　　　实 习 生：_____。

6. 完成下列对话

汪医生：卡奇，看过9床了吗？

卡　奇：按照您的_____，去看过了。

汪医生：情况有没有好转？

卡　奇：没有，家属说他又_____了。

汪医生：病人面色怎么样？

卡　奇：我们看见他_____。

汪医生：四肢_____？

卡　奇：跟刚来的时候一样，没有好转。

汪医生：嗯，严重的胃出血可能会引起_____。

卡　奇：那是不是很危险？

汪医生：是，所以要马上转到外科做_____。

卡　奇：好，我带家属去办_____吧。

7. 口语练习：复述成段表达的内容

向指导医生汇报病人的情况

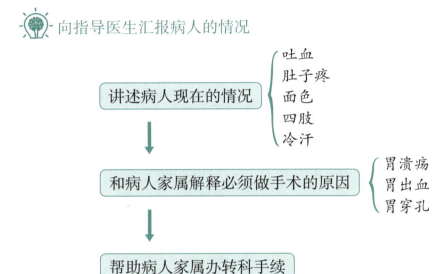

8. 节奏汉语

胃溃疡

面色苍白肚子疼，
四肢发冷出冷汗，
大口吐血胃出血，
情况严重胃穿孔，
大便检查潜血阳性，
快快转到外科做手术。

9. 写作练习：把课文的第一个对话改成对病人情况的叙述

常用专业词语

消化性胃溃疡	xiāohuàxìng wèikuìyáng	peptic gastric ulcer
顽固性胃溃疡	wángùxìng wèikuìyáng	refractory gastric ulcer
胃镜检查	wèijìng jiǎnchá	gastric endoscopy
胃肠道黏膜	wèichángdào niánmó	mucus of gastrointestinal tract
幽门螺杆菌感染	yōumén luógǎnjūn gǎnrǎn	helicobacter pylori infection
抗溃疡药	kàngkuìyáng yào	antiulcer drug
西咪替丁	xīmītìdīng	cimetidine
雷尼替丁	léinítìdīng	ranitidine

第八课　不能太激动

（心血管内科—冠心病）

扫码听

学习目标和重难点：
1. 与冠心病相关的词语
2. 向病人了解冠心病发作时的情况及发作原因
3. 指导医生向实习生分析病人的情况

一　生词

1.	血管	xuèguǎn	名	blood vessel
2.	彩票	cǎipiào	名	lottery
3.	中奖	zhòng jiǎng		to win a prize in a lottery
4.	含	hán	动	to keep in mouth
5.	硝酸甘油	xiāosuāngānyóu	名	nitroglycerin
6.	心前区	xīnqiánqū	名	pericardial region
7.	情绪	qíngxù	名	mood
8.	类似	lèisì	动	to be similar to
9.	劳累	láolèi	形	tired, overworked
10.	高血压	gāoxuèyā	名	hypertension
11.	冠心病	guānxīnbìng	名	coronary artery disease
12.	心音	xīnyīn	名	cardiac sound
13.	杂音	záyīn	名	murmur

103

14. 胆固醇	dǎngùchún	名	cholesterol
15. 甘油三酯	gānyóusānzhǐ	名	triglyceride
16. 胸片	xiōngpiàn	名	X-ray film
17. 心电图	xīndiàntú	名	electrocardiogram
18. 窦性心律	dòuxìng xīnlǜ		sinus rhythm
19. 心肌	xīnjī	名	cardiac muscle
20. 项	xiàng	量	item
21. 心绞痛	xīnjiǎotòng	名	angina

三 课文

人物： 指导 医生——谢 小平
rénwù: zhǐdǎo yīshēng Xiè Xiǎopíng

实习生——卡奇
shíxíshēng Kǎqí

护士——郭兰
hùshi Guō Lán

心血管 内科 20床 病人——钱冬明（男，65 岁）
xīnxuèguǎn nèikē èrshí chuáng bìngrén Qián Dōngmíng (nán, liùshíwǔ suì)

病人 家属——钱 永兴（钱 冬明 的儿子）
bìngrén jiāshǔ Qián Yǒngxīng (Qián Dōngmíng de érzi)

第八课　不能太激动

1. 会话

钱永兴：爸爸，告诉您一个好消息，您买的 彩票 中了
　　　　Bàba, gàosu nín yí ge hǎo xiāoxi, nín mǎi de cǎipiào zhòngle

　　　　一等奖，500 万 啊！
　　　　yīděngjiǎng, wǔbǎi wàn a!

钱冬明：一等奖？ 500 万？ 真的吗？ 啊！ 我 中 大奖
　　　　Yīděngjiǎng? Wǔbǎi wàn? Zhēnde ma? À! Wǒ zhòng dàjiǎng

　　　　了！我，我，哎哟……
　　　　le! Wǒ, wǒ, āiyō……

钱永兴：爸爸！爸爸！您怎么了？
　　　　Bàba! Bàba! Nín zěnme le?

　　　　护士！医生！快来人啊！
　　　　Hùshi! Yīshēng! Kuài lái rén a!

卡　奇：钱 爷爷，您是这里疼 吗？（钱　冬明　点头）
　　　　Qián yéye, nín shì zhèli téng ma?（Qián Dōngmíng diǎn tóu）

　　　　护士，快 给他含 硝酸甘油 片！
　　　　Hùshi, kuài gěi tā hán xiāosuāngānyóu piàn!

郭　兰：好。来，快 含上。
　　　　Hǎo. Lái, kuài hánshang.

（谢 医生 跑进 病房）
（Xiè yīshēng pǎojìn bìngfáng）

卡　奇：谢老师，20 床 心前区 疼痛 又 发作了，刚刚
　　　　Xiè lǎoshī, èrshí chuáng xīnqiánqū téngtòng yòu fāzuò le, gānggāng

給他含了 硝酸甘油 片。
gěi tā hánle xiāosuāngānyóu piàn.

谢小平: 好。钱爷爷，您现在舒服点儿了吗？
Hǎo. Qián yéye, nín xiànzài shūfu diǎnr le ma?

钱冬明: 舒服多了。刚才儿子告诉我彩票中了大奖，
Shūfu duō le. Gāngcái érzi gàosu wǒ cǎipiào zhòngle dàjiǎng,

太高兴了，结果胸口又疼了。
tài gāoxìng le, jiéguǒ xiōngkǒu yòu téng le.

谢小平: 哦，您以后可要注意了，情绪不能太激动。
Ò, nín yǐhòu kě yào zhùyì le, qíngxù bù néng tài jīdòng.

钱冬明: 唉，人老了，身体没用了，连太高兴也不
Ài, rén lǎo le, shēntǐ méi yòng le, lián tài gāoxìng yě bù

行啊。
xíng a.

2. 会话

谢小平: 钱爷爷，您现在这儿还疼吗？
Qián yéye, nín xiànzài zhèr hái téng ma?

钱冬明: 不疼了。
Bù téng le.

谢小平: 刚才疼痛持续了多长时间？
Gāngcái téngtòng chíxùle duō cháng shíjiān?

卡奇: 大概十分钟吧。他住院这三天，每天都
Dàgài shí fēnzhōng ba. Tā zhù yuàn zhè sān tiān, měi tiān dōu

第八课　不能太激动

会 发作 三四 次。
huì fāzuò sān-sì cì.

谢小平：以前 发生过 类似 的 情况 吗？
　　　　Yǐqián fāshēngguo lèisì de qíngkuàng ma?

钱冬明：两 年 前 发生过。那 时 疼 得 不 太 厉害，持续
　　　　Liǎng nián qián fāshēngguo. Nà shí téng de bú tài lìhai, chíxù

大概 三四 分钟，一个 星期 发作 两三 次。
dàgài sān-sì fēnzhōng, yí ge xīngqī fāzuò liǎng-sān cì.

谢小平：多 在 什么 情况 下 发作？
　　　　Duō zài shénme qíngkuàng xià fāzuò?

明钱冬：一般 是 劳累 或者 情绪 激动 的 时候，休息 后
　　　　Yìbān shì láolèi huòzhě qíngxù jīdòng de shíhou, xiūxi hòu

就 不 疼 了。
jiù bù téng le.

谢小平：您的病 一定要 注意 情绪，不能 太 激动。您
　　　　Nín de bìng yídìng yào zhùyì qíngxù, bù néng tài jīdòng. Nín

躺下，我 给 您 听听 心 和 肺 吧。
tǎngxia, wǒ gěi nín tīngting xīn hé fèi ba.

卡　奇：谢老师，他得的是 什么 病 啊？
　　　　Xiè lǎoshī, tā dé de shì shénme bìng a?

谢小平：你 跟 我 到 办公室，我们 分析分析。
　　　　Nǐ gēn wǒ dào bàngōngshì, wǒmen fēnxi fēnxi.

3. 成段表达（谢医生对卡奇说）

20床有三年的高血压病史，他的父亲也有冠心病。刚才听诊发现他心音有力，没听到杂音。血常规检查发现他的胆固醇和甘油三酯都比较高；胸片没发现心、肺异常。心前区出现疼痛时，心电图检查结果是窦性心律、心肌缺血。如果能及时含硝酸甘油片，疼痛可在几分钟内消失，疼痛消失后心电图可恢复正常。根据这位病人的病史、体征及各项检查结果，他得的是冠心病、心绞痛。

三 注释

1. 快含上（硝酸甘油片）

这里的"上"跟在某些动词后面做补语，有时候表示由低处到高处的方向，有时候表示有了结果或达到目的等。这里是后一种意思，即要使硝酸甘油片含进病人的嘴里。如：

"上", placed after some verbs is a complement. Used this way, it can have two meanings: direction from a lower place to a higher place; having had a result or achieved a goal. The second meaning is used here: to place the nitroglycerin under the patient's tongue. e.g.

（1）快拿上化验单去检查大便。（使化验单拿在手里）

（2）快给病人输上液。

2. 心前区

是心脏在身体表面投影的位置。

Pericardial region is the surface projection of the heart in body.

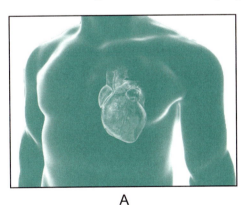
A

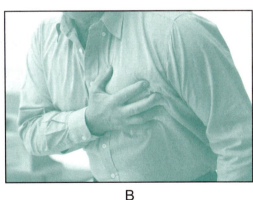
B

3. 连太高兴也不行啊。（连……也……）

这是一种强调句式。"连"和"也"之间是要强调的成分，"也"有时候也可以用"都"。如：

This is one way to show emphasis. Between "连" and "也" is the part to be emphasized. "也" is sometimes replaced by "都". e.g.

（1）连太晚睡觉也会对身体不好啊。
（2）连情绪太激动也会刺激心脏。
（3）连情绪激动都会引起心脏病发作。

4. 多在什么情况下发作？

医生了解病情的常用语，目的在于了解疾病发生的原因和诱因。

It is a usual expression used when a doctor wants to understand the conditions of a patient. The purpose is to find out the cause and incentive of the disease.

5. 卡　奇：谢老师，他得的是什么病？
　　谢小平：你跟我到办公室，我们分析分析。

一般情况下，医生不能在病人面前讨论该患者的病情，以免引起病人情绪的波动而加重病情，所以谢医生要卡奇到办公室讨论。

Normally, it is considered inappropriate to discuss a patient's state of illness in the presence of the patient, to avoid causing an anxious state of mind on the patient's part, and in turn aggravate his condition. For this reason, Dr. Xie demands that the discussion be held in the office.

6. 甘油三酯

又叫脂肪、三酯甘油，由一分子甘油和三分子脂肪酸脱水脂化而成。食物中的脂肪都是甘油三酯，进入人体后90％由肠道吸收。

Triglyceride is also called fat, synthesis of one molecule glycerin and three molecules fatty acid of esterification with dehydration. The fat in food is mainly glycerin, 90% of which is absorbed from intestine after entering the human body.

7. 窦性心律

是窦房结发出激动所形成的心律。窦房结是正常心脏的起搏点，位于右心房与上腔静脉交接处的心外膜下，细而长。窦性心律包括正常窦性心律、窦性心动过缓、窦性心动过速、窦性心律不齐及窦房结内游走性心律等。

Sinus rhythm is one kind of rhythms formed by the excited sinoatrial node. The sinoatrial node is long ellipse, located in the wall of the connection of the right atrium and superior vein and acts as a pacemaker. Sinus rhythm includes the normal sinus rhythm, sinus bradycardia, sinus tachycardia, sinus arrhythmia and wandering pacemaker within sinoatrial node and so on.

四 练习

（一）课堂练习

1. 听与读

| 心前区 | 心音 | 杂音 | 心肌 |
| 心前区疼痛 | 心音有力 | 心肺听诊有杂音 | 心肌缺血 |

高血压	胆固醇	硝酸甘油
心绞痛	甘油三酯	硝酸甘油片
冠心病	胆固醇和甘油三酯都增高	含硝酸甘油片
		快给他含硝酸甘油片

心电图

心电图检查

心电图检查结果

心电图检查结果是窦性心律

2. 替换与扩展

（1）2床心前区疼痛又发作了。

胸口	疼
血压	升高
情绪	激动

（2）这是硝酸甘油片，快含上。

血常规化验单	拿
心电图检查结果	写
办住院手续的钱	带

（3）连太高兴也不行。

太激动	会引起血压升高
呼吸	急促了
心肌缺血的症状	消失了
吃解痉止痛药	没有好转

（4）A：疼痛持续了多长时间？
　　 B：大概10分钟吧。

腹泻	大约两三天
高烧	一周左右
咳嗽	有半个月了
这种症状	差不多一年

第八课　不能太激动

（5）多在什么情况下发作？

> 呕吐
> 胸口痛
> 拉水样便
> 出现这些症状

（6）您的病一定要注意情绪，不能太激动。

> 注意休息　　　　　　　　劳累
> 少吃高胆固醇食物　　　　抽烟
> 注意饮食　　　　　　　　暴饮暴食
> 经常锻炼身体　　　　　　老是坐着躺着

3. 口语练习：交际活动

全班分为 A、B 两组，A 组看附录一，B 组看附录二，准备好后每次各组随机抽取一人进行有信息差的对话。

（二）课外练习

1. 看汉字，写拼音

血管_____　　硝酸甘油_____　　情绪_____

胆固醇_____　　甘油三酯_____　　窦性心律_____

冠心病_____　　心绞痛_____　　心肌_____

2. 看拼音，根据生词表写汉字

xiōngpiàn_____　　záyīn_____　　gāoxuèyā_____　　hán_____

lèisì＿＿＿＿　　láolèi＿＿＿＿　　xīndiàntú＿＿＿＿　　xiàng＿＿＿＿

cǎipiào＿＿＿＿　　zhòng jiǎng＿＿＿＿　　xīnqiánqū＿＿＿＿　　xīnyīn＿＿＿＿

3. 选择合适的词语填空，每个词语只能用一次

> 心绞痛　心血管　心肌　劳累　心前区　胆固醇
> 冠心病　甘油三酯　杂音　心电图　硝酸甘油片

（1）3床今天胸口又疼了，你给他做＿＿＿＿检查了吗？

（2）3床的心电图检查结果是心肌缺血，能诊断为＿＿＿＿吗？

（3）要不要把8床转到＿＿＿＿内科？

（4）你给2床含＿＿＿＿了吗？

（5）给病人听诊时，你听到＿＿＿＿了吗？

（6）5床的＿＿＿＿和＿＿＿＿都比较高，他得的是不是冠心病？

（7）心电图检查发现有＿＿＿＿缺血，可以诊断为冠心病吗？

（8）胸痛时心电图检查有心肌缺血，这种疼痛叫作＿＿＿＿。

（9）冠心病病人的疼痛常常发生在＿＿＿＿。

（10）冠心病病人不能太＿＿＿＿。

4. 根据病人的情况写出合适的问句

（1）病人手按着心前区说："哎哟，疼死了，疼死了……"

　　实习生：＿＿＿＿＿＿＿＿＿＿＿＿＿＿＿＿＿＿？

（2）病人含了一会儿硝酸甘油片。

　　实习生：＿＿＿＿＿＿＿＿＿＿＿＿＿＿＿＿＿＿？

（3）病人说以前发生过类似的疼痛。

　　　实习生：_____？

5. 完成下列对话

　　实习生：谢老师，20床的各项检查结果都出来了。

　　医　生：你先说说_____检查的结果吧。

　　实习生：胆固醇和_____都比较高。

　　医　生：胸片呢？

　　实习生：没有发现异常。

　　医　生：心前区疼痛时的心电图结果是什么？

　　实习生：_____心律，心肌_____。

　　医　生：听诊的情况呢？

　　实习生：_____有力，没听到_____。

　　医　生：根据各项检查结果，病人得的是_____、心绞痛。

6. 口语练习：复述成段表达的内容

指导医生向实习生分析病人的情况

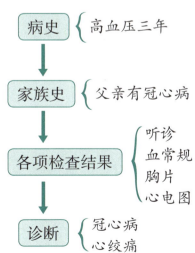

7. 节奏汉语

> **冠心病、心绞痛**
>
> 高血压病史已三年，
> 劳累过度、情绪激动，
> 心前区疼痛又发作，
> 心肺检查会发现，
> 心音有力无杂音，
> 血常规检查胆固醇，
> 甘油三酯都比较高，
> 胸片心、肺无异常，
> 心前区疼痛查心电图，
> 窦性心律和心肌缺血。
> 及时口含硝酸甘油，
> 疼痛消失恢复正常。

8. 写作练习：把课文的第二个对话改成对病人情况的叙述

常用专业词语

心房	xīnfáng	atrium
心室	xīnshì	ventricle
动脉粥样硬化	dòngmài zhōuyàng yìnghuà	atherosclerosis
二尖瓣	èrjiānbàn	bicuspid valve
收缩压	shōusuōyā	systolic pressure
舒张压	shūzhāngyā	diastolic pressure
心肌梗死	xīnjī gěngsǐ	myocardial infarction
心律失常	xīnlǜ shīcháng	arrhythmia
心内膜炎	xīnnèimóyán	endocarditis
心包炎	xīnbāoyán	pericarditis

第九课　快把病人转到心血管内科吧
（心血管内科—心肌梗死）

扫码听

学习目标和重难点：
1. 与心肌梗死相关的词语
2. 给老年心肌梗死病人做检查
3. 向另一位实习生讲述有些老年心肌梗死病人容易误诊的原因

一　生词

1.	下	xià	动	to draw, to deduce
2.	结论	jiélùn	名	conclusion
3.	测	cè	动	to take
4.	脉搏	màibó	名	pulse
5.	毫米汞柱	háomǐ-gǒngzhù		mmHg
6.	清晰	qīngxī	形	clear
7.	瓣膜	bànmó	名	valve
8.	病理性	bìnglǐxìng	形	pathological
9.	触诊	chùzhěn	动	to palpate
10.	胀	zhàng	动	to distend
11.	腹肌	fùjī	名	abdominal muscle
12.	反跳痛	fǎntiàotòng	名	rebound tenderness
13.	明显	míngxiǎn	形	evident, obvious, distinct
14.	怀疑	huáiyí	动	to suspect

15. 心肌梗死	xīnjī gěngsǐ		myocardial infarction
16. 赶紧	gǎnjǐn	副	without delay
17. 误诊	wùzhěn	动	to misdiagnose
18. 考虑	kǎolǜ	动	to think over, to consider
19. 临床	línchuáng	动	to be at the sicked providing medical services
20. 表现	biǎoxiàn	动	to manifest

二 课文

人物： 指导 医生——李 英
rénwù: zhǐdǎo yīshēng　　Lǐ Yīng

实习生——白瑞蒂、莎娜
shíxíshēng　Báiruìdì、Shānà

消化 内科 6 床 病人——吴心（女，72 岁）
xiāohuà nèikē liù chuáng bìngrén　Wú Xīn (nǚ, qīshí'èr suì)

病人 家属——吴雪（吴心的女儿）
bìngrén jiāshǔ　Wú Xuě (Wú Xīn de nǚ'ér)

1. 会话

（在办公室）
（zài bàngōngshì）

李 英： 白瑞蒂，新 来了 一位 病人，你 看了 没有？ 她
　　　　Báiruìdì, xīn láile yí wèi bìngrén, nǐ kànle méiyǒu? Tā

怎么样？
zěnmeyàng?

白瑞蒂： 我 刚才在 忙，还没去看她。听说 是县医院
Wǒ gāngcái zài máng, hái méi qù kàn tā. Tīngshuō shì xiàn yīyuàn

转来 的 急性 肠胃炎 病人。
zhuǎnlái de jíxìng chángwèiyán bìngrén.

李 英： 我们 先别 下 结论，去看看再说 吧。
Wǒmen xiān bié xià jiélùn, qù kànkan zài shuō ba.

（俩人进病房）
(liǎ rén jìn bìngfáng)

吴 雪： 大夫，刚才我 妈妈 肚子
Dàifu, gāngcái wǒ māma dùzi

又 疼 了。
yòu téng le.

李 英： 呕吐 没有？
Ǒutù méiyǒu?

吴 雪： 吐了，她还 觉得 恶心。
Tù le, tā hái juéde ěxin.

李 英： （对 白瑞蒂）测过 体温、脉搏、呼吸、血压 了吗？
(duì Báiruìdì) Cèguo tǐwēn, màibó, hūxī, xuèyā le ma?

白瑞蒂： 护士 测过了。（看病历）体温 36.5 度， 脉搏 每
Hùshi cèguo le. (kàn bìnglì) Tǐwēn sānshíliù diǎn wǔ dù, màibó měi

分钟 80 次，呼吸 每 分钟 24 次，血压 120/90
fēnzhōng bāshí cì, hūxī měi fēnzhōng èrshísì cì, xuèyā yìbǎi èrshí/jiǔshí

毫米汞柱。
háomǐ-gǒngzhù.

第九课　快把病人转到心血管内科吧

李　英：白瑞蒂，你给她做心肺听诊吧。
Báiruìdì, nǐ gěi tā zuò xīnfèi tīngzhěn ba.

白瑞蒂：好。双肺听诊呼吸音清晰，心律整齐，各瓣膜听诊区没听到病理性杂音。
Hǎo. Shuāng fèi tīngzhěn hūxīyīn qīngxī, xīnlǜ zhěngqí, gè bànmó tīngzhěnqū méi tīngdào bìnglǐxìng záyīn.

李　英：再给她的腹部做触诊。
Zài gěi tā de fùbù zuò chùzhěn.

白瑞蒂：好的。腹胀，但腹肌不紧张。
Hǎo de. Fùzhàng, dàn fùjī bù jǐnzhāng.

吴　心：这儿还有点儿疼。
Zhèr hái yǒudiǎnr téng.

白瑞蒂：腹部压痛和反跳痛都不明显。
Fùbù yātòng hé fǎntiàotòng dōu bù míngxiǎn.

李　英：在县医院有没有做过心电图？
Zài xiàn yīyuàn yǒu méiyǒu zuòguo xīndiàntú?

吴　雪：没做过。
Méi zuòguo.

李　英：（对白瑞蒂）我怀疑不是急性肠胃炎，给她查查心电图吧。
(duì Báiruìdì) Wǒ huáiyí bú shì jíxìng chángwèiyán, gěi tā chácha xīndiàntú ba.

（半小时后）
(bàn xiǎoshí hòu)

白瑞蒂：李老师，心电图结果出来了，是心肌梗死。
Lǐ lǎoshī, xīndiàntú jiéguǒ chūlai le, shì xīnjī gěngsǐ.

李　英：赶紧把病人转到心血管内科吧。
Gǎnjǐn bǎ bìngrén zhuǎndào xīnxuèguǎn nèikē ba.

白瑞蒂：好。
Hǎo.

2. 成段表达　（白瑞蒂对莎娜说）

莎娜，我们病房今天把一位病人转到心血管
Shānà, wǒmen bìngfáng jīntiān bǎ yí wèi bìngrén zhuǎndào xīnxuèguǎn
内科了。她是从县医院转来的，县医院的诊断是
nèikē le. Tā shì cóng xiàn yīyuàn zhuǎnlai de, xiàn yīyuàn de zhěnduàn shì
急性肠胃炎。我们科李英老师根据病人的各种情况
jíxìng chángwèiyán. Wǒmen kē Lǐ Yīng lǎoshī gēnjù bìngrén de gè zhǒng qíngkuàng
怀疑是急性心肌梗死，心电图检查的结果真的是这样。
huáiyí shì jíxìng xīnjī gěngsǐ, xīndiàntú jiǎnchá de jiéguǒ zhēn de shì zhèyàng.
我问李老师为什么会怀疑县医院误诊，李老师告诉
Wǒ wèn Lǐ lǎoshī wèishénme huì huáiyí xiàn yīyuàn wùzhěn, Lǐ lǎoshī gàosu
我，对病人做诊断时还要考虑病人的年龄。这是
wǒ, duì bìngrén zuò zhěnduàn shí hái yào kǎolǜ bìngrén de niánlíng. Zhè shì
个72岁的病人，这个年龄容易得心肌梗死。老年
ge qīshí'èr suì de bìngrén, zhège niánlíng róngyì dé xīnjī gěngsǐ. Lǎonián

急性心肌梗死的 临床 表现 与 中青年 有 明显 不同，

中青年 常常 表现 为 心绞痛，老年 心梗 有时候 的 主要 表现 是 上 腹部 疼痛、恶心、呕吐、腹胀 等，与 急性 肠胃炎 的 症状 类似，所以 容易 被 误诊。这 种 情况 占 老年 心肌 梗死 的 30%。

注释

1. 下

在这里，"下"是"做出"的意思，常带名词宾语。如下结论、下决心、下定义。

Here "下" means to draw (conclusion), to make (decision) etc. It is often followed by an object noun. e.g. "下结论""下决心""下定义".

2. 每分钟……次

中间加上数字，是某种单位名称的读法，但书写形式是 ×次/分钟。如"每分钟 90 次"写作"90 次/分"。这与英语的表达方式不同。

The number can be inserted in between, which is a way to express a certain unit, written as "×次/分钟". For example "每分钟 90 次" is written "90 次/分". Note that this way of expression is different from English.

3. 触诊

触诊是临床医学的一种检查方法，即医生用手指或触觉来进行体格检查。通过触、摸、按、压被检查局部，以了解体表（皮肤及皮下组织等）及脏器（心、肺、肝、脾、肾、子宫等）的物理特征，如大小、轮廓、硬度、触痛、移动度及液动感等，通过这些直观的依据可帮助医生判断检查部位及脏器是否发生病变。

Palpation is a method of examination in clinical which the doctor performs a physical examination with fingers or sense of touch. Medical doctors may palpate body parts through touching and pressing to check for physical characteristics of the body surface (skin and subcutaneous tissue, etc.) and organs (heart, lung, liver, spleen, kidney, uterus, etc.), such as size, shape, hardness, tenderness, mobility, fluid movement and so on. These intuitive basis can help doctors determine whether the examination part and viscera are diseased or not.

4. 反跳痛

医学名词，指医生给病人触诊时，在病人痛处轻轻按压，然后迅速抬手，在抬手的一瞬间，病人若有明显的痛感，便叫作"反跳痛"。

"反跳痛" (rebound pain) is a medical term. When a doctor makes palpation for the patient, he presses gently the place where the patient feels pain, then swiftly raises his hand. If at that very moment the patient feels obvious pain, this phenomenon is called "反跳痛".

5. 心肌梗死

病名。冠状动脉被血栓堵塞,造成部分心肌严重缺血而坏死。又叫心肌梗死,简称心梗。

A condition characterized by the formation of a dense wedge-shaped block of dead tissue in the myocardium following an interruption to its blood supply. Heart tissue dies when deprived of oxygen and the patient has a "heart attack". If the interruption to the blood supply is towards the end of a coronary artery, the heart attack may be very mild. If it is towards the beginning of the artery, however, the amount of tissue affected maybe large and the heart attack is severe. Its full name is "心肌梗死". The abbreviation is "心梗".

四 练习

(一)课堂练习

1. 听与读

听诊	心肺听诊	腹部触诊	肠胃炎
触诊	双肺听诊	胸部触诊	急性肠胃炎
误诊	各瓣膜听诊区	背部触诊	慢性肠胃炎

压痛	呼吸音清晰	胃肠道症状	心律整齐
反跳痛	呼吸杂音	呼吸道症状	心律不齐
胀痛	病理性杂音	消化道症状	腹肌紧张

临床表现	脉搏80次/分	心肌梗死
医学表现	呼吸24次/分	急性心肌梗死
		老年急性心肌梗死

2. 替换与扩展

（1）你给她做心肺听诊吧。

腹部触诊
背部触诊
双肺听诊

（2）护士刚才给她测过体温了。

脉搏
血压
呼吸

（3）病人是心肌梗死，快把病人转到心血管内科吧。

急性肺炎	呼吸内科
急性胰腺炎	消化内科
胃穿孔	外科

（4）我怀疑病人不是急性肠胃炎。

县医院误诊
他的诊断有问题
6床是心肌梗死
那个病人的肺有问题

（5）对病人做诊断时，还要考虑病人的年龄。

给病人开药	病人的身体情况
给病人开药	病人对这种药会不会过敏
让病人做CT检查	病人的经济状况
让病人拍X光片	病人最近是不是多次拍片

3. **口语练习：参考使用下列词语看图对话**

　　场景提示：大夫跟病人的对话。病人告诉大夫说肚子又疼了，大夫询问病情，并给病人做腹部触诊，一边触压病人腹部，一边与病人就痛与不痛的问题进行对话。

　　疼　呕吐　腹部触诊　腹胀　腹肌　压痛　反跳痛　明显

（二）课外练习

1. 看汉字，写拼音

触诊_____　　　误诊_____　　　腹肌_____

临床_____　　　瓣膜_____　　　脉搏_____

病理性_____　　反跳痛_____　　心肌梗死_____

2. 看拼音，根据生词表写汉字

zhàng_____　　biǎoxiàn_____　　kǎolǜ_____

míngxiǎn_____　qīngxī_____　　jiélùn_____

3. 词语搭配（每个词只能用一次）

测	胀
考虑	结论
下	表现
腹	病人的年龄
反跳痛	杂音
腹肌	脉搏
病理性	明显
临床	紧张

4. 选择合适的词语填空（每个词语只能用一次）

结论　触诊　脉搏　清晰　反跳痛　考虑　心肌梗死　胀　测　病理性

（1）白瑞蒂，刚才你给病人做检查的时候，有没有发现他腹　　　　？

（2）3床有明显的上腹痛，做腹部　　　　了吗？

（3）在心电图检查结果出来以前，还不好下　　　　。

（4）在心脏听诊区可听到　　　　杂音。

（5）病人的　　　　是76次/分。

（6）有些老年人　　　　的症状与急性肠胃炎类似，容易被误诊。

（7）对病人做诊断时还要　　　　病人的年龄。

（8）你给病人　　　　脉搏了吗？

（9）病人肺部听诊，双肺呼吸音　　　　。

（10）我觉得这位病人的　　　　不太明显。

5. 根据问句写出合适的应答句

（1）指导医生：新转来的病人，在县医院时的诊断是什么？

　　　实 习 生：＿＿＿＿＿＿＿＿＿＿＿＿＿＿＿＿＿＿＿＿＿＿＿＿＿＿。

（2）指导医生：心电图检查的结果是什么？

　　　实 习 生：＿＿＿＿＿＿＿＿＿＿＿＿＿＿＿＿＿＿＿＿＿＿＿＿＿＿。

（3）指导医生：腹部触诊发现什么问题？

　　　实 习 生：＿＿＿＿＿＿＿＿＿＿＿＿＿＿＿＿＿＿＿＿＿＿＿＿＿＿。

（4）实 习 生：老年心肌梗死为什么容易被误诊为急性肠胃炎？

　　　指导医生：＿＿＿＿＿＿＿＿＿＿＿＿＿＿＿＿＿＿＿＿＿＿＿＿＿＿。

6. 完成下列对话

（1）医　　生：根据心电图检查的结果，您患的是＿＿＿＿＿＿＿＿＿＿。

　　　病　　人：哦，原来不是急性肠胃炎。

　　　医　　生：我们要把您转到＿＿＿＿＿＿＿＿＿＿。

　　　病　　人：我现在要做什么？

　　　医　　生：让护士带家属去办＿＿＿＿＿＿＿＿＿＿吧。

　　　病　　人：好的。谢谢医生！

（2）医　　生：白瑞蒂，＿＿＿＿＿＿＿＿＿＿病人你看过了吗？

　　　白瑞蒂：看过了。

　　　医　　生：体温、＿＿＿＿＿＿＿＿、呼吸、＿＿＿＿＿＿＿＿都测过了？

　　　白瑞蒂：＿＿＿＿＿＿＿＿＿了：＿＿＿＿＿＿＿＿36.5度，脉搏80次/分，

　　　　　　　＿＿＿＿＿＿＿＿＿24次/分，血压120/90＿＿＿＿＿＿＿＿。

医　生：做过_____听诊了吗？

白瑞蒂：做过了。_____整齐，各瓣膜听诊区没听到_____ _____。

医　生：腹部触诊呢？

白瑞蒂：腹胀，但_____不紧张，腹部压痛和_____都不明显。

医　生：县医院做过_____吗？

白瑞蒂：没有。

医　生：马上去做心电图。

白瑞蒂：好。

7. 口语练习：复述成段表达的内容

向另一位实习生讲述病人的情况

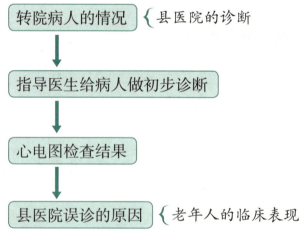

8. 节奏汉语

> **心肌梗死**
>
> 腹痛呕吐还恶心，
> 容易误诊肠胃炎。
> 病人年龄最重要，
> 临床表现有区别。
> 听诊呼吸音清晰，
> 心律整齐无杂音，
> 腹部触诊有腹胀，
> 但是腹肌不紧张。
> 压痛、反跳痛不明显，
> 心电图检查心肌梗死。

9. 写作练习：把练习6的第二个对话改成对病人情况的叙述

常用专业词语

动脉粥样硬化	dòngmài zhōuyàng yìnghuà	atherosclerosis
冠状动脉栓塞	guānzhuàng dòngmài shuānsè	coronary embolism
心力衰竭	xīnlì shuāijié	heart failure
心电监护室	xīndiàn jiānhùshì	CCH
阿托品	ātuōpǐn	atropine
美多心安	měiduōxīn'ān	betaloc, metoprololum
吗啡	mǎfēi	morphine
卡托普利	kǎtuōpǔlì	captopril
消心痛	xiāoxīntòng	isosorbide dinitrate

第十课　她是不是可以出院了？

（神经内科—脑中风）

扫码听

> 学习目标和重难点：
> 1. 与脑中风相关的词语
> 2. 了解脑中风病人的情况
> 3. 向病人家属交代脑中风病人出院后的注意事项

一　生词

1.	神经	shénjīng	名	ncrve
2.	摘要	zhāiyào	名	summary, abstract
3.	病情	bìngqíng	名	state of an illness
4.	稳定	wěndìng	形	stable
5.	安排	ānpái	动	to arrange
6.	肢体	zhītǐ	名	limb
7.	心率	xīnlǜ	名	heart rate
8.	昏迷	hūnmí	动	to be in a coma
9.	尿	niào	名	urine
10.	失禁	shī jìn		to suffer from incontinence
11.	脑出血	nǎochūxuè	名	cerebral hemorrhage
12.	血肿	xuèzhǒng	名	hematoma
13.	大脑	dànǎo	名	brain
14.	额叶	éyè	名	frontal lobe

第十课　她是不是可以出院了？

15. 热量	rèliàng	名	heat
16. 保暖	bǎo nuǎn		to keep warm
17. 降压药	jiàngyāyào	名	antihypertensive drugs
18. 头晕	tóu yūn		to feel dizzy
19. 脑中风	nǎozhòngfēng	名	apoplexy
20. 先兆	xiānzhào	名	sign, omen

二 课文

人物：　指导医生——史平
rénwù:　zhǐdǎo yīshēng　Shǐ Píng

实习生——李力、莎娜
shíxíshēng　Lǐ Lì、Shānà

神经　内科　9 床　病人——李江宁（女，68 岁）
shénjīng nèikē jiǔ chuáng bìngrén　Lǐ Jiāngníng (nǚ, liùshíbā suì)

病人　家属——王建军（李江宁的儿子）
bìngrén jiāshǔ　Wáng Jiànjūn (Lǐ Jiāngníng de érzi)

1. 会话

史　平：李力、莎娜，你们先看看9 床的病历摘要。
　　　　Lǐ Lì、Shānà, nǐmen xiān kànkan jiǔ chuáng de bìnglì zhāiyào.

李　力：好的。她是2月15日住院的，住院已经
　　　　Hǎo de. Tā shì èr yuè shíwǔ rì zhù yuàn de, zhù yuàn yǐjīng

一个月了。

史平：对，最近她的病情比较稳定。

莎娜：那她是不是可以出院了？

史平：你们先了解一下儿她的病情，然后跟我去看看她，如果检查后没什么问题，就安排她明天出院。

莎娜：好的。李力，我们一起看。

李力：好，我先念：李江宁，女，68岁。患高血压10年。2月15日喝酒后头疼、恶心、呕吐、左侧肢体不能动。

莎 娜：是不是就是左边的手和脚都不能动了？
Shì bu shì jiùshì zuǒbiān de shǒu hé jiǎo dōu bù néng dòng le?

李 力：对，你的汉语挺不错的。
Duì, nǐ de Hànyǔ tǐng búcuò de.

莎 娜：入院时测血压为 220/120 毫米汞柱，
Rù yuàn shí cè xuèyā wéi èrbǎi èrshí / yìbǎi èrshí háomǐ-gǒngzhù,

心率 108 次/分。
xīnlǜ yìbǎi líng bā cì měi fēn.

李 力：我来念：病人深昏迷，尿失禁。CT 检查
Wǒ lái niàn: bìngrén shēn hūnmí, niào shī jìn. CT jiǎnchá

确诊为脑出血，血肿位于大脑额叶，出血量
quèzhěn wéi nǎochūxuè, xuèzhǒng wèiyú dànǎo éyè, chūxuèliàng

约 20 ml。
yuē 20 háoshēng.

莎 娜：史医生，我们已经初步了解这位病人的
Shǐ yīshēng, wǒmen yǐjīng chūbù liǎojiě zhè wèi bìngrén de

情况了。
qíngkuàng le.

史 平：好，我们现在去看看她。
Hǎo, wǒmen xiànzài qù kànkan tā.

2. 成段表达 （李力对病人家属说）

您母亲明天可以出院了。出院以后要注意饮食，不要喝酒，少吃高蛋白、高脂肪、高热量的食品，要多吃豆类、水果和蔬菜。冬天注意保暖。每天坚持吃降压药，不要看到血压正常就停药。病人还要保持稳定的情绪，不能太激动。如果突然出现比较厉害的头痛、头晕、恶心、呕吐等症状，或血压突然升高，可能是脑中风的先兆，病人应该保持安静，躺下来休息。你们要尽量少搬动病人，更不能摇她的头。如果病人感觉越来越不舒服，就打120叫救护车。或者托住病人头部，几个人一起让病人保持平卧送医院治疗。

注释

1. 脑出血

   脑血管发生病变,血液流出管壁,使脑功能遭到破坏,叫做脑出血。血管硬化、血压突然上升等都能引起脑出血,发病前有头痛、头晕、麻木、抽搐等症状。也叫脑溢血。

   The lesion develops in the brain blood vessels, so blood flows out vessel walls and affects the function of the brain. Atherosclerosis or sudden rising of blood pressure and so on may cause cerebral hemorrhage. The signs are headache, dizziness, numbness and convulsion. It is also called "脑溢血".

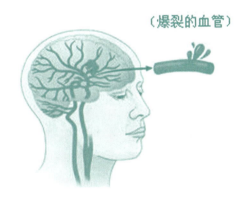

(爆裂的血管)

2. 血肿

   血管壁破裂,血液流出血管,聚积在软组织内所形成的肿块。

   Due to rupture of blood vessels, blood flows out vessels and accumulates in the soft tissue to form a mass.

3. 保暖

医生告诉病人要注意保暖，是要病人多穿衣服、多盖一些被子。

When a doctor reminds a patient to keep warm, he means the patient needs to put on enough clothes or to cover up well at night.

4. 脑中风

多由脑血栓、脑出血等引起。初起时突然头痛、眩晕，短时间内失去知觉。得病后半身不遂或截瘫，严重时很快死亡。又叫"脑卒中"，简称"中风"或"卒中"。

It is caused by brain thromboembolism or brain hemorrhage. At the first stage, the patient feels sudden headache and dizziness. The patient may even lose consciousness temporarily. After the patient falls ill, the result is hemiplegia or paraplegia. Severe case can result in death shortly afterwards. It is called "脑卒中". The abbreviation is "中风" 或 "卒中".

5. 先兆

指病人得病之前身体不适的反应。

Here "先兆" refers to the discomfort in the body felt by a patient before he falls ill.

四 练习

（一）课堂练习

1. 听与读

神经	心率	肢体	病历摘要	病情稳定
神经内科	心率正常	上肢	病史摘要	病情不稳定
神经外科	心率过慢	下肢		病情基本稳定
	心率过快	四肢	尿失禁	情绪基本稳定
			大小便失禁	情绪不稳定

昏迷	平卧	吃药	脑中风
深昏迷	让病人平卧	吃降压药	脑出血
	让病人保持平卧	要按时吃降压药	脑中风的先兆
		要坚持吃降压药	脑出血的先兆

2. 替换与扩展

（1）A：最近李江宁的病情怎么样？
　　B：最近李江宁的病情<u>基本稳定</u>。

> 不太稳定
> 已经好转
> 比较正常

（2）A：你感觉身体怎么样？
　　B：我感觉好多了，<u>心率、血压都正常了</u>。

> 头也不晕了
> 四肢也能活动了
> 病情稳定了

（3）CT检查确诊为脑出血。

脑血肿
脑梗死
脑中风

（4）出院以后要注意饮食，不要喝酒。

不要抽烟
少吃高热量、高脂肪的食品
多吃水果、蔬菜
常吃些粗粮

3. 口语练习：参考使用下列词语看图对话

场景一提示：李力和莎娜在办公室看病人李江宁入院时的病历。

心率　昏迷　失禁　脑出血　血肿　大脑额叶

第十课　她是不是可以出院了？

场景二提示：病人李江宁出院时，李力对她说回家以后要注意什么。

饮食　热量　保暖　降压药　脑中风　先兆

（二）课外练习

1. 看汉字，写拼音

神经_____　　心率_____　　昏迷_____

额叶_____　　失禁_____　　热量_____

肢体_____　　先兆_____　　血肿_____

2. 看拼音，根据生词表写汉字

bìngqíng_____　　ānpái_____　　wěndìng_____

bǎo nuǎn_____　　tóu yūn_____　　dànǎo_____

jiàngyāyào_____　　nǎozhòngfēng_____　　niào_____

3. 选择合适的词语填空（每个词语只能用一次）

> 神经内科　病情　肢体　昏迷　失禁　脑出血
> 大脑额叶　降压药　先兆　心率　稳定　血压

（1）脑CT检查病人脑内有出血症状，确诊为_____。

（2）高血压病人有脑中风的_____时，应平卧在床上。

（3）病人的左侧_____不能动。

（4）把病人安排在_____病房。

（5）神经内科9床的病人大小便_____。

（6）病人刚送到医院的时候是深_____，自己什么都不知道。

（7）这个病人_____过快，_____比较高。

（8）病人的血肿位于_____。

（9）高血压病人要按时吃_____。

（10）最近她的_____比较_____。

4. 根据病人情况写出合适的问句

（1）病人说他头痛得很厉害，恶心、呕吐。

　　实习生：_____？

（2）病人说他左边的手和脚都不能动了。

　　实习生：_____？

（3）病人家属说他妈妈大小便失禁，已经昏迷了。

　　实习生：_____？

5. 完成下列对话

（1）李力：病人入院时的情况你清楚吗？

　　莎娜：病人当时的＿＿＿＿＿很严重，血压＿＿＿＿＿＿＿，心率＿＿＿＿＿＿＿。

　　李力：病人当时是不是＿＿＿＿＿＿＿？

　　莎娜：对，而且大小便＿＿＿＿＿，左侧＿＿＿＿＿不能动。

　　李力：CT检查结果是什么？

　　莎娜：CT检查确诊为＿＿＿＿＿＿＿。

　　李力：有没有＿＿＿＿＿＿＿？

　　莎娜：有，血肿位于＿＿＿＿＿＿＿。

（2）医生：这几天你感觉怎么样？

　　病人：好多了，每天按时吃药，现在＿＿＿＿＿可以活动了。

　　医生：昨天的身体检查没有发现什么问题。＿＿＿＿＿和＿＿＿＿＿都正常。从CT片上看，脑部的＿＿＿＿＿差不多完全消失了，你明天就可以出院了。

　　病人：非常感谢你们，一个月的时间就治好了我的＿＿＿＿＿。

6. 口语练习：复述成段表达的内容

　　💡 向病人家属交代出院后的注意事项

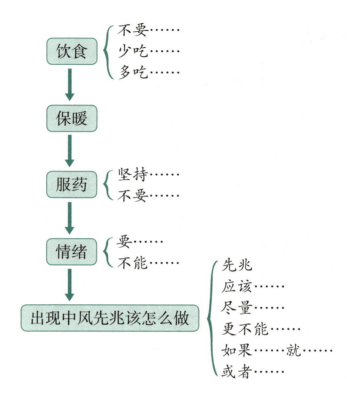

7. 节奏汉语

脑中风

病人高血压已十年，
酒后头疼又恶心，
呕吐肢体不能动。
深昏迷、尿失禁，
CT检查脑出血，
大脑额叶有血肿。
注意饮食别饮酒，
少食"三高"类食品，
多吃豆类、水果和蔬菜。
冬天特别注意要保暖，
每天坚持吃降压药。
保持稳定情绪别激动，

第十课　她是不是可以出院了？

> 如果感到头痛又头晕，
> 恶心、呕吐、血压升高，
> 可能是脑中风的先兆。
> 保持安静，平卧休息，
> 不要随意搬动病人，
> 更不要摇动她的头，
> 不舒服 120 来急救。

8. 写作练习：把练习 5 的第一个对话改成对病人情况的叙述

常用专业词语

脑震荡	nǎozhèndàng	concussion of the brain
脑硬化	nǎoyìnghuà	cerebrosclerosis, encephalosclerosis
脑炎	nǎoyán	encephalitis
脑出血	nǎochūxuè	brain hemorrhage
脑栓塞	nǎoshuānsè	cerebral embolism
脑水肿	nǎoshuǐzhǒng	brain edema, cerebral edema
脑积水	nǎojīshuǐ	hydrencephalus
脑电图	nǎodiàntú	electroencephalogram
脑病	nǎobìng	cerebrosis
脑膜炎	nǎomóyán	cerebral meningitis, encephalomeningitis

第十一课　检查结果出来了
（血液科—急性白血病）

扫码听

学习目标和重难点：
1. 与急性白血病相关的词语
2. 向病人家属了解病人的情况
3. 与指导医生讨论病人的检查结果
4. 向病人家属讲述指导医生的治疗意见

一　生词

1.	血液病	xuèyèbìng	名	blood disorder
2.	氨苄西林	ānbiànxīlín	名	ampicillin
3.	病毒唑	bìngdúzuò	名	ribavirin
4.	月经	yuèjīng	名	menstrual cycle
5.	白细胞	báixìbāo	名	white blood cell (leukocyte)
6.	红细胞	hóngxìbāo	名	red blood cell (erythrocyte)
7.	血红蛋白	xuèhóngdànbái	名	hemoglobin
8.	血小板	xuèxiǎobǎn	名	blood platelet (thrombocyte)
9.	贫血	pínxuè	名	anaemia
10.	骨髓	gǔsuǐ	名	bone marrow
11.	涂片	túpiàn	名	smear slide (biopsy)
12.	型	xíng		style
13.	象	xiàng	名	symptom, syndrome
14.	白血病	báixuèbìng	名	leukemia

第十一课 检查结果出来了

15.	非淋巴细胞	fēilínbā xìbāo		nonlymphocyte
16.	类	lèi	名	kind
17.	化疗	huàliáo	动	to chemotherapy
18.	疗程	liáochéng	名	therapy of treatment
19.	照顾	zhàogù	动	to look after
20.	效果	xiàoguǒ	名	effect
21.	移植	yízhí	动	to transplant

三 课文

人物： 指导 医生——江 海涛
rénwù: zhǐdǎo yīshēng Jiāng Hǎitāo

实习 生——卡奇
shíxíshēng Kǎqí

血液病 科19 床 病人——陈 丽敏（女，15 岁）
xuèyèbìng kē shíjiǔ chuáng bìngrén Chén Lìmǐn (nǚ, shíwǔ suì)

病人 家属——张 敏（陈 丽敏 的妈妈）
bìngrén jiāshǔ Zhāng Mǐn (Chén Lìmǐn de māma)

1. 会话

卡 奇： 张 阿姨，我是 实习生卡奇。您女儿是 昨天
Zhāng āyí, wǒ shì shíxíshēng Kǎqí. Nín nǚ'ér shì zuótiān

住 院 的 吗？以前 看过 医生 吗？
zhù yuàn de ma? Yǐqián kànguo yīshēng ma?

张　敏：对。以前在区医院
　　　　Duì. Yǐqián zài qū yīyuàn

　　　　看过，医生说是
　　　　kànguo, yīshēng shuō shì

　　　　上呼吸道炎症。
　　　　shàng hūxīdào yánzhèng.

卡　奇：那时候她有什么症状？
　　　　Nà shíhou tā yǒu shénme zhèngzhuàng?

张　敏：一个月前是面色苍白，全身无力，有时候
　　　　Yí ge yuè qián shì miànsè cāngbái, quánshēn wúlì, yǒu shíhou

　　　　头晕。
　　　　tóu yūn.

卡　奇：发热吗？
　　　　Fā rè ma?

张　敏：没有。可是半个月前开始发热，最低 37.5 度，
　　　　Méiyǒu. Kěshì bàn ge yuè qián kāishǐ fā rè, zuì dī sānshíqī diǎn wǔ dù,

　　　　最高 39 度。咳嗽，但没有痰。
　　　　zuì gāo sānshíjiǔ dù. Késou, dàn méiyǒu tán.

卡　奇：用过什么药？
　　　　Yòngguo shénme yào?

张　敏：用过氨苄西林、病毒唑。用药后不咳了，
　　　　Yòngguo ānbiànxīlín、bìngdúzuò. Yòng yào hòu bù ké le,

　　　　不过还是反复低烧，一般在 38 度左右。
　　　　búguò háishi fǎnfù dīshāo, yìbān zài sānshíbā dù zuǒyòu.

卡　奇：最近一次 月经 跟以前一样吗?
　　　　Zuìjìn yí cì yuèjīng gēn yǐqián yíyàng ma?

张　敏：不一样。以前持续五天，这次持续了八天，
　　　　Bù yíyàng. Yǐqián chíxù wǔ tiān, zhè cì chíxùle bā tiān,

　　　　出血也特别多。
　　　　chū xuè yě tèbié duō.

卡　奇：谢谢您。我去看看她入院后的检查结果
　　　　Xièxiè nín. Wǒ qù kànkan tā rù yuàn hòu de jiǎnchá jiéguǒ

　　　　出来没有。
　　　　chūlai méiyǒu.

2. 会话

卡　奇：江老师，19床的检查结果出来了。
　　　　Jiāng lǎoshī, shíjiǔ chuáng de jiǎnchá jiéguǒ chūlai le.

江海涛：血常规的结果是什么?
　　　　Xuèchángguī de jiéguǒ shì shénme?

卡　奇：白细胞 8.4 × 10^9 / L，红细胞
　　　　Báixìbāo bā diǎn sì chéng shí de jiǔcìfāng měi shēng, hóngxìbāo

　　　　1.74 × 10^{12} / L，血红蛋白
　　　　yī diǎn qī sì chéng shí de shí'èrcìfāng měi shēng, xuèhóng dànbái

　　　　57 g / L，血小板 29 × 10^9 / L。
　　　　wǔshíqī kè měi shēng, xuèxiǎobǎn èrshíjiǔ chéng shí de jiǔcìfāng měi shēng.

江海涛：这是贫血。骨髓涂片的结果呢?
　　　　Zhè shì pínxuè. Gǔsuǐ túpiàn de jiéguǒ ne?

卡　奇：是 ANLL-M₂ 型 骨髓象。
　　　　Shì ANLL-M èr xíng gǔsuǐxiàng.

江海涛：病人 入院 时我们 的初步 诊断 是急性 白血病，
　　　　Bìngrén rù yuàn shí wǒmen de chūbù zhěnduàn shì jíxìng báixuèbìng,

　　　　检查 结果 说明 这个初步 诊断 是 对 的。
　　　　jiǎnchá jiéguǒ shuōmíng zhège chūbù zhěnduàn shì duì de.

卡　奇：江 老师，ANLL 的 汉语 病 名 叫 什么？
　　　　Jiāng lǎoshī, ANLL de Hànyǔ bìng míng jiào shénme?

江海涛：叫 急性 非淋巴 细胞 白血病，是 急性 白血病 的
　　　　Jiào jíxìng fēilínbā xìbāo báixuèbìng, shì jíxìng báixuèbìng de

　　　　一个大 类。
　　　　yí ge dà lèi.

卡　奇：白血病 有 哪些主要 的 症状？
　　　　Báixuèbìng yǒu nǎxiē zhǔyào de zhèngzhuàng?

江海涛：头晕、无力、贫血、发热、出血 等。女性 病人
　　　　Tóu yūn、wúlì、pínxuè、fā rè、chū xuè děng. Nǚxìng bìngrén

　　　　月经 比以前多也很 常见。
　　　　yuèjīng bǐ yǐqián duō yě hěn chángjiàn.

3. 成段表达　（卡奇对张敏说）

张阿姨，您女儿的检查结果出来了，她得的不是上呼吸道炎症，是急性白血病，这是一种比较危险的病。刚才江医生说，您的女儿要进行化疗。请你们考虑一下儿，如果同意，第一个疗程要住院，后面的疗程可以回家。化疗期间您女儿的身体会很不舒服，感觉非常难受，还会掉头发，所以你们要多照顾她。治疗这种病花的时间比较长，一般都要好几年。您女儿年龄还小，治好的希望比较大，你们要有信心。如果化疗的效果不好，再考虑进行骨髓移植。

三 注释

1. 氨苄西林

青霉素类抗生素，用于治疗敏感细菌所致的呼吸道感染、胃肠道感染、尿路感染、软组织感染、脑膜炎、败血症、心内膜炎等。

Ampicillin is a penicillin-type antibiotics used to treat infections caused by susceptible bacteria such as respiratory tract infection, the gastrointestinal tract infection, the urinary tract infection, the soft tissue infection, meningitis, septicemia, and endocarditis.

2. 涂片

把需要检查的血、痰、分泌物等样本涂在玻璃片上，再根据要求放在显微镜下检查，以发现或排除某些疾病。

Smear is a sample, as of blood, sputum or secretion, spread on a glass slide for microscopic examination and diagnosis of diseases.

3. 急性非淋巴细胞白血病

急性白血病中的一种。白血病的症状是白细胞异常增多、贫血、出血、脾脏肿大、眩晕等，俗称"血癌"。

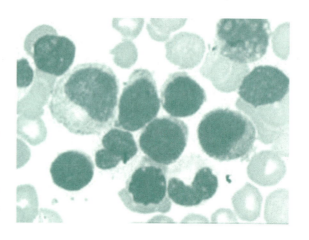

Acute nonlymphocytic leukemia is one type of acute leukemia. Leukemia is also called "血癌" in spoken Chinese, the symptoms of which include leukocytosis, anaemia, bleeding, splenomegaly and vertigo.

非～，前缀。用在一些名词性成分的前面，表示不属于某种范围。如：非淋巴细胞、非典型性肺炎。

A prefix used in front of some nouns which means not belonging to some range. e.g. "非淋巴细胞" "非典型性肺炎".

4. 化疗

名词用法时是化学疗法的简称，如"做化疗"。动词用法指用化学疗法进行治疗，特指治疗恶性肿瘤，如"手术后又化疗了三个疗程"。

It is the abbreviation of chemotherapy in Chinese. When it is used as a noun, it goes with the verb "做". e.g. "做化疗". When it is used as a verb, it means to treat cancer with anticancer therapy. e.g. "手术后又化疗了三个疗程".

"疗"前加上单音节词语，常用来表示某些治疗方法的简称。如：放疗（放射疗法）、理疗（物理疗法）。

"疗" is also the abbreviation of some therapy methods when it has monosyllabic word as prefix. e.g. "放疗（放射疗法）" "理疗（物理疗法）".

四 练习

（一）课堂练习

1. 听与读

贫血	血液病	骨髓	月经
血红蛋白	白血病	骨髓移植	月经正常
血小板	急性白血病	骨髓象	月经比以前多
红细胞	急性非淋巴细胞白血病	骨髓涂片	
白细胞	得了急性非淋巴细胞白血病		

化疗	疗程	炎症	氨苄西林
做化疗	一个疗程	有什么炎症	病毒唑
需要化疗	第一个疗程	上呼吸道炎症	用过氨苄西林
	做三个疗程的化疗		用病毒唑治疗

淋巴细胞	
非淋巴细胞	全身无力
典型性肺炎	面色苍白
非典型性肺炎	

2. 替换与扩展

（1）A：诊断结果是什么？
　　 B：诊断结果是<u>急性白血病</u>。

　糖尿病
　高血压
　肺炎
　急性非淋巴细胞白血病
　急性肠炎

（2）你入院后要进行<u>血常规</u>检查。

　X光
　尿常规
　B超
　骨髓涂片

（3）刚才江医生吩咐说，您的女儿要进行<u>化疗</u>。

　放疗
　手术治疗
　骨髓移植
　理疗

（4）化疗的时候她会感觉非常难受，还会掉头发。

觉得很不舒服	吃不下饭
变得全身无力	恶心、呕吐
非常痛苦	情绪不稳定

3. 口语练习：参考使用下列词语看图对话

（1）场景提示：医生江海涛在病房问病人陈丽敏住院前身体有什么症状。

住院　以前　炎症　头晕　发热

（2）场景提示：卡奇在病房拿着病人陈丽敏的检查结果，向病人的妈妈介绍她的检查结果。

炎症　急性　白血病　化疗　疗程　移植

(二) 课外练习

1. 看汉字，写拼音

氨苄西林_____   病毒唑_____   血红蛋白_____

血小板_____   骨髓_____   涂片_____

非淋巴细胞_____   移植_____   疗程_____

2. 看拼音，根据生词表写汉字

xuèyèbìng_____   hóngxìbāo_____   báixuèbìng_____

pínxuè_____   yuèjīng_____   huàliáo_____

lèi_____

3. 选择合适的词语填空（每个词语只能用一次）

> 急性白血病 白细胞 疗程 红细胞 骨髓移植 化疗 贫血 骨髓涂片

（1）最近她有些_____，脸色苍白，全身无力。

（2）从化验结果看，我的_____、_____、血小板都不正常。

（3）大夫说我是_____，需要_____。

（4）化疗的第一个_____要住院。

（5）_____的结果是 ANLL-M_2 型骨髓象。

（6）如果化疗的效果不好，再考虑进行_____。

4. 根据问句写出合适的应答句

（1）指导医生：病人最近有什么症状？

　　卡　　奇：_____。

（2）指导医生：病人以前用过什么药？

　　卡　　奇：_____。

（3）指导医生：病人用药后病情有没有好转？

　　卡　　奇：_____。

（4）指导医生：病人最近一次月经跟以前一样吗？

　　卡　　奇：_____。

5. 完成下列对话

江医生：19床病人血常规的检查结果是什么？

卡　奇：_____

　　　　_____。

江医生：这是贫血，_____涂片结果呢？

卡　奇：是_____。

江医生：我们现在可以确诊了，病人得的是_____。

卡　奇：ANLL 的汉语_____叫什么？

江医生：叫_____，是_____的一个大类。

卡　奇：江老师，白血病有哪些主要的症状？

江医生：_____、_____、_____、发热、出血等。女性病人月经_____。

6. 口语练习：复述成段表达的内容

向病人家属讲述指导医生的治疗意见

```
诊断结果
   ↓
治疗方法及治疗过程中的注意事项
   ↓
鼓励病人家属
```

7. 节奏汉语

急性白血病

急性白血病很危险，
面色苍白全身无力，
头晕、发热，反复低烧，
咳嗽没痰得吃药，
氨苄西林、病毒唑。
女性患者月经期，
时间增长出血多。
血常规检查是贫血，
骨髓涂片 ANLL-M_2，
急性非淋巴细胞白血病，
化疗难受掉头发，
效果差要骨髓移植。

8. 写作练习：把练习5的对话改成对病人情况的叙述

常用专业词语

造血系统	zàoxuè xìtǒng	hematopoietic system
造血功能不全	zàoxuè gōngnéng bù quán	deshematopoietic
浆细胞	jiāng xìbāo	phlogocyte, plasmacyte
巨噬细胞	jùshì xìbāo	macrophage, macrophagocyte
黄疸血红蛋白尿	huángdǎn xuèhóngdànbái niào	icterohemoglobinuria
血浆	xuèjiāng	blood plasma
凝血因子	níngxuè yīnzǐ	coagulation factors
抗凝血酶	kàngníngxuè méi	antithrombin
免疫球蛋白	miǎnyì qiúdànbái	immunoglobulin

第十二课　她不是胖，是浮肿

（肾内科—肾炎）

扫码听

学习目标和重难点：
1. 与肾小球肾炎和肾功能不全相关的词语
2. 和指导医生讨论病人的情况
3. 向病人讲述病情及治疗意见
4. 向病人家属讲述病人的情况及治疗意见

一　生词

1.	肾	shèn	名	kidney
2.	浮肿	fúzhǒng	动	dropsy
3.	眼睑	yǎnjiǎn	名	eyelid
4.	睁	zhēng	动	to open
5.	精神	jīngshen	名	vitality
6.	乏力	fálì	形	hypodynamic
7.	酸	suān	形	sour, acid
8.	量	liàng	名	quantity
9.	减少	jiǎnshǎo	动	to decrease
10.	尿频	niàopín	形	frequent micturition
11.	尿急	niàojí	形	urgent micturition
12.	尿痛	niàotòng	形	odynuria
13.	食欲	shíyù	名	appetite

第十二课　她不是胖，是浮肿

14. 慢性	mànxìng	形	chronic
15. 肾小球肾炎	shènxiǎoqiú shènyán		glomerulonephritis
16. 肾功能不全	shèngōngnéng bù quán		renal insufficiency
17. 巩固	gǒnggù	动	to consolidate
18. 定期	dìngqī	形	regular
19. 积极	jījí	形	active
20. 配合	pèihé	动	to cooperate
21. 控制	kòngzhì	动	to control
22. 鼓励	gǔlì	动	to encourage

二 课文

人物： 指导 医生——张 力
rénwù: zhǐdǎo yīshēng　Zhāng Lì

实习生——白瑞蒂
shíxíshēng　Báiruìdì

肾 内科 1 床 病人——邓 梅（女，28 岁）
shèn nèikē yī chuáng bìngrén　Dèng Méi (nǚ, èrshíbā suì)

病人 家属——李 先生（邓 梅 的 丈夫）
bìngrén jiāshǔ　Lǐ xiānsheng (Dèng Méi de zhàngfu)

1. 会话

白瑞蒂: 张老师，我已经按
Zhāng lǎoshī, wǒ yǐjīng àn

您的吩咐叫1床去
nín de fēnfù jiào yī chuáng qù

验尿和验血了。
yàn niào hé yàn xiě le.

张　力: 你跟我说说她的
Nǐ gēn wǒ shuōshuo tā de

情况吧。
qíngkuàng ba.

白瑞蒂: 我觉得她胖得不正常。
Wǒ juéde tā pàng de bú zhèngcháng.

张　力: 她那样不是胖，是浮肿。昨天她入院时我
Tā nàyàng bú shì pàng, shì fúzhǒng. Zuótiān tā rù yuàn shí wǒ

就看见她全身浮肿了。
jiù kànjiàn tā quánshēn fúzhǒng le.

白瑞蒂: 哦。她的面部浮肿比较厉害，特别是眼睑，
Ò. Tā de miànbù fúzhǒng bǐjiào lìhai, tèbié shì yǎnjiǎn,

连眼睛都睁不开了。
lián yǎnjīng dōu zhēng bu kāi le.

第十二课　她不是胖，是浮肿

张　力：她的 精神 怎么样？
　　　　Tā de jīngshen zěnmeyàng?

白瑞蒂：我 看 她 没 什么 精神，她 自己 说 觉得 很 累、
　　　　Wǒ kàn tā méi shénme jīngshen, tā zìjǐ shuō juéde hěn lèi、

　　　　乏力、腰 酸。
　　　　fálì、 yāo suān.

张　力：她 排 尿 的 情况 呢？
　　　　Tā pái niào de qíngkuàng ne?

白瑞蒂：她 说 尿量 比 平时 明显 减少，颜色 深黄。
　　　　Tā shuō niàoliàng bǐ píngshí míngxiǎn jiǎnshǎo, yánsè shēnhuáng.

　　　　没有 尿频、尿急、尿痛。
　　　　Méiyǒu niàopín、niàojí、niàotòng.

张　力：她的 食欲 好不好？
　　　　Tā de shíyù hǎo bu hǎo?

白瑞蒂：她 觉得 恶心，两 天 前 开始 呕吐，还 出现 腹
　　　　Tā juéde ěxin, liǎng tiān qián kāishǐ ǒutù, hái chūxiàn fù

　　　　胀，没 什么 食欲。
　　　　zhàng, méi shénme shíyù.

2. 会话

白瑞蒂：邓小姐，你的检查结果出来了。
　　　　Dèng xiǎojiě, nǐ de jiǎnchá jiéguǒ chūlai le.

邓　梅：我得的是什么病？
　　　　Wǒ dé de shì shénme bìng?

白瑞蒂：根据尿常规和血常规的检查结果，还有
　　　　Gēnjù niàochángguī hé xuèchángguī de jiǎnchá jiéguǒ, hái yǒu

　　　　你的各种症状，张医生诊断是慢性
　　　　nǐ de gè zhǒng zhèngzhuàng, Zhāng yīshēng zhěnduàn shì mànxìng

　　　　肾小球肾炎和慢性肾功能不全。
　　　　shènxiǎoqiú shènyán hé mànxìng shèngōngnéng bù quán.

邓　梅：这种病好治吗？
　　　　Zhè zhǒng bìng hǎo zhì ma?

白瑞蒂：治疗这种病要花比较长的时间。
　　　　Zhìliáo zhè zhǒng bìng yào huā bǐjiào cháng de shíjiān.

邓　梅：那是不是治不好了？
　　　　Nà shì bu shì zhì bu hǎo le?

白瑞蒂：别太担心。住院治疗一段时间后，病情是
　　　　Bié tài dānxīn. Zhù yuàn zhìliáo yí duàn shíjiān hòu, bìngqíng shì

　　　　可以稳定下来的。
　　　　kěyǐ wěndìng xiàlái de.

邓　梅：我需要住院多长时间？
　　　　Wǒ xūyào zhù yuàn duō cháng shíjiān?

白瑞蒂：大概需要一个月，然后回家巩固治疗，定期到医院来检查。

邓　梅：你这么说我就不害怕了，谢谢您。治疗的时候我一定好好儿配合。

3. 成段表达 （白瑞蒂对病人家属说）

李先生，前天入院时您说您的妻子十二天前发热，五天后尿量明显减少、眼睑浮肿，后来全身浮肿；这段时间感觉腰酸、乏力、头晕、腹胀、恶心、食欲差。入院两天前开始呕吐，每天两到三次；体重增加约八公斤。16岁时曾经有尿少、全身浮肿的症状，当时诊断为肾炎。昨天我们给您

妻子 验了 尿 和 血。根据 您 妻子 的 症状 和 检查 结果，
qīzi yànle niào hé xiě. Gēnjù nín qīzi de zhèngzhuàng hé jiǎnchá jiéguǒ,

张 医生 诊断 是 慢性 肾小球 肾炎 和 慢性 肾功能
Zhāng yīshēng zhěnduàn shì mànxìng shènxiǎoqiú shènyán hé mànxìng shèngōngnéng

不 全。这 种 病 的 治疗 要 花 比较 长 的 时间，也 不
bù quán. Zhè zhǒng bìng de zhìliáo yào huā bǐjiào cháng de shíjiān, yě bù

一定 能 完全 治 好。不过 如果 病人 能 积极 配合 医生
yídìng néng wánquán zhì hǎo. Búguò rúguǒ bìngrén néng jījí pèihé yīshēng

的 治疗，就 可以 控制 住 病情。希望 您 多 关心 和 鼓励
de zhìliáo, jiù kěyǐ kòngzhì zhù bìngqíng. Xīwàng nín duō guānxīn hé gǔlì

您 的 妻子，让 她 积极 配合 治疗。
nín de qīzi, ràng tā jījí pèihé zhìliáo.

注释

1. 她那样不是胖，是浮肿。(不是……，是……)

"不是……，是……"句式常用于说明、解释原因等，有时有申辩的意味，例如：

The pattern of "不是……，是……" is often used for offering explanations and corrections. e.g.

（1）他不是学中医的，是学西医的。
（2）她得的不是上呼吸道炎症，是急性白血病。

2. 肾小球肾炎

肾小球肾炎是以肾小球损害为主的变态反应性炎症，临床表现主要有蛋白尿、血尿、水肿和高血压等。早期症状常不明显，容易被忽略，发展到晚期可引起肾功能衰竭，严重威胁病人的健康和生命。

Glomerulonephritis is an allergic inflammation which damages renal glomerulus. The clinical manifestations include albuminuria, hematuria, edema, high blood pressure, etc. The incipient symptoms are usually not obvious, and can be easily ignored. Renal failure may occur at the advanced stage, which can seriously threaten the patients' health and lives.

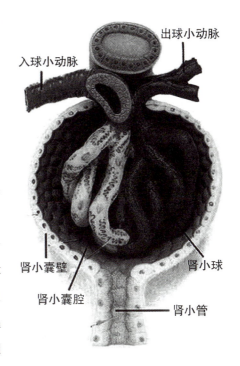

3. 肾功能不全

肾脏是人体的重要排泄器官，其主要的功能是排泄体内代谢产物、药物、毒物和解毒产物，调节体内水、电解质、酸碱平衡。当各种病因引起肾功能严重障碍时，人体内环境就会发生紊乱，其主要表现为代谢产物在体内蓄积，水、电解质和酸碱平衡紊乱，并伴有尿量和尿质的改变以及由肾脏内分泌功能障碍引起的一系列病理生理变化，这就是肾功能不全。

The kidneys are very important excretory organs of the human body, and the main function of them is to excrete metabolic wastes, drugs, poison, and products of detoxification, and to regulate the body's water, electrolyte, and acid-base balance. When a serious loss of kidney function occurs due to various causes, disorders of internal environment will be present. The clinical manifestations are that the waste products of metabolism are cumulated in the body; water, electrolyte and acid-base balance is disturbed, accompanied by a change of urine quantity and quality and by a series of pathological and physiological changes caused by the endocrine dysfunction of the kidneys. Based on the above symptoms renal insufficiency can be diagnosed.

4. 大概需要（住院）一个月，然后回家巩固治疗，定期到医院来检查。

这是对慢性肾炎的一般治疗方法。肾炎通常分为急性与慢性两大类。急性肾炎起病快，来势较猛，各种症状也比较齐全，但病程相对短些；慢性肾炎起病慢，症状来势缓慢，病程很长，有时可迁延一辈子。所以慢性肾炎通常都是在医院控制住病情后就让病人出院，回家后继续吃药，定期检查。

This is the general treatment of chronic nephritis. Nephritis can be acute or chronic. Acute nephritis develops rather suddenly and fiercely, and with nearly all the symptoms of nephritis. The course is relatively shorter compared with that of chronic nephritis. Chronic nephritis develops over longer course, and in some cases, the length of treatment could be life long. So the patient with chronic nephritis could leave hospital after the symptoms get controlled, and keep on taking medicine, and have regular examinations.

第十二课　她不是胖，是浮肿

四　练习

（一）课堂练习

1. 听与读

肾	眼睑浮肿	尿急	配合治疗
肾小球	四肢浮肿	尿频	积极配合治疗
肾功能	全身浮肿	尿痛	积极配合医生进行治疗
肾小球肾炎	面部浮肿	尿量减少	积极配合医生进行巩固治疗
肾功能不全			

慢性肾小球肾炎	控制病情	定期检查	排尿	各项检查
慢性肾功能不全	控制住病情	定期到医院检查	排痰	各项安排
	控制住情绪	定期检查肾功能	排汗	各项治疗
		定期验尿	排毒	各项体征

2. 替换与扩展

（1）她不是<u>胖</u>，是<u>浮肿</u>。

头疼	胃疼
病了	累了
肝炎	肾炎
肠胃炎	心肌梗死
消化不良	胃溃疡

169

（2）A：她的 精神 怎么样？
　　　B：她觉得 很累、乏力、腰酸。

病情　　　　　　没有好转
感觉　　　　　　恶心、腹胀
恢复情况　　　　身体越来越好了
尿量　　　　　　比平时明显减少了

（3）A：她排尿的情况呢？
　　　B：她说 尿量明显减少，颜色深黄。

尿量比平时增多
尿液白色
尿液呈淡红色
尿频、尿痛

3. 口语练习：交际活动

全班分为A、B两组，A组看附录一，B组看附录二，准备好后每次各组随机抽取一人进行有信息差的对话。

（二）课外练习

1. 看汉字，写拼音

肾小球肾炎＿＿＿＿＿＿　　浮肿＿＿＿＿＿＿　　眼睑＿＿＿＿＿＿

乏力＿＿＿＿＿＿　　　　　慢性＿＿＿＿＿＿　　食欲＿＿＿＿＿＿

尿频＿＿＿＿＿＿　　　　　肾功能不全＿＿＿＿＿＿

第十二课　她不是胖，是浮肿

2. 看拼音，根据生词表写汉字

jiǎnshǎo_____　　pèihé_____　　kòngzhì_____　　dìngqī_____

gǔlì_____　　gǒnggù_____　　jījí_____　　zhēng_____

3. 词语搭配（可多选）

（1）
睁　排　各　腰　尿

酸　频　项　眼　尿

（2）
眼睑　积极　巩固　定期　控制

检查　治疗　病情　配合　浮肿

4. 选择合适的词语填空（每个词语只能用一次）

鼓励　巩固　减少　浮肿　配合　控制　积极　睁　食欲　定期

（1）他最近得了胃炎，觉得一点儿_____都没有。

（2）医生要多_____病人，这样对病人的身体恢复有好处。

（3）为了_____病情的发展，医生给他开了许多药。

（4）医生让病人出院后_____来医院检查。

（5）他的病情已经控制住了，不过还要继续吃药，进行_____治疗。

（6）我好几天都没好好儿睡觉了，上课时困得连眼睛都_____不开。

（7）她全身_____得很厉害，医生建议她先做一次尿常规和血常规检查。

（8）病人应该主动_____医生的治疗。

（9）医生，我最近食欲不好，尿量也_____了。

（10）如果病人_____配合治疗，一定可以控制住病情。

5. 根据病人的情况写出合适的问句

（1）病　人：我的面部浮肿得比较厉害。

　　实习生：_____？

（2）病　人：我觉得很累，乏力、腰酸。

　　实习生：_____？

（3）病　人：我的尿量比平时明显减少。

　　实习生：_____？

6. 完成下列对话

（1）李先生：我妻子的_____出来了吗？

　　白瑞蒂：出来了。

　　李先生：我妻子_____？

　　白瑞蒂：根据你妻子的尿常规和_____的结果，

　　　　　　张医生诊断是_____和_____。

　　李先生：这种病能治好吗？

　　白瑞蒂：治疗的时间可能会比较长，也不一定能_____。

　　李先生：现在我们家属能做什么？

　　白瑞蒂：多关心和_____她，让她_____。

　　李先生：好，我们一定好好儿配合。谢谢你！

（2）白瑞蒂：你哪儿不舒服？

　　邓　梅：十二天前开始_____，五天后_____。

　　白瑞蒂：尿的_____呢？

　　邓　梅：深黄色。

第十二课　她不是胖，是浮肿

白瑞蒂：你浮肿的情况比较严重。还有其他不舒服的感觉吗？

邓　梅：我还觉得腰_____、_____力、头_____、_____胀、恶心。

白瑞蒂：_____怎么样？

邓　梅：很差，不想吃东西。

白瑞蒂：有没有呕吐？

邓　梅：两天前开始_____。

白瑞蒂：每天_____？

邓　梅：两到三次。

白瑞蒂：_____有没有变化？

邓　梅：大概增加了八公斤。

白瑞蒂：你以前有过这样的_____吗？

邓　梅：16岁时曾经有尿少、全身_____的症状。

白瑞蒂：当时的_____是什么？

邓　梅：肾炎。

7. 根据课文的内容回答下列问题

（1）1床病人有哪些体征？

（2）1床病人精神怎么样？

（3）1床病人的排尿情况如何？

（4）根据尿常规和血常规的检查结果，1床病人得的是什么病？

（5）医生说1床病人需要住院多长时间？

8. 口语练习：复述成段表达的内容

向病人家属讲述病人的情况及这种病的治疗特点

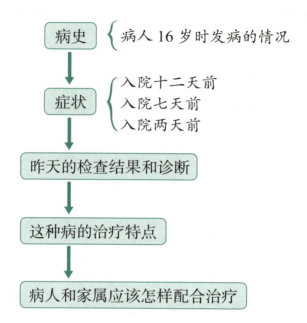

病史 { 病人16岁时发病的情况

症状 { 入院十二天前
入院七天前
入院两天前

昨天的检查结果和诊断

这种病的治疗特点

病人和家属应该怎样配合治疗

9. 节奏汉语

慢性肾小球肾炎和慢性肾功能不全

眼睑、面部浮肿很厉害，
腰酸、乏力、头晕还腹胀，
恶心、呕吐、食欲差，
体重增加，尿减少，色深黄，
尿常规、血常规来检查，
慢性肾小球肾炎，
并慢性肾功能不全。
治疗一个月后巩固，
定期回医院来检查。

10. 写作练习：把课文的第一个对话改成对病人情况的叙述

与泌尿系统炎症有关的术语

少尿	shǎo niào	oliguria
血尿	xuèniào	hematuria
脓尿	nóngniào	pyuria
尿比重	niào bǐzhòng	specific gravity, SG
管型	guǎnxíng	cast
膀胱炎	pángguāngyán	cystitis

第十三课　这是不是肾病综合征？

（肾内科—肾病综合征）

扫码听

学习目标和重难点：
1. 与肾病综合征相关的词语
2. 与指导医生和其他实习生一起向病人了解患病的情况
3. 与指导医生讨论病人的检查结果
4. 向另一位实习生讲述病人的情况、检查及诊断结果

一　生词

1.	患者	huànzhě	名	patient
2.	在……之间	zài……zhījiān		between
3.	泡沫	pàomò	名	foam
4.	肾病综合征	shènbìng zōnghézhēng		nephritic syndrome
5.	泼尼松	pōnísōng	名	prednisone (又名"强的松")
6.	消退	xiāotuì	动	to vanish
7.	服	fú	动	to take (medicines)
8.	维持	wéichí	动	to maintain
9.	生化	shēnghuà	名	biochemistry
10.	肝功能	gāngōngnéng	名	liver function
11.	定量	dìngliàng	名	quantification
12.	凹陷	āoxiàn	动	to depress
13.	疲倦	píjuàn	形	tired

第十三课　这是不是肾病综合征？

14. 气促	qì cù		shortness of breath
15. 视诊	shìzhěn	动	to inspect
16. 纹	wén	名	vein, line
17. 粗	cū	形	harsh
18. 水泡音	shuǐpàoyīn	名	bubble sound
19. 干啰音	gānluóyīn	名	dry rales
20. 代谢性酸中毒	dàixièxìng suān zhòng dú		metabolic acidosis
21. 低钾血症	dījiǎxuèzhèng	名	hypokalemia
22. 低钠血症	dīnàxuèzhèng	名	hyponatremia

二 课文

人物：　指导　医生——陈　小廷
rénwù:　zhǐdǎo yīshēng　　Chén Xiǎotíng

　　　实习生——李力、白瑞蒂、莎娜、卡奇
　　　shíxíshēng　　Lǐ Lì、Báiruìdì、Shānà、Kǎqí

　　　肾　内科　病人——伍立伟（男，38 岁）
　　　shèn nèikē bìngrén　　Wǔ Lìwěi (nán, sānshíbā suì)

1. 会话

陈小廷：这个 患者 刚 从 门诊 转 过来，你们 先
　　　　Zhège huànzhě gāng cóng ménzhěn zhuǎn guolai, nǐmen xiān

　　　　问问 他的 病史 吧。
　　　　wènwen tā de bìngshǐ ba.

177

卡奇：伍先生，您是什么时候开始觉得不舒服的？
Wǔ xiānsheng, nín shì shénme shíhou kāishǐ juéde bù shūfu de?

伍立伟：一个星期前劳累后呼吸很急，发烧，体温在37.5度到38.5度之间，最高的时候39度。
Yí ge xīngqī qián láolèi hòu hūxī hěn jí, fā shāo, tǐwēn zài sānshíqī diǎn wǔ dù dào sānshíbā diǎn wǔ dù zhījiān, zuì gāo de shíhou sānshíjiǔ dù.

莎娜：咳嗽吗？
Késou ma?

伍立伟：咳嗽，但没有痰。
Késou, dàn méiyǒu tán.

莎娜：您的眼睑浮肿很明显，让我们看看您的腿。
Nín de yǎnjiǎn fúzhǒng hěn míngxiǎn, ràng wǒmen kànkan nín de tuǐ.

白瑞蒂：双腿的浮肿也很明显。尿量正常吗？
Shuāngtuǐ de fúzhǒng yě hěn míngxiǎn. Niàoliàng zhèngcháng ma?

伍立伟：比平时少多了，大概每天600至800毫升，有比较多的泡沫。
Bǐ píngshí shǎo duō le, dàgài měitiān liùbǎi zhì bābǎi háoshēng, yǒu bǐjiào duō de pàomò.

卡　奇： 以前有过这样的症状吗？
Yǐqián yǒuguo zhèyàng de zhèngzhuàng ma?

伍立伟： 两年前有过，但没发烧。
Liǎng nián qián yǒuguo, dàn méi fā shāo.

莎　娜： 去医院看过吗？
Qù yīyuàn kànguo ma?

伍立伟： 在当地医院看过，验了尿，说是肾病
Zài dāngdì yīyuàn kànguo, yànle niào, shuō shì shènbìng

综合征。
zōnghézhēng.

白瑞蒂： 我看看您的病历——尿蛋白"＋＋＋"，用
Wǒ kànkan nín de bìnglì —— niàodànbái "sān ge jiā", yòng

的药是泼尼松。
de yào shì pōnísōng.

莎　娜： 用药后效果怎么样？
Yòng yào hòu xiàoguǒ zěnmeyàng?

伍立伟： 用药一周后浮肿消退，尿量增加，但
Yòng yào yì zhōu hòu fúzhǒng xiāotuì, niàoliàng zēngjiā, dàn

尿蛋白还是"＋＋＋"。坚持服药一年半，
niàodànbái háishi "sān ge jiā". Jiānchí fú yào yì nián bàn,

尿蛋白维持在"＋"。
niàodànbái wéichí zài "yí ge jiā".

卡　奇： 您停药多长时间了？
Nín tíng yào duō cháng shíjiān le?

伍立伟： 大概 半 年 了。这 是 在 这里 看 门诊 的 验 尿
Dàgài bàn nián le. Zhè shì zài zhèli kàn ménzhěn de yàn niào

结果，尿蛋白"＋＋＋＋"。
jiéguǒ, niàodànbái "sì ge jiā".

莎 娜： 陈 老师，这是不是 肾病 综合征？
Chén lǎoshī, zhè shì bu shì shènbìng zōnghézhēng?

陈小廷： 对，可能 还 有 别 的 病。
Duì, kěnéng hái yǒu bié de bìng.

卡 奇： 现在 该 怎么 办？
Xiànzài gāi zěnme bàn?

陈小廷： 先 给 他 开 血常规、 尿常规、 生化、
Xiān gěi tā kāi xuèchángguī、niàochángguī、shēnghuà、

肝功能、 二十四 小时 尿蛋白 定量 等 检查
gāngōngnéng、èrshísì xiǎoshí niàodànbái dìngliàng děng jiǎnchá

的 化验单。
de huàyàndān.

2. 成段表达 （卡奇对李力说）

李力，我们 肾 内科 前天 收了 一 位 患者。他 来 的
Lǐ Lì, wǒmen shèn nèikē qiántiān shōule yí wèi huànzhě. Tā lái de

时候发低烧， 37.8 度， 眼睑 和 双 下肢 都 有 明显
shíhou fā dīshāo, sānshíqī diǎn bā dù, yǎnjiǎn hé shuāng xiàzhī dōu yǒu míngxiǎn

的凹陷性浮肿，精神疲倦。他告诉我们一周前劳累后开始发热、咳嗽、气促，尿量比平时明显减少，食欲差。视诊发现他的腹部胀大，腹部和双下肢皮肤有紫纹。听诊发现双肺呼吸音比较粗，右下肺听到细小的水泡音，没有干啰音。我们给他做了血常规、尿常规、生化、肝功能、24小时尿蛋白定量等检查。根据他的症状和检查结果，陈老师诊断为肾病综合征、急性肾功能不全、代谢性酸中毒、低钾血症、低钠血症、右下肺炎。我想看看陈老师对这样的病人是怎么治疗的。

注释

1. 肾病综合征

这是多种病因引起的一种临床综合征。临床表现为"三高一低"四大症状：水肿、大量蛋白尿、高脂血症、低蛋白血症。

Nephritic syndrome is a clinical syndrome caused by various factors. It involves four symptoms called "三高一低": edema, large amount of proteinuria, hyperlipemia and hypoproteinemia.

2. 从门诊转过来

如果门诊病人的病情比较严重，或者情况比较特殊，需要住院做深入检查或全面治疗，门诊部的医生会建议病人住院，将病人转到住院部。

If the outpatient needs to be hospitalized for thorough examination or comprehensive treatment because of his/her comparatively serious or peculiar illness, the doctor will suggest that the patient be transferred to the inpatient department.

"从……转过来"：在医院里，指从一个科室转到另外一个科室。如：从心内科转过来、从口腔科转过来。

"从……转过来" means that the patient is transferred from one department to another in hospital. e.g. "从心内科转过来" "从口腔科转过来".

3. 肝功能

肝脏具有代谢、解毒、排泄等多种功能。临床上常通过验血来检测肝功能是否正常。

Liver has various functions such as metabolism, detoxification and excretion. The liver function is often measured by blood tests to determine how well it performs.

4. 水泡音

即湿啰音。它是吸气时气体通过呼吸道内的稀薄分泌物,形成水泡破裂所产生的声音。

It is also called moist rales, a bubble crackling sound produced due to passage of air through thin secretions in the respiratory tract during inspiration.

5. 代谢性酸中毒

代谢性酸中毒是因体内酸性物质积聚过多或碱性物质丢失而引起的。对于轻度代谢性酸中毒病人一般采用适当补液纠正脱水的方法,对严重的患者必须用碱性药物治疗。

Metabolic acidosis is caused by an abnormal accumulation of acids or by depletion of bicarbonates. Mild metabolic acidosis can be treated with the administration of intravenous fluids to correct dehydration, but the severe one should be treated with bicarbonate drugs.

6. 低钾血症

指血清钾浓度低于正常值(3.5mmol/L),由钾盐经消化道或肾脏丢失过多、血清钾转入细胞内及长期未进食等原因引起。临床表现为肌肉软弱无力甚至软瘫、腹胀、肠麻痹、心律失常,严重时可猝死。治疗方法是静脉点滴或口服钾盐。

Hypokalemia means serum or plasma levels of potassium ions that fall below 3.5 mmol/L. It is caused by losing too much potassium in the digestive tract or the kidneys, the serum potassium shifting into the cell, or by prolonged fasting and starvation. The clinical manifestations include myasthenia or soft paralysis, abdominal enlargement, enteroparalysis, arrhythmia and even sudden death. The treatment involves the intravenous administration of potassium or oral consumption of potassium chloride pills.

7. 低钠血症

指血清钠浓度低于正常值（130mmol/L）。主要由严重呕吐、腹泻等大量丢失钠盐及血清钠稀释（如水中毒）等引起。临床表现主要为头痛、嗜睡、肌痉挛、昏迷甚至死亡。治疗方法是补充钠盐及治疗原发病。

Hypokalemia is a condition of below normal levels (130 mmol/L) of sodium in the blood serum, caused by severe loss of sodium or diluting of serum sodium due to severe vomit or diarrhea. The clinical manifestations include headache, drowsiness, myospasm, coma or even death. Treatments include the infusion of sodium and targetting the underlying disease causing the decline in plasma sodium levels.

四 练习

（一）课堂练习

1. 听与读

听诊	生化检查	水泡音	泼尼松
视诊	肝功能检查	干啰音	抗生素
触诊	尿蛋白定量检查	湿啰音	解痉止痛药
问诊	24小时尿蛋白定量检查	哮鸣音	硝酸甘油
		呼吸音	降压药
			氨苄西林
			病毒唑

肾病综合征	浮肿消退
低钠血症	疼痛消退
低钾血症	炎症消退
代谢性酸中毒	皮肤上的紫色斑消退
急性肾功能不全	双下肢皮肤上的紫纹消退

2. 替换与扩展

（1）让我们<u>看看</u>你的<u>腿</u>。

听听	心脏
量量	血压
测测	脉搏
检查检查	肾功能

（2）<u>尿量</u>正常吗？

食欲
睡眠
体温
肝功能

（3）你是什么时候开始<u>觉得不舒服</u>的？

出现这种症状
觉得气促
接受化疗
用泼尼松

（4）<u>视诊</u>发现他<u>腹部胀大</u>。

听诊	肺部有水泡音
触诊	右上腹有压痛
问诊	已有多年高血压病史

3. 口语练习：交际活动

全班分为 A、B 两组，A 组看附录一，B 组看附录二，准备好后每次各组随机抽取一人进行有信息差的对话。

（二）课外练习

1. 看汉字，写拼音

肾病综合征_____　　　代谢性酸中毒_____

低钠血症_____　　　低钾血症_____

泼尼松_____　　水泡音_____　　定量_____

2. 看拼音，根据生词表写汉字

shēnghuà_____　　huànzhě_____　　qì cù_____

wéichí_____　　píjuàn_____　　āoxiàn_____

xiāotuì_____　　gāngōngnéng_____

3. 选择适当的词语填空（每个词只能用一次）

> 肝功能　维持　粗　患者　定量　疲倦　视诊　服　消退　凹陷

（1）医生对待_____一定要耐心、细心。

（2）听诊发现，病人的呼吸音很_____。

（3）病人最近精神不好，常常觉得_____，想睡觉。

（4）_____发现，病人腹部胀大，腹部和双下肢皮肤有紫纹。

（5）经过一周的治疗，病人皮肤上的紫纹已经_____了。

（6）患者最近病情已经得到控制，尿蛋白_____在"+"。

（7）大夫，这种药我每天_____几次？

（8）你的脸色有点儿黄，去做个_____检查吧。

（9）病人入院时比较瘦，脸部_____，没有精神。

（10）你记住要坚持每天定时_____服药。

4. 根据问句写出合适的应答句

（1）指导医生：病人一个星期前有什么症状？

实 习 生：_____。

（2）指导医生：病人身体哪些部位浮肿了？

实 习 生：_____。

（3）指导医生：病人排尿情况怎么样？

实 习 生：_____。

（4）指导医生：病人用泼尼松后的效果怎么样？

实 习 生：_____。

5. 完成对话

（1）指导医生：病人今天的_____？

实 习 生：在37.5度～38.5度之间，最高的时候39度。

指导医生：_____吗？

实 习 生：咳嗽比较厉害，但没痰。

指导医生：还有_____吗？

实 习 生：眼睑的浮肿好些了，但腿部浮肿还很明显。

指导医生：_____的结果怎么样？

实 习 生：尿蛋白"＋＋＋"。

（2）白瑞蒂：听说你们肾内科新来了一个病人，＿＿＿＿＿＿＿＿＿＿？

卡　奇：来的时候＿＿＿＿＿＿，37.8度，眼睑和双腿有明显浮肿。

白瑞蒂：＿＿＿＿＿＿＿＿＿＿？

卡　奇：腹部胀大，皮肤能看见紫纹。

白瑞蒂：听诊的情况呢？

卡　奇：＿＿＿＿＿＿，右下肺听到＿＿＿＿＿＿，没有干啰音。

白瑞蒂：是肾病综合征吗？

卡　奇：现在还不能确诊，我们给他做了血常规、＿＿＿＿＿＿、生化、＿＿＿＿＿＿、二十四小时＿＿＿＿＿＿等检查，还要看结果。

6. 根据课文内容判断正误

（1）病人以前没有得过肾病综合征。　　　　　　　　　（　　）

（2）病人眼睑和双下肢的浮肿都很明显。　　　　　　　（　　）

（3）病人的尿量比平时多，每天600～800毫升。　　　（　　）

（4）病人两年前服用过泼尼松，效果很好。　　　　　　（　　）

（5）视诊发现胸部和双下肢皮肤有紫纹。　　　　　　　（　　）

（6）听诊发现左下肺有水泡音，没有干啰音。　　　　　（　　）

7. 口语练习：复述成段表达的内容

向中国实习生介绍一位肾病综合征病人的病情、检查结果和医生的诊断。

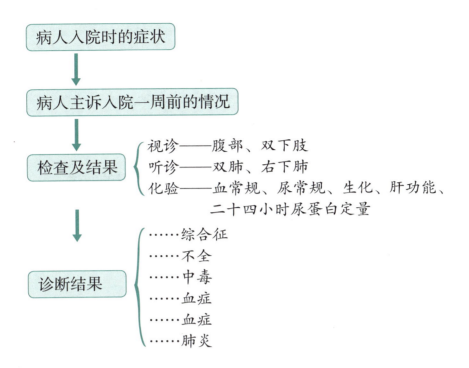

8. 节奏汉语

肾病综合征

劳累后低烧、咳嗽又气促，
眼睑、双下肢凹陷性浮肿，
尿量明显减少，食欲差，
坚持服药泼尼松，
消肿、增加尿量、尿蛋白维持在"+"。
视诊发现腹部胀大，
腹部、双下肢皮肤有紫纹。
听诊双肺呼吸音较粗，
右下肺听到细小水泡音。
确诊需要一系列检查，
血常规、尿常规、生化肝功能、
二十四小时尿蛋白定量。

> 根据症状和检查结果，
> 确诊肾病综合征、急性肾功能不全、
> 代谢性酸中毒、低钾血症、低钠血症、右下肺炎。

9. 写作练习：把练习5的第二个对话改成对病人情况的叙述

与肾脏疾病有关的术语

蛋白尿	dànbáiniào	proteinuria
糖尿	tángniào	glycosuria
肾小球肾炎	shènxiǎoqiú shènyán	glomerulonephritis
肾盂肾炎	shènyú shènyán	pyelonephritis
尿毒症	niàodúzhèng	uremia
腹膜透析	fùmó tòuxī	peritoneal dialysis
血液透析	xuèyè tòuxī	hemodialysis

第十四课　甲亢病人发病时会有哪些典型症状？
（内分泌科—甲亢）

扫码听

> 学习目标和重难点：
> 1. 与甲亢相关的词语
> 2. 向病人了解病史及最近的情况
> 3. 与指导医生讨论病人的情况
> 4. 向病人讲述治疗方法及需要注意的事项

一　生词

1.	内分泌	nèifēnmì	名	incretion
2.	旺盛	wàngshèng	形	rich, abundant
3.	下降	xiàjiàng	动	to decrease, to fall
4.	甲亢 / 甲状腺功能亢进症	jiǎkàng/ jiǎzhuàngxiàn gōngnéng kàngjìnzhèng	名	hyperthyroidism
5.	他巴唑	tābāzuò	名	tapazole
6.	心得安	xīndé'ān	名	propranolol
7.	维生素	wéishēngsù	名	vitamin
8.	监测	jiāncè	动	to monitor
9.	减轻	jiǎnqīng	动	to relieve
10.	心悸	xīnjì	动	to heart-throb
11.	复发	fùfā	动	to relapse

12.	胸闷	xiōngmèn	动	to have chest tightness
13.	抖	dǒu	动	to shiver, to shake
14.	失眠	shī mián		to have insomnia
15.	震颤	zhènchàn	动	to shiver, to tremble
16.	眼球	yǎnqiú	名	eyeball
17.	突出	tūchū	动	to protrude
18.	甲亢平	jiǎkàngpíng	名	carbimazole
19.	调整	tiáozhěng	动	to modify, to rectify
20.	淡水	dànshuǐ	名	fresh water
21.	碘	diǎn	名	iodine

二 课文

人物： 指导 医生——黄　明
rénwù: zhǐdǎo yīshēng　Huáng Míng

　　　实习生——白瑞蒂
　　　shíxíshēng　Báiruìdì

内分泌科3　床　病人——周 荷亭（女，28 岁）
nèifēnmì kē sān chuáng bìngrén　Zhōu Hétíng (nǚ, èrshíbā suì)

1. 会话

白瑞蒂: 周小姐,你好。我是实习生白瑞蒂。黄医生让我详细了解一下儿你的病史。

周荷亭: 哦。五年前我曾经因为怕热、多汗、食欲旺盛、体重下降,被诊断为甲亢。

白瑞蒂: 当时吃过什么药?

周荷亭: 吃过他巴唑、心得安、维生素C等。

白瑞蒂: 有没有定期对甲状腺功能进行监测?

周荷亭： 没有 坚持 定期 监测。吃药 三 年 左右 我 觉得
Méiyǒu jiānchí dìngqī jiāncè. Chī yào sān nián zuǒyòu wǒ juéde

症状 减轻 就 停药 了。
zhèngzhuàng jiǎnqīng jiù tíng yào le.

白瑞蒂： 最近 感觉 怎么样？
Zuìjìn gǎnjué zěnmeyàng?

周荷亭： 两 个 月 前 体重 开始 持续 下降，到 现在 下降 了
Liǎng ge yuè qián tǐzhòng kāishǐ chíxù xiàjiàng, dào xiànzài xiàjiàngle

大概 十 公斤，可是 食欲 非常 旺盛。
dàgài shí gōngjīn, kěshì shíyù fēicháng wàngshèng.

白瑞蒂： 还 有 哪 些 症状 呢？
Hái yǒu nǎ xiē zhèngzhuàng ne?

周荷亭： 多 汗、心悸、月经量 减少。大便 次数 比较 多，
Duō hàn、 xīnjì、 yuèjīngliàng jiǎnshǎo. Dàbiàn cìshù bǐjiào duō,

每 天 三 次，黄色，像 水 一样。
měi tiān sān cì, huángsè, xiàng shuǐ yíyàng.

2. 会话

黄 明： 白瑞蒂，你 来 看看 3 床 的 甲状腺 功能
Báiruìdì, nǐ lái kànkan sān chuáng de jiǎzhuàngxiàn gōngnéng

检查 结果。
jiǎnchá jiéguǒ.

白瑞蒂： 根据 这个 结果 可以 确诊 为 甲亢 吧？
Gēnjù zhège jiéguǒ kěyǐ quèzhěn wéi jiǎkàng ba?

第十四课　甲亢病人发病时会有哪些典型症状？

黄　明：对。她五年前就得过甲亢，这次复发比较严重，需要住院治疗。

白瑞蒂：黄老师，甲亢病人发病时会有哪些典型症状呢？

黄　明：心悸、胸闷、怕热、多汗、手抖、失眠、食欲旺盛、体重下降、乏力、腹泻、甲状腺肿大，血管有杂音和震颤、眼球突出等。

白瑞蒂：哦，我看见3床的眼球明显往外突出，还以为她原先就那样呢。

黄　明：也有一些患者眼球突出不明显或没有突出的。

白瑞蒂：治疗这种病一般用他巴唑和甲亢平吗？

黄　明：对。但还要看看患者有没有其他疾病，
　　　　Duì. Dàn hái yào kànkan huànzhě yǒu méiyǒu qítā jíbìng,

　　　　再根据具体情况调整用药。
　　　　zài gēnjù jùtǐ qíngkuàng tiáozhěng yòng yào.

3. 成段表达　（白瑞蒂对周荷亭说）

周小姐，根据入院后对你做的各项身体检查和
Zhōu xiǎojiě, gēnjù rù yuàn hòu duì nǐ zuò de gèxiàng shēntǐ jiǎnchá hé

甲状腺功能检查的结果，你得的是甲亢，也可以
jiǎzhuàngxiàn gōngnéng jiǎnchá de jiéguǒ, nǐ dé de shì jiǎkàng, yě kěyǐ

说是甲亢复发了。这次的病情比较重，需要住院
shuō shì jiǎkàng fùfā le. Zhè cì de bìngqíng bǐjiào zhòng, xūyào zhù yuàn

接受治疗，等病情减轻以后再出院服药治疗。甲亢
jiēshòu zhìliáo, děng bìngqíng jiǎnqīng yǐhòu zài chū yuàn fú yào zhìliáo. Jiǎkàng

病人特别需要增加营养，要多吃高热量、高蛋白
bìngrén tèbié xūyào zēngjiā yíngyǎng, yào duō chī gāorèliàng、gāodànbái

和维生素丰富的食物。所以你在接受治疗的同时，
hé wéishēngsù fēngfù de shíwù. Suǒyǐ nǐ zài jiēshòu zhìliáo de tóngshí,

要多吃牛肉、猪肉、羊肉、淡水鱼和含维生素丰富
yào duō chī niúròu、zhūròu、yángròu、dànshuǐyú hé hán wéishēngsù fēngfù

的水果、蔬菜。像你这样年轻的患者，还要多吃
de shuǐguǒ、shūcài. Xiàng nǐ zhèyàng niánqīng de huànzhě, hái yào duō chī

脂肪类食物，不要怕胖，要想办法增加体重。要少吃辣椒，少吃含碘多的食品和海产品，不吸烟，不喝酒，少喝浓茶、咖啡。平时要注意休息，保持愉快的心情。

三 注释

1. 内分泌

人和高等动物体内有些腺体或器官能分泌激素，不通过导管，由血液带到全身，从而调节机体的生长、发育和生理机能，这种分泌叫作内分泌。

Some glands and organs of human beings and higher animals can secrete hormones which are delivered through the body by blood, rather than by a duct, in which way regulates the growth and development and physiological functioning of a living organism. This kind of secretion is called incretion.

2. 他巴唑

他巴唑是一种治疗甲状腺功能亢进的药品。

Tapazole is a medicine for treating hyperthyroidism. It is used to inhibit the synthesis of tetraiodothyronine, and can be applied to hyperthyroidism caused by variety of factors.

3. 心得安

心得安是一种肾上腺素 β 受体阻滞剂，可以降低交感神经的张力，并减慢心脏的传导，从而可以减轻交感神经兴奋症状和心跳频率。

Propranolol is a kind of β-adrenergic blocking agents, used to palliate the tension of sympathetic nerves and lower the conduction speed of heart, and thus reduce the excitability of sympathetic nerves and the heart rate.

4. 心悸

心悸是一种自觉心脏跳动的不适感或心慌感。当心率加快时感到心脏跳动不适，心率缓慢时则感到搏动有力。心悸时，心率可快、可慢，也可有心律失常，心率和心律正常者亦可有心悸。

Palpitation is a sensation in which a person is aware of an irregular, hard, or rapid heart beat. When the heart rate increases, one feels the irregular beat; when the heart rate decreases, one may feel the heart beats heavily. When palpitation occurs, the heart rate can be either inappropriately fast or slow, and the rhythm of heart may also become irregular. Palpitation may occur to people with normal heart rate and rhythm.

5. 复发

同一种病反复发作，称作复发。如"甲亢复发""糖尿病复发"。

Relapse means the return of signs and symptoms of a disease after a patient has enjoyed a remission. For examples: "甲亢复发" "糖尿病复发".

6. 我看见3床的眼球明显往外突出，还以为她原先就那样呢。

"眼球明显往外突出"：甲亢往往会引起脂肪或肌肉发生水肿，这种体积的增大往往会造成眼球突出，而且这种眼球突出大多数情况下是双侧性的。

"Protruding eyeballs": hyperthyroidism may result in waterlogged fat and muscles and the enlargement thus resulted may lead to abnormal eyeball protrusion. In most cases protrusion will happen to both eyeballs simultaneously.

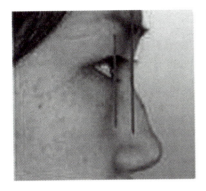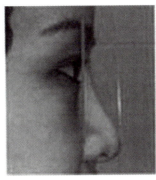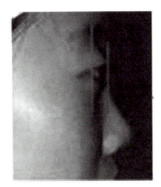

眼球凸度

7. 甲亢平

一种治疗甲亢的常见药,是他巴唑的衍生物,在体内水解可逐渐游离出他巴唑,其作用、副作用等与他巴唑类似,但作用较缓慢、维持时间较长。

Carbimazole is a common medicine used for hyperthyroidism. It is the ramification of tapazole which can dissociate from carbimazole, as carbimazole hydrolyzes in the body. The effects and side-effects of carbimazole are similar to those of tapazole. It takes time to begin its effects, but they generally last long.

四 练习

（一）课堂练习

1. 听与读

食欲旺盛	多汗	手抖	用药
体重下降	心悸	失眠	用甲亢平
眼球突出	胸闷	乏力	用他巴唑
月经量减少	怕热	腹泻	用心得安

甲状腺	调整用药
甲状腺肿大	根据具体情况调整用药
甲状腺功能	
甲状腺功能亢进症（甲亢）	

2. 替换与扩展

（1）甲亢病人发病时会有哪些典型症状呢？

- 肺炎
- 脑中风
- 急性胰腺炎
- 胃出血

（2）这次复发比较严重，需要住院治疗。

感冒	用抗生素治疗
胃出血	进行手术治疗
高血压发作	立即服降压药

第十四课　甲亢病人发病时会有哪些典型症状？

（3）在 接受治疗 的同时，要 多吃肉。

> 接受化疗　　　　吃些中药
> 增加营养　　　　多锻炼身体
> 吃降压药　　　　保持稳定的情绪

3. 口语练习：交际活动

全班分为 A、B 两组，A 组看附录一，B 组看附录二，准备好后每次各组随机抽取一人进行有信息差的对话。

（二）课外练习

1. 看汉字，写拼音

他巴唑_____　　心得安_____　　维生素_____

碘_____　　甲亢平_____　　震颤_____

失眠_____　　旺盛_____　　调整_____

2. 看拼音，根据生词表写汉字

jiǎkàng_____　　fùfā_____　　xiōngmèn_____

xīnjì_____　　xiàjiàng_____　　jiāncè_____

dǒu_____　　yǎnqiú_____　　nèifēnmì_____

3. 选择合适的词语填空（每个词只能用一次）

> 眼球　调整　失眠　他巴唑　旺盛　复发　下降　监测　甲亢平　抖　甲亢

（1）根据这位患者的病情，我们要对她的用药进行_____。

（2）病人两个月前体重开始_____，可是食欲非常_____。

（3）停药一年后，她的甲亢又_____了。

（4）出院后你要定期来医院检查，对甲状腺功能进行_____。

（5）3床的_____明显向外突出。

（6）最近你常常_____吗？

（7）根据你的症状和检查结果，你得的是_____。

（8）治疗这种病一般用_____和_____。

（9）张医生，6床病人的手_____得很厉害。

4. 根据病人的情况写出合适的问句

（1）病　人：我曾经因为怕热、多汗、食欲旺盛、体重下降被诊断为甲亢。

　　　实习生：_____？

（2）病　人：我吃过他巴唑和心得安。

　　　实习生：_____？

（3）病　人：我最近大便次数比较多。

　　　实习生：_____？

5. 完成下列对话

（1）病人：5年前我曾经被诊断为甲亢。

医生：当时吃过什么药？

病人：吃过_____、心得安、_____等。

医生：有没有定期对_____进行监测？

病人：没有坚持定期_____。吃药三年左右我觉得症状减轻就停药了。

医生：最近感觉怎么样？

病人：两个月前体重开始_____，到现在下降了大概十公斤，可是食欲非常_____。

医生：还有哪些症状呢？

病人：多汗、_____、月经量减少。大便次数也比较多，每天三次，黄色，_____。

（2）医　生：白瑞蒂，你了解了3床的_____了吗？

白瑞蒂：了解过了。病人说她五年前得过甲亢。

医　生：_____的检查结果出来了吗？

白瑞蒂：出来了，您看看。

医　生：根据这个结果，可以确诊为_____了。

白瑞蒂：那这是甲亢_____了吧？

医　生：对。你说说甲亢病人发病时会有哪些_____？

白瑞蒂：心悸、_____、怕热、多汗、_____、_____、食欲_____、体重下降。

医　　生：你再想想，还有其他症状吗？

白瑞蒂：还有乏力、腹泻、＿＿＿＿＿＿＿＿＿＿肿大，血管有杂音和

　　　　　＿＿＿＿＿＿＿＿＿＿、＿＿＿＿＿＿＿＿＿＿突出等。

医　　生：不错。

6. 根据课文内容判断正误

（1）周荷亭五年前被确诊为甲亢，她当时的症状是怕热、　　　（　　）
　　　多汗、食欲不振、体重下降。

（2）周荷亭服药三年左右觉得症状减轻就停药了。　　　　　　（　　）

（3）甲亢病人发病时有心悸、胸闷、失眠、咯血、杵状指等　　（　　）
　　　典型症状。

（4）甲亢病人要少吃高热量、高蛋白和含维生素丰富的食物。　（　　）

（5）年轻的甲亢病人要多吃脂肪类食物，想办法增加体重。　　（　　）

7. 口语练习：复述成段表达的内容

💡 告诉病人检查结果及诊断、治疗方法及注意事项

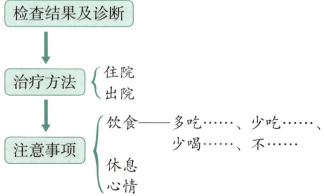

8. 节奏汉语

> **甲亢（甲状腺功能亢进症）**
>
> 甲亢症状很典型，
> 心悸、胸闷、怕热且多汗，
> 手抖、失眠、食欲太旺盛，
> 体重下降、乏力又腹泻，
> 甲状腺肿大、眼球突出，
> 血管杂音和震颤，
> 女性患者月经量减少。
>
> 他巴唑、心得安、
> 维 C 药物来治疗。
> 定期监测很重要，
> 症状减轻别停药。
> 复发严重得住院。
>
> 病人特别需要增加营养，
> 高热量、高蛋白、维生素丰富，
> 此类食物要多吃。
> 比如猪羊和牛肉，
> 淡水鱼、水果和蔬菜。
> 年轻患者别怕胖，
> 多吃脂肪类食物，
> 想办法增加体重。
> 少吃辣椒、海产品，
> 含碘多食物也别碰。
> 不吸烟、不喝酒，
> 少喝浓茶和咖啡。
> 注意休息要愉快。

9. 写作练习：把课文的第二个对话改成对病人情况的叙述

常用专业词语

甲状腺肿瘤	jiǎzhuàngxiàn zhǒngliú	thyroid tumor
甲状腺腺瘤	jiǎzhuàngxiàn xiànliú	thyroid adenoma
甲状腺囊肿	jiǎzhuàngxiàn nángzhǒng	thyroid cyst
甲状腺癌	jiǎzhuàngxiàn'ái	thyroid cancer
甲减	jiǎjiǎn	hypothyroidism

第十五课　他怎么又来了？

（内分泌科—糖尿病）

扫码听

> 学习目标和重难点：
> 1. 与糖尿病相关的词语
> 2. 与其他实习生讨论病人的情况
> 3. 指导医生向病人及家属了解病人的情况
> 4. 向病人及家属交代出院后的注意事项

一　生词

1.	低血糖	dīxuètáng	名	hypoglycemia
2.	输	shū	动	to transfuse
3.	葡萄糖	pútaotáng	名	glucose
4.	静脉	jìngmài	名	vein
5.	注射液	zhùshèyè	名	injection
6.	2型糖尿病	èrxíng tángniàobìng		2-diabetes mellitus
7.	剂量	jìliàng	名	dosage
8.	优降糖	yōujiàngtáng	名	glibenclamide
9.	降糖药	jiàngtángyào	名	blood glucose lowering drug
10.	反应	fǎnyìng	名	reaction
11.	补充	bǔchōng	动	to supplement
12.	碳水化合物	tànshuǐ-huàhéwù		carbohydrate

13.	听信	tīngxìn	动	to believe what one hears
14.	轻度	qīngdù	形	mild
15.	谷物	gǔwù	名	cereal
16.	适当	shìdàng	形	proper
17.	随身	suíshēn	形	(take) with one
18.	携带	xiédài	动	to carry, to take along
19.	饥饿	jī'è	形	hungry
20.	心慌	xīn huāng		(of the heart) beating rapidly
21.	以免	yǐmiǎn	连	in order to avoid, so as not to

二 课文

人物： 指导 医生——谢 文龙
rénwù: zhǐdǎo yīshēng　Xiè Wénlóng

实习生——卡奇、莎娜
shíxíshēng　Kǎqí、Shānà

内分泌科 30 床 病人——邓 新（男，56 岁）
nèifēnmì kē sānshí chuáng bìngrén　Dèng Xīn (nán, wǔshíliù suì)

病人 家属——王 水仙
bìngrén jiāshǔ　Wáng Shuǐxiān

1. 会话

（在 医生 办公室）
（zài yīshēng bàngōngshì）

卡 奇： 莎娜，30 床 不是
Shānà, sānshí chuáng bú shì

中午 一定要 回家
zhōngwǔ yídìng yào huí jiā

的 那个 病人 吗？
de nàge bìngrén ma?

怎么 又 来了？
Zěnme yòu lái le?

莎 娜： 又 是 低血糖 昏迷！在 给 他 输 葡萄糖 静脉
Yòu shì dīxuètáng hūnmí! Zài gěi tā shū pútaotáng jìngmài

注射液 呢。
zhùshèyè ne.

卡 奇： 听说 他 患有 2型 糖尿病。
Tīngshuō tā huànyǒu èrxíng tángniàobìng.

莎 娜： 对。三 天 前 他 看 门诊，医生 叫 他 先 不 吃 药，
Duì. Sān tiān qián tā kàn ménzhěn, yīshēng jiào tā xiān bù chī yào,

注意 饮食 和 运动，可 他 自己 听 朋友 介绍，按
zhùyì yǐnshí hé yùndòng, kě tā zìjǐ tīng péngyou jièshào, àn

最 大 剂量 吃了 优降糖。
zuì dà jìliàng chīle yōujiàngtáng.

卡奇：这应该是服降糖药引起的低血糖反应。
Zhè yīnggāi shì fú jiàngtángyào yǐnqǐ de dīxuètáng fǎnyìng.

（走进病房）
（zǒujìn bìngfáng）

莎娜：你看，30床醒了。我们去叫谢老师过来吧。
Nǐ kàn, sānshí chuáng xǐng le. Wǒmen qù jiào Xiè lǎoshī guòlai ba.

谢文龙：邓先生，现在感觉好多了吧？
Dèng xiānsheng, xiànzài gǎnjué hǎo duō le ba?

邓新：好多了。医生，早上您说我的昏迷是吃了
Hǎo duō le. Yīshēng, zǎoshang nín shuō wǒ de hūnmí shì chīle

优降糖，可是中午回家后我就没吃了，为
yōujiàngtáng, kěshì zhōngwǔ huí jiā hòu wǒ jiù méi chī le, wèi

什么还会昏迷？
shénme hái huì hūnmí?

谢文龙：您回家后吃午饭了吗？
Nín huí jiā hòu chī wǔfàn le ma?

王水仙：他一回家就说累，想睡觉，没吃午饭就睡
Tā yì huí jiā jiù shuō lèi, xiǎng shuìjiào, méi chī wǔfàn jiù shuì

了。三个多小时后，我们发现喊不醒他了，
le. Sān ge duō xiǎoshí hòu, wǒmen fāxiàn hǎn bu xǐng tā le,

只好又把他送来了。
zhǐhǎo yòu bǎ tā sònglai le.

谢文龙：哦，那是因为没吃午饭引起低血糖昏迷了。
Ò, nà shì yīnwèi méi chī wǔfàn yǐnqǐ dīxuètáng hūnmí le.

第十五课　他怎么又来了？

邓　新：为什么会这样呢？
　　　　Wèi shénme huì zhèyàng ne?

谢文龙：您虽然上午注射了葡萄糖，后来也没有再
　　　　Nín suīrán shàngwǔ zhùshèle pútaotáng, hòulái yě méiyǒu zài

　　　　服优降糖，但优降糖的作用时间可持续
　　　　fú yōujiàngtáng, dàn yōujiàngtáng de zuòyòng shíjiān kě chíxù

　　　　二十四小时以上，由于中午您没有及时补充
　　　　èrshísì xiǎoshí yǐshàng, yóuyú zhōngwǔ nín méiyǒu jíshí bǔchōng

　　　　碳水化合物，所以再次出现了低血糖反应。
　　　　tànshuǐ-huàhéwù, suǒyǐ zàicì chūxiànle dīxuètáng fǎnyìng.

卡　奇：吃优降糖的患者都会出现低血糖昏迷
　　　　Chī yōujiàngtáng de huànzhě dōu huì chūxiàn dīxuètáng hūnmí

　　　　吗？
　　　　ma?

谢文龙：不，每个人的情况不同，所以治疗糖尿病
　　　　Bù, měi ge rén de qíngkuàng bù tóng, suǒyǐ zhìliáo tángniàobìng

　　　　不能急，一定要在医生指导下用药。不能
　　　　bù néng jí, yídìng yào zài yīshēng zhǐdǎo xià yòng yào. Bù néng

　　　　随便听信别人的话。
　　　　suíbiàn tīngxìn biérén de huà.

2. 成段表达 （莎娜对邓新、王水仙说）

你们好！今天邓先生可以出院了，我真高兴
Nǐmen hǎo! Jīntiān Dèng xiānsheng kěyǐ chū yuàn le, wǒ zhēn gāoxìng

啊！邓先生虽然得了糖尿病，但只是轻度的。谢医生
a! Dèng xiānsheng suīrán déle tángniàobìng, dàn zhǐshì qīngdù de. Xiè yīshēng

说暂时不用吃药，一个月后来医院复查血糖。您的
shuō zànshí bú yòng chī yào, yí ge yuè hòu lái yīyuàn fùchá xuètáng. Nín de

身体比较胖，一定要注意控制好饮食。您主要的食物
shēntǐ bǐjiào pàng, yídìng yào zhùyì kòngzhì hǎo yǐnshí. Nín zhǔyào de shíwù

应该是谷物和蔬菜，少吃高蛋白、高脂肪、高糖的
yīnggāi shì gǔwù hé shūcài, shǎo chī gāodànbái、gāozhīfáng、gāotáng de

食品。每天要有适当的运动，饭后要坚持散步。外出
shípǐn. Měi tiān yào yǒu shìdàng de yùndòng, fànhòu yào jiānchí sàn bù. Wàichū

时要随身携带一些食物，如果有饥饿、心慌等低血糖
shí yào suíshēn xiédài yìxiē shíwù, rúguǒ yǒu jī'è、xīn huāng děng dīxuètáng

反应，要及时补充，以免发生低血糖昏迷。只要您能
fǎnyìng, yào jíshí bǔchōng, yǐmiǎn fāshēng dīxuètáng hūnmí. Zhǐyào nín néng

做好上面几点，您的糖尿病就能很好地控制
zuòhǎo shàngmiàn jǐ diǎn, nín de tángniàobìng jiù néng hěn hǎo de kòngzhì

住。王阿姨，您平时可以多注意邓先生的身体
zhù. Wáng āyí, nín píngshí kěyǐ duō zhùyì Dèng xiānsheng de shēntǐ

变化。如果他出现多尿、多饮、多食和体重下降这
biànhuà. Rúguǒ tā chūxiàn duō niào、duō yǐn、duō shí hé tǐzhòng xiàjiàng zhè

种 "三多一少" 的 糖尿病 典型 症状，就要 马上
zhǒng "sānduō-yìshǎo" de tángniàobìng diǎnxíng zhèngzhuàng, jiù yào mǎshàng

让 他 到 医院 来 检查。
ràng tā dào yīyuàn lái jiǎnchá.

注释

1. 又是低血糖昏迷！

在临床上，如果某个病人反复出现一种症状，或者多个病人患同一种病，我们常常用到"又是"的句式。如：

We often use the pattern of "又是" to mean that a symptom or an illness recurs in the same patient or several patients have the same disease. e.g.

（1）又是重感冒！
（2）又是发高烧！

"血糖"是指血液中所含的葡萄糖，是机体的能源之一，主要来源于食物中的淀粉以及肝中的糖原。

"低血糖昏迷"是一组多种病因引起的综合征。临床表现为饥饿感、乏力、出汗、面色苍白、心悸、嗜睡、昏迷。血糖测定可以及时确诊。低血糖急性发作时应静脉注射或点滴葡萄糖。

"血糖" refers to glucose contained in blood which mainly originates from the starch in food and glycogen in liver. It is one kind of the body's energy sources.

"低血糖昏迷" is a syndrome caused by various factors. The clinical manifestations include hunger sensation, hypodynamia, pallor, palpitation, drowsiness and coma. It can be diagnosed by a blood glucose test. An acute attack of hypoglycemia should be treated with intravenous injection or continuous infusion of glucose.

2. 听说他患有2型糖尿病。（v. + 有）

"有"用在单音节动词后面，表示具有或存在，常见的动词为"写""装""含""涂""患"等，这些动词跟"有"结合紧密，类似于一个动词，但后面一般不出现"着""了""过"。如：

"有" is often used behind monosyllable verbs to mean having, possessing or being existent. Verbs such as "写""装""含""涂""患" can combine with "有" to act like one verb, but they will not be followed by words such as "着""了""过".
e.g.

（1）山本患有重感冒。

（2）这种水果含有丰富的维生素。

"糖尿病"是以慢性高血糖为特征的一种疾病。临床上分为1型（胰岛素依赖型）和2型（非胰岛素依赖型）。典型症状是多饮、多尿、多食及体重降低的"三多一少"症状。其诊断依据是临床症状、血糖、尿糖检查及口服葡萄糖耐量试验等。

"糖尿病" is a disease characterized by chronic hyperglycaemia. There are two types of diabetes: type I (insulin dependent diabetes) and type II (non-insulin dependent diabetes). Typical symptoms are called "三多一少", including polydipsia , polyuria, polyphagia and loss of weight. The diagnosis is made based on clinical symptoms, blood and urine glucose tests, oral glucose tolerance test and so on.

3. 这应该是服降糖药引起的低血糖反应。（"应该是" + 推测的病因 + "引起的" + 症状）

医生在确诊之前，往往会根据临床经验对病人发病原因作出推测，这时常用这个句式。如：

Usually the doctor will use this pattern to speculate on the cause of a patient's disease based on his clinical experiences before a definite diagnosis is made. e.g.

（1）这应该是感冒引起的发烧。

（2）这应该是过敏引起的红疹。

4. 他一回家就说累，想睡觉。（一……就……）

"一……就……"格式表示两个动作或情况紧接着发生。前一个动作或情况常常是后一个动作或情况发生的条件。如：

"一……就……" means that two actions or things happen one after another. The former part, i.e. the part preceding "就" supplies the condition for the latter part. e.g.

（1）他一激动就胸口痛。

（2）张医生一上班就去看昨天的病历记录。

5. 要及时补充（食物），以免发生低血糖昏迷。

"以免"，连词，用在下半句的开头，表示上半句所做事情的目的是使下半句所说的情况不至于发生。如：

"以免" is a conjunction which is often used at the beginning of the latter half of a sentence. It means for the purpose of not letting something happen as illustrated in the latter half of the sentence. e.g.

（1）你要注意控制好情绪，以免血压升高。

（2）你要及时补充碳水化合物，以免出现低血糖反应。

四 练习

（一）课堂练习

1. 听与读

又是高血压昏迷　　出现低血糖反应　　补充碳水化合物
又是低血糖昏迷　　出现过敏反应　　　补充蛋白质
又是中风昏迷　　　出现中毒反应　　　补充维生素

患有糖尿病　　葡萄糖　　最大剂量
患有肺炎　　　优降糖　　最小剂量
患有胆囊炎　　低血糖　　正常剂量
　　　　　　　降糖药　　按最大剂量服用
　　　　　　　糖尿病　　适当加大剂量

2. 替换与扩展

（1）听说他患有<u>2型糖尿病</u>。

　　心肌梗死
　　冠心病
　　胆囊炎
　　慢性肾炎

（2）这应该是<u>服降糖药</u>引起的<u>低血糖反应</u>。

高血压	头疼
甲亢	眼球突出
支气管扩张	杵状指
慢性肾小球肾炎	浮肿

第十五课　他怎么又来了？

（3）他要<u>及时补充食物</u>，以免<u>发生低血糖昏迷</u>。

```
注意保暖      哮喘再次发作
注意饮食      再得急性肠胃炎
控制好情绪    心绞痛发作
```

（4）他不是那个<u>低血糖昏迷</u>的病人吗？怎么<u>又来了</u>？

```
昨天刚出院的          又来住院了
得了糖尿病            不注意控制饮食呢
发生过低血糖昏迷      不随身携带一些食物
```

（5）他一<u>回家</u>就<u>说累</u>。

```
吃油腻的东西          胃痛
服降压药              不头晕了
吃优降糖              有低血糖反应
补充碳水化合物        不感到心慌了
```

3. 口语练习：参考使用下列词语看图对话

场景提示：实习生和糖尿病人家属的对话。病人出现低血糖昏迷，实习生向病人家属询问病人昏迷的过程，找出昏迷原因：服降糖药引起的低血糖反应。然后给病人输葡萄糖静脉注射液。家属在旁边与实习生对话，内容是病人醒后要注意的问题。

糖尿病　优降糖　碳水化合物　注射液　低血糖昏迷
低血糖反应　携带　以免

（二）课外练习

1. 看汉字，写拼音

低血糖_____　　葡萄糖_____　　优降糖_____

降糖药_____　　静脉_____　　饥饿_____

心慌_____　　携带_____　　注射液_____

碳水化合物_____　　2 型糖尿病_____

第十五课　他怎么又来了？

2. 看拼音，根据生词表写汉字

fǎnyìng_____　　yǐmiǎn_____　　jìliàng_____

bǔchōng_____　　qīngdù_____　　shìdàng_____

3. 词语搭配（可多选）

服	食物
补充	反应
患有	别人的话
控制	降糖药
输	糖尿病
出现	液
听信	饮食
携带	碳水化合物

4. 选择适当的词语填空（每个词语只能用一次）

葡萄糖　补充　昏迷　饮食　剂量　适当　反应　以免　引起　携带

（1）30床病人出现了低血糖_____，这应该是服降糖药_____的。

（2）5床病人要马上做手术，_____出现生命危险。

（3）病人这次_____是因为吃了优降糖。

（4）医生说得了轻度糖尿病可以先不用药，注意_____和运动就可以了。

（5）他自己按最大_____吃了优降糖。

（6）护士在给他输_____静脉注射液呢。

（7）甲亢病人要适当_____维生素C。

（8）患冠心病的人应该随身_____硝酸甘油片。

（9）糖尿病人要注意控制饮食和_____运动。

5. 根据问句写出合适的应答句

（1）病人家属：我丈夫吃了降糖药为什么会昏迷呢？

实习生：_____。

（2）病人家属：我丈夫中午没吃饭，也没有再吃优降糖，为什么又昏迷了？

实习生：_____。

（3）指导医生：你还记得优降糖的作用可持续多长时间吗？

实习生：_____。

（4）指导医生：糖尿病"三多一少"的典型症状指的是什么？

实习生：_____。

6. 完成下列对话

医生：现在_____好多了吧？

病人：好多了，谢谢医生。早上您说我的昏迷是吃了优降糖，可是中午回家后我没吃了，为什么_____？

医生：您回家后_____？

病人：我很累，没吃午饭就睡了。

医生：可能是由于您中午没有及时补充碳水化合物，所以出现了_____。

第十五课　他怎么又来了？

病人：是不是吃优降糖的患者都会出现_____呢？

医生：不，每个人的情况不同，所以治疗_____不能急，一定要在医生的指导下_____，不能随便_____别人的话。

7. 根据课文内容判断正误

（1）优降糖的作用时间可持续 24 小时以上。　　　　　　（　）

（2）吃优降糖的患者都会出现低血糖昏迷。　　　　　　　（　）

（3）"三多一少"的糖尿病典型症状是：多尿、多饮、多食和饭量减少。　　　　　　　　　　　　　　　　　　　（　）

（4）糖尿病人要多吃高蛋白、高脂肪、高糖的食品，每天饭后要坚持散步。　　　　　　　　　　　　　　　　　　（　）

（5）糖尿病人如果有饥饿、心慌等低血糖反应，要及时补充食物，以免发生低血糖昏迷。　　　　　　　　　　　　（　）

8. 口语练习：复述成段表达的内容

告诉病人诊断结果、出院后的注意事项

诊断结果
↓
出院后病人的注意事项 { 用药 / 复查 / 饮食——主要食物、少吃…… / 运动 / 外出
↓
出院后家属的注意事项 { 病人的身体变化——如果……就……

9. 节奏汉语

> **2型糖尿病**
>
> 糖尿病典型"三多一少",
> 多饮、多尿和多食,
> 体重下降得注意。
> 注意饮食和运动,
> 主食谷物和蔬菜,
> 少吃三高类食品。
> (高蛋白、高脂肪、高糖)
> 饭后坚持多散步,
> 随身携带小食物,
> 及时补充碳水化合物。
> 饥饿、心慌、低血糖,
> 及时补充别昏迷。
> 降糖药有优降糖,
> 用药一定遵医嘱。

10. 写作练习:把练习6的对话改成对病人情况的叙述

第十五课　他怎么又来了？

常用专业词语

1 型糖尿病	yīxíng tángniàobìng	1-diabetes mellitus
胰岛素	yídǎosù	insulin
胰岛素缺乏	yídǎosù quēfá	insufficient insulin
空腹血糖	kōngfù xuètáng	fasting blood glucose, FBG
糖耐量	tángnàiliàng	sugar tolerance

第十六课　我们现在有了新疗法

（普外科—胆石症）

扫码听

学习目标和重难点：

1. 与胆石症相关的词语
2. 与病人家属讨论病人的情况
3. 向指导医生报告病人的情况
4. 向病人及家属解释医生的治疗方案及术后注意事项

一 生词

1.	绞痛	jiǎotòng	形	angina, colicky pain
2.	隐痛	yǐntòng	名	dull heavy ache
3.	肩部	jiānbù	名	shoulder
4.	胆石症	dǎnshízhèng	名	gallstone, cholelithiasis
5.	放射痛	fàngshètòng	形	radiating pain
6.	伴	bàn	动	to be accompanied by
7.	实性感	shíxìnggǎn	名	palpability
8.	直径	zhíjìng	名	diameter
9.	厘米	límǐ	名	centimeter
10.	尽早	jǐnzǎo	副	as early as possible
11.	尽快	jǐnkuài	副	as soon as possible
12.	切除术	qiēchúshù	名	resection
13.	疗法	liáofǎ	名	therapy

第十六课　我们现在有了新疗法

14. 腹腔镜	fùqiāngjìng	名	laparoscope
15. 普伐他汀钠	pǔfátātīngnà	名	pravastatin sodium
16. 加强	jiāqiáng	动	to promote
17. 平常	píngcháng	名	usually
18. 含量	hánliàng	名	content
19. 内脏	nèizàng	名	internal organ, viscus
20. 有效	yǒuxiào	动	to have effects
21. 预防	yùfáng	动	to prevent

二　课文

人物：　指导 医生——周　梅
rénwù:　zhídǎo yīshēng　Zhōu Méi

　　　　实习生——卡奇
　　　　shíxíshēng　Kǎqí

　　　　普外科　21　床　病人——章　萍（女，45 岁）
　　　　pǔwàikē èrshíyī chuáng bìngrén　Zhāng Píng (nǚ, sìshíwǔ suì)

1. 会话

卡　奇：您好，您 哪儿 不 舒服？
　　　　Nín hǎo! Nín nǎr bù shūfu?

章　萍：医生，我肚子疼得 很厉害。
　　　　Yīshēng, wǒ dùzi téng de hěn lìhai.

卡　奇：是 上腹 疼 还是 下腹 疼？
　　　　Shì shàngfù téng háishi xiàfù téng?

章 萍： 上腹，靠右边。
Shàngfù, kào yòubian.

卡 奇： 是 什么样 的痛？是 绞痛 还是 隐痛？
Shì shénmeyàng de tòng? Shì jiǎotòng háishi yǐntòng?

章 萍： 一开始 是 隐痛，后来 越来越 严重， 变成了
Yì kāishǐ shì yǐntòng, hòulái yuèláiyuè yánzhòng, biànchéngle

绞痛， 特别 是 吃过 饭 以后， 还 感觉 恶心，
jiǎotòng, tèbié shì chīguo fàn yǐhòu, hái gǎnjué ěxin,

想 吐。
xiǎng tù.

卡 奇： 是不是吃过油腻 的 东西 以后 疼 得 更 厉害？
Shì bu shì chīguo yóunì de dōngxi yǐhòu téng de gèng lìhai?

章 萍： 是。
Shì.

卡 奇： 还 有其他 地方 不 舒服 吗？
Hái yǒu qítā dìfang bù shūfu ma?

章 萍： 有，我的 右 肩部 和 腰背部 也 疼。
Yǒu, wǒ de yòu jiānbù hé yāo-bèibù yě téng.

卡 奇： 这样 的 情况 持续了多 长 时间？
Zhèyàng de qíngkuàng chíxùle duō cháng shíjiān?

章 萍： 有一个星期了。我 会 不 会 是 得了胃病啊？
Yǒu yí ge xīngqī le. Wǒ huì bu huì shì déle wèibìng a?

卡　奇：不太像。您躺下来，我来给您做一下儿胆囊
　　　　Bú tài xiàng. Nín tǎng xiàlai, wǒ lái gěi nín zuò yíxiàr dǎnnáng

　　　　触诊 吧。
　　　　chùzhěn ba.

2. 会话

卡　奇：周 老师，我怀疑 21 床 病人 得了 胆石症。
　　　　Zhōu lǎoshī, wǒ huáiyí èrshíyī chuáng bìngrén déle dǎnshízhèng.

周　梅：她有哪些 症状？
　　　　Tā yǒu nǎxiē zhèngzhuàng?

卡　奇：患者 主诉 右上腹 绞痛，还有肩部和背部的
　　　　Huànzhě zhǔsù yòu-shàngfù jiǎotòng, hái yǒu jiānbù hé bèibù de

　　　　放射痛。 伴 有 恶心、呕吐。
　　　　fàngshètòng. Bàn yǒu ěxin、 ǒutù.

周　梅：你给 她做 胆囊 触诊了 吗？
　　　　Nǐ gěi tā zuò dǎnnáng chùzhěn le ma?

卡　奇：做过 了，患者 胆囊 肿大，有 触痛，而且 有
　　　　Zuòguo le, huànzhě dǎnnáng zhǒngdà, yǒu chùtòng, érqiě yǒu

　　　　实性感。
　　　　shíxìnggǎn.

周　梅：胆囊 有 触痛，说明 病人 可能 是 胆结石，
　　　　Dǎnnáng yǒu chùtòng, shuōmíng bìngrén kěnéng shì dǎnjiéshí,

　　　　还 伴 有 胆囊炎。
　　　　hái bàn yǒu dǎnnángyán.

卡 奇: 患者 的 B超 结果
Huànzhě de B-chāo jiéguǒ

已经出来了，您看看。
yǐjīng chūlai le. nín kànkan.

周 梅: 嗯，你看，患者 胆囊
Ǹg, nǐ kàn, huànzhě dǎnnáng

里有结石，直径大约有3到4厘米。现在可以
li yǒu jiéshí, zhíjìng dàyuē yǒu sān dào sì límǐ. Xiànzài kěyǐ

确诊 了。
quèzhěn le.

卡 奇: 这位 病人需要做手术 吗？
Zhè wèi bìngrén xūyào zuò shǒushù ma?

周 梅: 她的 症状 非常 明显，结石也比较大，应
Tā de zhèngzhuàng fēicháng míngxiǎn, jiéshí yě bǐjiào dà, yīng

尽早 手术。你去 通知 一下儿 病人 吧。
jǐnzǎo shǒushù. Nǐ qù tōngzhī yíxiàr bìngrén ba.

3. 成段表达 （卡奇对章萍说）

章 女士，我们 根据您的 临床 症状 和 B超
Zhāng nǚshì, wǒmen gēnjù nín de línchuáng zhèngzhuàng hé B-chāo

检查 的结果，现在 确诊 您得了胆囊 结石。但您也不必太
jiǎnchá de jiéguǒ, xiànzài quèzhěn nín déle dǎnnáng jiéshí. Dàn nín yě búbì tài

担心，这是一种比较常见的疾病。我们建议您尽快接受胆囊切除术，这是治疗胆结石的最好方法。您可以放心，我们现在有了新疗法，可以用腹腔镜胆囊切除术，您不会有什么痛苦。这两天您放松心情，准备手术。另外，手术后您要按时服用普伐他汀钠，加强胆固醇代谢。平常要多吃维生素含量高的绿色蔬菜、水果，少吃动物内脏、蛋黄、肥肉这些胆固醇和脂肪含量比较高的食物。要保持精神愉快，经常做些运动，不要坐太长时间，这样就能有效地预防胆结石的复发了。

注释

1. 绞痛　隐痛　放射痛

"绞痛"指体内产生的剧烈疼痛，疼痛的部位像被用力扭着、拉着一样。

"绞痛" means very severe pain in the body. It feels like being twisted or pulled very hard.

"隐痛"指隐隐约约的疼痛。

"隐痛" means dull pain.

"放射痛"指远离病变部位的疼痛。如肝胆疾病的疼痛放射至右肩，心绞痛放射至左肩及左臂内侧，非腹部器官疼痛放射至腹部等。

"放射痛" means that the pain extends to other parts of the body, well away from the part that causes the pain. For example, the pain caused by liver and gallbladder diseases radiates to the right shoulder. Angina pectoris radiates to the left shoulder or inside of the left arm. Non-abdominal pain radiates to the abdomen.

2. 是不是吃过油腻的东西以后疼得更厉害？

胆结石患者不能吃过于油腻的东西，也不能吃动物的内脏，因为这些食物胆固醇含量太高了，不易消化，也会刺激胆道的收缩，容易诱发胆道结石病。所以如果医生怀疑患者得了胆石症时，问诊的时候一般会问患者是否吃过此类食物，或者吃过此类食物后的反应，以帮助诊断。

Cholelithiasis patients can neither eat greasy food nor the internal organs of animals, because these foods contain a high level of cholesterol and they are not easily digested. In addition, they can stimulate the bile duct to contract, and thus induce the occurrence of cholelithiasis. If we suspect that the patient has cholelithiasis, during interrogation we usually ask him if he ate the foods mentioned or had any reactions after eating them to facilitate our diagnosis.

3. 胆石症

胆石症包括胆囊结石和胆管结石。胆囊结石常合并急性、慢性胆囊炎，患者表现为右上腹或心窝部痛，进食油腻食物后易出现症状，不少胆囊结石患者主诉有"胃痛"，有时还会有右肩背部痛及发热症状。

Cholelithiasis includes gallbladder stone and bile duct stone. Gallbladder stone is often accompanied by acute or chronic gallbladder inflammation, and the patient has pain in the right upper quadrant or in the pit of the stomach. The symptom easily appears after eating greasy food. Many patients with gallbladder stone complain of stomachache. Sometimes they have symptoms of fever and right shoulder or back pain.

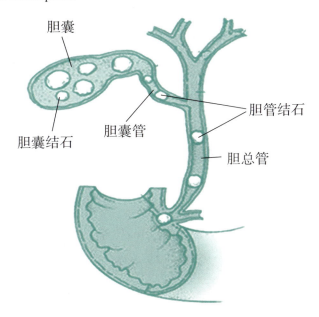

4. 患者主诉右上腹绞痛，还有肩部和背部的放射痛。伴有恶心、呕吐。

医生在陈述或记录患者病情时，如有多个症状同时出现，常在主要症状后用"伴有"一词来表示还有其他症状。如：

When the doctor describes or writes down the patient's condition, "伴有" is used to express that there are other symptoms to follow the chief complaint. For examples:

（1）病人可能是胆结石还伴有胆囊炎。

（2）他得了急性肠胃炎伴有重感冒。

5. 实性感

指可触摸到的或有硬块的感觉。

"实性感"（palpability） means the feeling that something or a hard lump is tangible by touch.

6. 尽早 / 尽快

"尽"，常放在别的词前面，表示力求在一定范围内达到最大限度。

"尽早"，副词，表示尽可能地提前。如：

Here "尽" is usually placed before other words to express doing one's best to reach a maximum.

"尽早" is an adverb which means as early as possible, e.g.

（1）我想尽早出院。

"尽快"，副词，表示尽量加快。如：

"尽快" is an adverb which means as quickly as possible, e.g.

（2）他疼得这么厉害，尽快把他送到医院吧。

7. 腹腔镜胆囊切除术

腹腔镜是一种带有微型摄像头的医疗器械。腹腔镜胆囊切除术就是利用腹腔镜及其相关器械，通过腹部细小的穿刺口进入腹腔进行的胆囊切除手术。它可以减轻病人开刀的痛苦，同时使病人的恢复期缩短，大部分进行了腹腔镜胆囊切除术的病人术后当天就可以回家，可以正常饮食和活动。而进行开腹胆囊切除术的病人术后则要留院5～7天，一周后才能正常饮食，

4～6周后才能正常活动。

Laparoscope is a medical apparatus with microcamera. Laparoscope cholecystectomy is the operation performed by laparoscope and its related devices which go through small incision into the peritoneal cavity. This operation can relieve the pain caused by lancet operation; meanwhile it can shorten the patients' recovery time. Most of the patients who undergo the laparoscope cholecystectomy can go home the same day after the operation and can eat a normal diet and return to normal activity. However, the patient undergoing operation by opening peritoneal cavity must be hospitalized for 5 to 7 days, get back to a normal diet one week after the operation and return to normal activity 4 to 6 weeks after the operation.

四 练习

（一）课堂练习

1. 听与读

绞痛	胆囊	结石	上腹
剧痛	胆囊炎	胆结石	下腹
隐痛	胆囊肿大	胆囊结石	右肩部
压痛	胆囊触诊	肾结石	腰背部
放射痛		胆石症	
反跳痛		得了胆石症	

腹腔镜	胆固醇	普伐他汀钠
胆囊切除术	胆固醇代谢	服用普伐他汀钠
腹腔镜胆囊切除术	加强胆固醇代谢	
接受腹腔镜胆囊切除术		

2. 替换与扩展

（1）我怀疑21床病人得了<u>胆石症</u>。

　　急性肠胃炎
　　肺炎
　　甲亢
　　低钾血症

（2）你给她做<u>胆囊触诊</u>了吗？

　　腹部触诊
　　腹腔镜检查
　　B超检查
　　心肺听诊

（3）我们建议您尽快<u>接受胆囊切除手术</u>。

　　做一次支气管造影
　　进行肝功能检查
　　进行肾功能检查
　　输葡萄糖静脉注射液

（4）这样就能有效地预防<u>胆结石</u>的复发了。

　　甲亢
　　哮喘病
　　胰腺炎
　　支气管扩张

3. 口语练习：交际活动

　　全班分为A、B两组，A组看附录一，B组看附录二，准备好后每次各组随机抽取一人进行有信息差的对话。

（二）课外练习

1. 看汉字，写拼音

厘米＿＿＿＿＿　　直径＿＿＿＿＿　　疗法＿＿＿＿＿

胆石症＿＿＿＿＿　　切除术＿＿＿＿＿　　腹腔镜＿＿＿＿＿

实性感＿＿＿＿＿　　普伐他汀钠＿＿＿＿＿　　内脏＿＿＿＿＿

2. 看拼音，根据生词表写汉字

jiǎotòng＿＿＿＿＿　　yǐntòng＿＿＿＿＿　　fàngshètòng＿＿＿＿＿

jiānbù＿＿＿＿＿　　yǒuxiào＿＿＿＿＿　　yùfáng＿＿＿＿＿

jiāqiáng＿＿＿＿＿　　hánliàng＿＿＿＿＿

3. 选择合适的词语填空（每个词语只能用一次）

> 直径　预防　尽快　加强　胆结石　伴有　隐痛　含量　疗法　肩部

（1）一开始是＿＿＿＿＿，后来越来越严重，变成了绞痛。

（2）胆囊有触痛，说明病人可能是＿＿＿＿＿，还＿＿＿＿＿胆囊炎。

（3）结石＿＿＿＿＿有3～4厘米。

（4）是不是＿＿＿＿＿和腰背部也疼？

（5）我们建议您＿＿＿＿＿接受胆囊切除术。

（6）您要按时服用普伐他汀钠，＿＿＿＿＿胆固醇代谢。

（7）绿色蔬菜、水果的维生素＿＿＿＿＿特别高。

（8）这样就能有效地_____胆结石的复发了。

（9）使用这种_____，患者的痛苦少，术后可以正常饮食和活动。

4. 根据问句写出合适的应答句

（1）指导医生：21床病人有哪些症状？

实 习 生：_____。

（2）指导医生：21床病人是什么样的痛？绞痛还是隐痛？

实 习 生：_____。

（3）指导医生：你给她做胆囊触诊了吗？

实 习 生：_____。

（4）指导医生：这样的情况持续多长时间了？

实 习 生：_____。

（5）指导医生：患者的B超结果怎么样？

实 习 生：_____。

5. 完成对话

周梅：卡奇，21床病人有哪些主要症状？

卡奇：患者主诉_____，还有肩部和背部的_____，伴有恶心、呕吐。

周梅：你给她做_____了吗？

卡奇：做过了，触诊发现胆囊_____，有触痛，而且有_____。

周梅：这说明病人可能是_____，还伴有_____。她的B超结果出来了吗？

卡奇：哦，已经出来了，您看看。

周梅：患者胆囊里有结石，＿＿＿＿＿＿大约有3到4厘米。现在可以确诊病人得了＿＿＿＿＿＿。

6. 根据课文内容判断正误

（1）章萍的下腹很疼。　　　　　　　　　　　　　　　（　）

（2）章萍得了胆囊结石。　　　　　　　　　　　　　　（　）

（3）章萍的胆囊肿大，有触痛，而且有实性感。　　　　（　）

（4）服用普伐他汀钠，可以减少胆固醇代谢。　　　　　（　）

（5）动物内脏、蛋黄、肥肉这些食物的胆固醇含量比较低。（　）

（6）多休息、少做运动，可以有效地预防胆结石的复发。（　）

7. 口语练习：复述成段表达的内容

告诉病人检查结果及诊断、治疗方法及注意事项

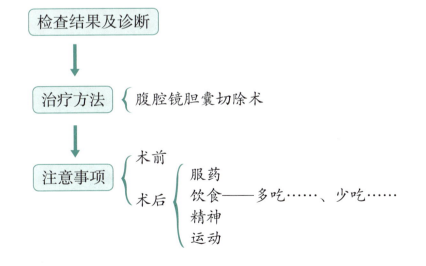

8. 节奏汉语

> **胆囊结石**
>
> 患者主诉右上腹绞痛,
> 肩部、背部放射痛,
> 伴有恶心和呕吐,
> 胆囊触诊来检查。
> 胆囊肿大有触痛,
> 而且还有实性感。
> B超检查有结石,
> 直径较大应手术。
> 胆囊切除术是最好方法,
> 现在又有了新疗法,
> 腹腔镜胆囊切除术,
> 病人不会感觉到痛苦。
> 术后服用普伐他汀钠,
> 加强胆固醇代谢。
> 油腻东西要少吃,
> 多吃蔬菜和水果。
> 精神愉快多运动,
> 有效防止病复发。

9. 写作练习:把课文的第二个对话改成对病人情况的叙述

第十六课　我们现在有了新疗法

常用专业词语

胆固醇结石	dǎngùchún jiéshí	cholesterol stone
胆色素结石	dǎnsèsù jiéshí	bilirubin pigment stone
混合型结石	hùnhéxíng jiéshí	mixed stone
胆囊结石	dǎnnáng jiéshí	gallbladder stone
肝外胆管结石	gānwài dǎnguǎn jiéshí	extrahepatic gallstone

第十七课　饭后运动不会直接诱发阑尾炎
（普外科—阑尾炎）

扫码听

> 学习目标和重难点：
> 1. 与阑尾炎相关的词语
> 2. 向病人了解病情
> 3. 向指导医生报告病人的情况
> 4. 向中国实习生转述病人的情况

一　生词

1.	转移	zhuǎnyí	动	to shift
2.	肚脐	dùqí	名	umbilicus
3.	一阵子	yízhènzi	数量	a period of time
4.	直接	zhíjiē	形	direct
5.	诱发	yòufā	动	to induce
6.	阑尾炎	lánwěiyán	名	appendicitis
7.	叩诊	kòuzhěn	动	percussion
8.	麦氏点	màishìdiǎn	名	McBurney's point
9.	腹膜	fùmó	名	peritoneum
10.	刺激	cìjī	动	to stimulate
11.	征象	zhēngxiàng	名	sign
12.	波及	bōjí	动	to spread to

13.	难怪	nánguài	副	no wonder
14.	肠鸣音	chángmíngyīn	名	bowel sound
15.	减弱	jiǎnruò	动	to weaken, to attenuate
16.	计数	jìshù	动	to count
17.	避免	bìmiǎn	动	to avoid
18.	并发症	bìngfāzhèng	名	complication
19.	判断	pànduàn	动	to decide
20.	盲肠	mángcháng	名	cecum
21.	剧烈	jùliè	形	intense
22.	吸收	xīshōu	动	to absorb

二 课文

人物： 指导 医生——王 瑶
rénwù: zhǐdǎo yīshēng　　Wáng Yáo

实习生——莎娜、李力
shíxíshēng　　Shānà、Lǐ Lì

普外科 13 床 病人——齐晖（男，25 岁）
pǔwàikē shísān chuáng bìngrén　　Qí Huī (nán, èrshíwǔ suì)

1. 会话

王瑶：莎娜，你去看看 13 床的病人，问一下儿病史和症状。
Shānà, nǐ qù kànkan shísān chuáng de bìngrén, wèn yíxiàr bìngshǐ hé zhèngzhuàng.

莎娜：好的。
Hǎo de.

齐晖：大夫，我肚子很不舒服。
Dàifu, wǒ dùzi hěn bù shūfu.

莎娜：你不要着急，我马上给你做检查。你肚子哪里不舒服？
Nǐ búyào zháojí, wǒ mǎshàng gěi nǐ zuò jiǎnchá. Nǐ dùzi nǎli bù shūfu?

齐晖：一开始是上腹部疼，现在又转移到肚脐了。
Yì kāishǐ shì shàng fùbù téng, xiànzài yòu zhuǎnyí dào dùqí le.

莎娜：经过多长时间才转移到脐部的？
Jīngguò duō cháng shíjiān cái zhuǎnyí dào qíbù de?

齐晖：七到八个小时吧。
Qī dào bā ge xiǎoshí ba.

莎娜：疼得厉害吗？
Téng de lìhai ma?

齐　晖：大多数时候是隐痛，有一阵子疼得很厉害。
Dàduōshù shíhou shì yǐntòng, yǒu yízhènzi téng de hěn lìhai.

另外我还感觉恶心，不想吃东西。
Lìngwài wǒ hái gǎnjué ěxin, bù xiǎng chī dōngxi.

莎　娜：量过体温了吗？
Liángguo tǐwēn le ma?

齐　晖：量过了，39度。
Liángguo le, sānshíjiǔ dù.

莎　娜：我怀疑你得了急性阑尾炎。
Wǒ huáiyí nǐ déle jíxìng lánwěiyán.

齐　晖：阑尾炎？是不是因为我前天一吃完午饭就
Lánwěiyán? Shì bu shì yīnwèi wǒ qiántiān yì chīwán wǔfàn jiù

去打篮球了？
qù dǎ lánqiú le?

莎　娜：饭后运动不会直接诱发阑尾炎。现在还不
Fànhòu yùndòng bú huì zhíjiē yòufā lánwěiyán. Xiànzài hái bù

能确诊，我再给你做些别的检查吧。
néng quèzhěn, wǒ zài gěi nǐ zuò xiē bié de jiǎnchá ba.

2. 会话

王　瑶：13床病人的情况怎么样？
Shísān chuáng bìngrén de qíngkuàng zěnmeyàng?

莎　娜：他有典型的转移性腹痛，还有高热和胃肠道
Tā yǒu diǎnxíng de zhuǎnyíxìng fùtòng, hái yǒu gāorè hé wèichángdào

症状。我怀疑他是急性阑尾炎。
zhèngzhuàng. Wǒ huáiyí tā shì jíxìng lánwěiyán.

王 瑶：还有其他的体征吗？
Hái yǒu qítā de tǐzhēng ma?

莎 娜：我给他做了叩诊，他的麦氏点有压痛。这是
Wǒ gěi tā zuòle kòuzhěn, tā de màishìdiǎn yǒu yātòng. Zhè shì

急性阑尾炎的重要体征吧？
jíxìng lánwěiyán de zhòngyào tǐzhēng ba?

王 瑶：是的。病人有腹膜刺激征象吗？
Shì de. Bìngrén yǒu fùmó cìjī zhēngxiàng ma?

莎 娜：有。病人不但有压痛，还有反跳痛。
Yǒu. Bìngrén búdàn yǒu yātòng, hái yǒu fǎntiàotòng.

王 瑶：这说明病人阑尾的炎症已经波及腹膜了。
Zhè shuōmíng bìngrén lánwěi de yánzhèng yǐjīng bōjí fùmó le.

莎 娜：哦，难怪病人的腹肌非常紧张，而且肠鸣音
Ò, nánguài bìngrén de fùjī fēicháng jǐnzhāng, érqiě chángmíngyīn

也减弱了。
yě jiǎnruò le.

王 瑶：病人的血常规检查结果出来了吗？
Bìngrén de xuèchángguī jiǎnchá jiéguǒ chūlai le ma?

莎 娜：出来了，白细胞计数升高，达到了 15 ×
Chūlai le, báixìbāo jìshù shēng gāo, dádàole shíwǔ chéng

10^9／L，炎症反应很明显。
shí de jiǔcìfāng měi shēng, yánzhèng fǎnyìng hěn míngxiǎn.

王 瑶：现在可以确诊病人得了急性阑尾炎了。为了避免发生更严重的并发症，要尽快给病人做阑尾切除手术。

3. 成段表达 （莎娜对李力说）

李力，我们科今天来了一位腹痛的患者，王老师叫我去了解他的病情。患者告诉我他有转移性腹痛，我对他进行检查后还发现他的麦氏点有压痛，血常规的白细胞计数已经升得很高。我判断这个患者得了急性阑尾炎，王老师也同意我的判断，建议病人立即接受阑尾切除手术。你知道吗？病人以为是因为几天前刚吃过午饭就去打篮球引起急性阑尾炎的。学医以前，我也担心饭后参加体育活动会把食物掉到盲肠里，引起阑尾炎，现在才知道这种担心是没有必要的。我明天还要提醒那个病人，虽然饭后运动不会得阑尾炎，但是饭后还是不要进行剧烈运动。因为这样对胃肠道的消化和吸收都不好，对健康没有好处。

注释

1. 阑尾炎

阑尾发炎的病，多由于病菌、寄生虫或其他异物侵入阑尾引起。主要症状是右下腹疼痛、恶心、呕吐等。俗称盲肠炎。

The etiology of appendicitis is multiple; mostly it is caused by bacteria, parasites and invasive foreign bodies. The main symptoms are the pain in the right lower quadrant, nausea, vomiting and so on. Its popular name is "盲肠炎".

2. 叩诊

指用手指或锤状器械叩击人体胸、腹等部位，借以诊断疾病的方法。

Percussion is a method used by the doctor. With fingers or percussion hammer the doctor taps at the patient's chest, abdomen and so on to make diagnosis.

3. 麦氏点

麦氏点又称阑尾点，位于右髂前上棘与脐连线的中外 1/3 交界处。急性阑尾炎是外科常见病，在外科急腹症中占首位，所以麦氏点压痛在急性阑尾炎的诊断中具有重要作用。

McBurney's point is the projection of the surface of appendix root, usually in umbilical and right anterosuperior iliac spine of attachment, and the third point of intersection (McBurney's point) for mark, sometimes also in left and right anterosuperior iliac spines of attachment right of a third intersection point (Lanz point). The pressing pain of McBurney's point is clinically important sign and symptom of acute appendicitis.

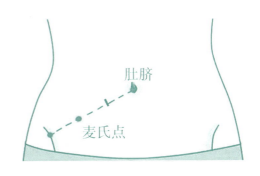

4. 腹膜

腹腔内包着胃肠等脏器的薄膜，由结缔组织构成。

The peritoneum is the thin membrane which covers the stomach, intestines and other organs of peritoneal cavity. It consists of connective tissue.

5. 病人不但有压痛，还有反跳痛。（不但……，还／也……）

连词"不但"和副词"还／也"用在表示递进的复句里，"不但"用在前一分句，"还／也"用在后一分句。如果两个分句的主语相同，主语在"不但"前边；如果主语不同，主语要放在"不但"后边。后一分句所说的情况比前一分句有所增加或在前一分句的范围之外有所补充时，用"还"；前后分句所说的情况一样时，用"也"。

Here the conjunction "不但" and the adverb "还/也" are used in the compound clause to express progressive meaning, "不但" is used in the former clause and "还/也" is used in the latter. If the subjects of the two clauses are different, the subject must be put behind "不但". If the condition mentioned in the latter clause is more severe than that in the former or is supplementary to that in the former, we use "还". If the conditions in both clauses are the same, we use "也".

6. 肠鸣音

肠蠕动时，肠管内气体和液体随之流动，产生一种断断续续的咕噜声（或气过水声），这种声音叫作"肠鸣音"。正常情况下，肠鸣音大约为4～5次/分钟。如果持续3～5分钟以上才听到一次肠鸣音或听不到肠鸣音，称为肠鸣音减弱或消失，可见于急性腹膜炎、肠麻痹等。

In the process of peristalsis, intraluminal gas and water move along, and thus produce a rumbling or gurgling sound intermittently. This sound is referred to as "肠鸣音". Normally bowel sounds can be heard 4 to 5 times per minute. If bowel sounds are absent or occasional as in once every 3 to 5 minutes, absence or decreased of bowel sound are present. These are symptoms for acute peritoneum inflammation and intestinal paralysis.

7. 并发症

一种疾病在发展过程中引起另一种疾病或症状的发生，后者即为前者的并发症。如胃溃疡可能引起胃穿孔或胃出血等并发症。

Complication is a secondary disease or symptoms which occur in the process of the existing disease. For example, perforation or bleeding is the complications of gastric ulcer.

8. 转移性腹痛

转移指病痛从一个部位转往另一个部位。典型的急性阑尾炎病人，腹痛开始的部位多在上腹部，剑突下或脐周围，经6～8小时或十几个小时后，腹痛部位逐渐下移，最后固定于右下腹部。这种腹痛部位的变化，在临床上称之为转移性右下腹痛，是急性阑尾炎所独有的特征，也是和其他急腹症鉴别的主要依据之一，绝大多数的病人具有这一特点。

Shifting abdominal pain means that the pain migrates from one part to another part. In the patient with typical appendicitis, the abdominal pain mostly starts in epigastrium, subxiphoid area or umbilicus. After 6 to 8 hours or longer than 10 hours, the pain migrates to the lower abdomen, at last it is localized in the right lower quadrant. Clinically this phenomenon is called shifting right lower abdominal pain. This is the unique feature of acute appendicitis and it is the major evidence for differentiating it from other acute abdominal diseases.

9. 盲肠

大肠的一段，下端有阑尾。

The cecum is a part of the large intestine and its low end is appendix.

四 练习

（一）课堂练习

1. 听与读

腹痛	阑尾炎	波及
转移	急性阑尾炎	波及腹膜
转移性腹痛	诱发急性阑尾炎	波及盲肠
典型的转移性腹痛	阑尾切除手术	波及阑尾

征象 ： 麦氏点
有腹膜刺激征象 ： 麦氏点有压痛

肠鸣音 ： 并发症
肠鸣音减弱 ： 发生严重的并发症

2. 替换与扩展

（1）一开始是<u>左肩</u>疼，现在又转移到<u>背部</u>了。

右下腹	胃部
上腹部	脐部
手臂	肩部
左腿	右腿

（2）<u>饭后运动不会直接</u>诱发<u>阑尾炎</u>。

冠心病病人情绪激动容易	心绞痛
暴饮暴食可能	胰腺炎
吃了不干净的东西可能	急性肠胃炎

（3）我判断这个患者得了<u>急性阑尾炎</u>。

糖尿病
支气管扩张
胆囊炎
急性白血病

3. 口语练习：参考使用下列词语看图对话

场景说明：两位实习生的对话。讨论一位急性阑尾炎病人的病情和治疗方法等。

上腹部　转移　肚脐　隐痛　厉害　怀疑　急性阑尾炎　麦氏点　肠鸣音

（二）课外练习

1. 看汉字，写拼音

阑尾炎＿＿＿＿＿＿　　诱发＿＿＿＿＿＿　　刺激＿＿＿＿＿＿

腹膜＿＿＿＿＿＿　　　盲肠＿＿＿＿＿＿　　麦氏点＿＿＿＿＿＿

肠鸣音＿＿＿＿＿＿　　肚脐＿＿＿＿＿＿　　并发症＿＿＿＿＿＿

2. 看拼音，根据生词表写汉字

zhuǎnyí＿＿＿＿　xīshōu＿＿＿＿　nánguài＿＿＿＿　zhíjiē＿＿＿＿

bìmiǎn＿＿＿＿　　pànduàn＿＿＿＿　bōjí＿＿＿＿　　kòuzhěn＿＿＿＿

3. 选择合适的词语填空（每个词语只能用一次）

> 判断　阑尾炎　难怪　减弱　诱发　直接　叩诊　剧烈　避免　转移

（1）她听诊时发现患者的肠鸣音＿＿＿＿＿了。

（2）我＿＿＿＿＿这个患者得了急性阑尾炎。

（3）饭后不要进行＿＿＿＿＿运动。

（4）病人的疼痛＿＿＿＿＿到肚脐了。

（5）我怀疑你得了急性＿＿＿＿＿。

（6）我给她做了＿＿＿＿＿，她的麦氏点有压痛。

（7）饭后运动不会直接＿＿＿＿＿阑尾炎。

（8）为了＿＿＿＿＿脑中风的发生，您要特别注意饮食，不要喝酒。

（9）你应该＿＿＿＿＿跟病人说清楚化疗后会出现的不良反应。

（10）8床得的是阑尾炎，＿＿＿＿＿血常规的白细胞计数这么高。

4. 根据病人的情况写出合适的问句

（1）病　　人：我一开始是上腹部疼，现在又转移到肚脐了。

　　　实 习 生：＿＿＿＿＿＿＿＿＿＿＿＿＿＿＿＿＿＿＿＿？

（2）病　　人：我大多数时候是隐痛，有一阵子疼得很厉害。

　　　实 习 生：＿＿＿＿＿＿＿＿＿＿＿＿＿＿＿＿＿＿＿＿？

（3）指导医生：病人的麦氏点有压痛，白细胞计数升高。

　　　实 习 生：＿＿＿＿＿＿＿＿＿＿＿＿＿＿＿＿＿＿＿＿？

5. 完成对话

（1）病　　人：大夫，我感觉_____。

　　　医　　生：肚子哪里疼？

　　　病　　人：一开始是_____，现在又_____到了肚脐。

　　　医　　生：经过多长时间才转移到_____的？

　　　病　　人：七八个小时吧。

　　　医　　生：疼得厉害吗？

　　　病　　人：大多数时候是_____，有一阵子疼得_____。

（2）实　习　生：老师，13床有典型的_____腹痛，还有_____和胃肠道症状。

　　　指导医生：你给他做了哪些检查？

　　　实　习　生：做了_____，他的麦氏点有_____。

　　　指导医生：病人有腹膜刺激_____吗？

　　　实　习　生：有，病人不但有压痛，还有_____。

　　　指导医生：这说明病人的阑尾炎症已经_____到腹膜了。

　　　实　习　生：难怪病人的腹肌_____，而且_____也减弱了。

　　　指导医生：血常规结果如何？

　　　实　习　生：_____计数很高，炎症反应很_____。

　　　指导医生：现在可以_____病人得了急性阑尾炎了，要尽快给他做_____。

6. 口语练习：复述成段表达的内容

> 向中国实习生转述病人的主诉、检查结果、诊断、治疗方法，并解释人们对急性阑尾炎病因的误解。

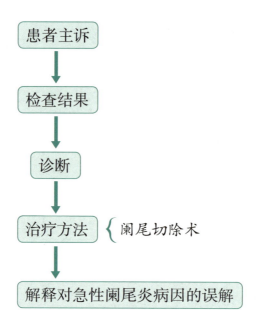

7. 节奏汉语

急性阑尾炎

病人患了急性阑尾炎，
转移性腹痛很典型，
高热、胃肠道不舒服，
叩诊麦氏点有压痛，
同时还有反跳痛。
炎症一旦波及腹膜，
血常规白细胞升很高，
为了避免严重并发症，
立即接受阑尾切除术。
饭后最好别剧烈运动，
对胃肠道消化、吸收都不好。

8. 写作练习：把课文的第二个对话改成对病人情况的叙述

常用专业词语

慢性阑尾炎	mànxìng lánwěiyán	chronic appendicitis
早期急性阑尾炎	zǎoqī jíxìng lánwěiyán	early acute appendicitis
急性化脓性阑尾炎	jíxìng huànóngxìng lánwěiyán	acute purulent appendicitis
阑尾脓肿	lánwěi nóngzhǒng	appendiceal abscess
阑尾穿孔	lánwěi chuānkǒng	appendiceal perforation

附录一　交际活动 A

第 2 课：

你是印度尼西亚实习生马奔。负责 17 床的哮喘病人。你还不认识他,他昨天晚上哮喘病发作入院,有呼吸急促、唇指发绀等症状。现在你要去问问他的身体情况,还要给他做肺部听诊等。

第 4 课：

你是实习生,负责 8 床。8 床病人住院三天了,昨天白天身体已经好多了,可是昨晚肠胃炎又急性发作了。你去问他昨晚的身体情况和再次发作的原因,告诉病人饮食方面要注意的问题,并为他开化验单。

第 6 课：

你是实习生。负责消化内科 9 床病人。刚才你对 9 床进行了体格检查,初步诊断他得了胆囊结石和胆囊炎。讨论病情时你回答指导医生的问题。

第 8 课：

你是实习生。你看了 3 床的心电图、胸片、血常规等检查结果,初步诊断他得了冠心病、心绞痛。你向指导医生报告 3 床的病情。

第 12 课：

你是实习生。你向 1 床了解病史、这次发病的情况、现在的症状。告诉病人医生的诊断,并解答病人的问题。

第 13 课：

你是住院部肾内科的实习生。有一位病人刚从门诊转来，你要问他的病情和病史，并检查他的身体。尽量用上"浮肿、尿量、效果、凹陷、粗、水泡音、泼尼松、紫纹"等词。

第 14 课：

你是内分泌科 8 床病人，30 岁。你最近两个月怕热、多汗、心悸、食欲旺盛、体重持续下降，月经量减少，大便每天约 3 次。你今天刚住院，实习生来问你病情，你要好好儿回答他的问题。

第 16 课：

你是实习生。21 床的 B 超结果出来了，初步诊断他得了胆石症。你要向你的指导医生报告 21 床的 B 超结果、治疗方法、手术后病人要注意的问题。

附录二　交际活动 B

第 2 课：

你叫李卫。昨天因为哮喘病发作住院,在呼吸内科 17 号病床。今天你觉得好多了,呼吸不太急,唇指的颜色也恢复了正常,可以躺一会儿了。

第 4 课：

你是 8 床的病人,住院三天了。你昨天白天已经好多了,下午跟朋友一起出去吃海鲜,昨晚又拉了七八次,大便像水一样。你把这些情况告诉实习生。

第 6 课：

你是消化内科的副主任医师,也是实习生的指导医生。你让实习生对 9 床病人做体格检查,他做完检查后你问他检查的情况,指导他进行诊断。

第 8 课：

你是指导医生。实习生向你报告 3 床病人的检查结果,你和他分析病史、病情,指导他进行诊断。

第 12 课：

你是 1 床病人。实习生向你了解病史、现在的症状。你向实习生了解自己得了什么病、应该怎样治疗等。

第 13 课：

你是刚从门诊转到住院部肾内科的病人。你 1 个星期前劳累后气促、发热,体温在 37.5 度到 38.5 度之间,最高的时候 39 度。咳嗽没痰,尿量 600～800 ml,有泡沫。眼睑和双腿浮肿。两年前有过这样的症状，但没发热。服过泼尼松。到住院部后，实习生问你的病情和病史，你要回答他的问题。

第14课：

你是内分泌科的实习生。今天有一位病人刚住院，你看见她多汗、手抖、眼球明显向外突出。你要问她的病情，并根据指导医生的意见，安排她进行身体检查和甲状腺功能检查。

第16课：

你是实习生的指导医生。你让实习生对21床病人的B超结果进行分析，并根据实习生说的情况，指导他进行诊断，提出治疗方案以及手术后病人要注意的问题。

附录三 英文翻译

Lesson 1

Text

Persons

Director—Ma Wen

Intern—Shana

Inpatient of the Department of Respiratory—Jiang Haishan

1. Dialogue

Ma Wen: Good morning!

Jiang Haishan: Good morning! Dr. Ma.

Ma Wen: Allow me to make an introduction. This is the intern Shana. This is Jiang Haishan, the patient of bed No.5.

Shana: How do you do!

Jiang Haishan: How do you do!

Ma wen: Jiang Haishan, Shana is responsible for your bed. If you have any trouble, you can contact her.

Jiang Haishan: All right! Where are you from, Dr. Shana?

Shana: I am Pakistani. My Chinese is not very good. Could you please speak slowly to me?

Jiang Haishan: Your Chinese is very good. I can understand you.

Shana: Thanks! I have read your case record. When you were admitted to the hospital yesterday, the diagnosis was pneumonia. How are you feeling today?

Jiang Haishan: I feel a little better after I got injection and took medicine.

2. Dialogue

Shana: Mr. Jiang. Do you still have any pain in the chest or sputum today?

Jiang Haishan: I still have chest pain when I cough, mainly hacking cough with scanty sputum production.

Shana: Let me listen to your lungs again. Hmm, there is still moist rale.

Jiang Haishan: What problem does this moist rale show?

Shana: It means you still have inflammation in your lungs. Now let me take your temperature.

After ten minutes

Jiang Haishan: Oh, doctor, I still have a fever. The temperature is 38.9°C.

Shana: Your temperature is quite high, which also means you still have inflammation. Do you have a headache?

Jiang Haishan: A little.

Shana: How about your breathing?

Jiang Haishan: Still short of breath, and my cough is still serious.

Shana: Now you have a rest, and continue your injection and drug therapy. I'll tell your condition to Dr. Ma.

3. Express the whole period (Shana speaks to Dr. Ma)

Dr. Ma, I have read the medical record of the patient in bed No.5, and asked him about today's condition. When he was admitted to our hospital, his temperature was 40°C. He felt short of breath and his cough was serious. When he coughed, he felt a chest pain, but mainly hacking cough with scanty sputum production. There is moist rale in both his lungs. The X-ray taken yesterday revealed small patches of unclear shadow in his lungs, and pneumonia was diagnosed. I asked him about today's condition, he said he felt better after injection and drug therapy, but he still has headache, dry cough, shortness of breath, chest pain and so on. I listened to his lungs, and there is moist rale. The temperature is 38.9 °C. I asked him to take a good rest, continue to have injections and take pills.

Lesson 2

Text

Persons

Intern supervisor—Chen Dong

Interns—Kaqi and Li Li

Inpatient of the Department of Respiratory—Zhang Yingmei (female, 54 years old)

1. Dialogue

Chen Dong: Kaqi, please pay special attention to the patient in bed No. 23 today.

Kaqi: What's the matter with her?

Chen Dong: The doctor on duty says that she had asthma breaking out last night because she caught a cold while bathing.

Kaqi: What symptoms did she have?

Chen Dong: She breathed rapidly, had cold sweat on forehead and cyanotic in lips and figures. And she couldn't be in supine position.

Kaqi: Then, I'd better go to take a look and have lung auscultation for her now.

Chen Dong: Oh, all right.

Kaqi: Dr. Chen, what should I pay attention to while having auscultation?

Chen Dong: Please be careful to find out whether or not she has wheeze stridor at expiration.

2. Dialogue

Kaqi: Mrs. Zhang, how are you? How do you feel now?

Mrs. Zhang: I feel much better.

Kaqi: Let me have lung auscultation for you.

Mrs. Zhang: Ok. Thank you!

Kaqi: Now, breathe in—, breathe out—. Very well. There's no wheeze stridor now.

Mrs. Zhang: I felt terrible at midnight last night.

Kaqi: How did you feel at that moment?

Mrs. Zhang: I couldn't lie down. I breathed rapidly and had cold sweat on the forehead. I only felt a little better while at sitting position.

Kaqi: You must take care not to catch a cold again, because it is dangerous for asthma patients.

Mrs. Zhang: Ok, I certainly will be more careful; it feels terrible to have asthama break out.

Kaqi: You were lucky to have it break out while being in hospital this time. It would be even more terrible if you were at home.

3. Connected Speech (Kaqi to Li Li)

Li Li, today we have a patient at Respiratory Department who had an asthma break out last night due to catching a cold while bathing. It is said that she breathed rapidly, had cold sweat on the forehead, cyanotic in lips and figures, couldn't be in supine position, and had wheeze stridor at expiration. It was very serious. Today Dr. Chen asks me to pay special attention to her condition. I went to have lung auscultation for her. She no longer has wheeze stridor in lungs while breathing, and the color of her lips and fingers have been back to normal. She doesn't feel uncomfortable in supine position and feels much better now. I told her to take care not to catch cold again, because it would be terrible if asthma had broken out while she had been at home and couldn't have been treated in time.

Lesson 3

Text

Persons

Intern supervisor—Liu Chuanhua

Intern—Bairuidi

Bed No.2 inpatient of the Department of Respiratory Medicine—Su Jun (male, 39 years old)

The family member of the patient—He Tao, Su Jun's wife

1. Dialogue

Liu Chuanhua: Bairuidi, have you seen bronchiectasis case?

Bairuidi: Yes, I saw it on the table. I'll get it to you (She goes and gets the medical record of bed No. 2 to Liu.)

Liu Chuanhua: Ah? No, no. I meant the medical case of the disease bronchiectasis, not the medical record of patient's condition.

Bairuidi: (Blushing) Oh! I am sorry! I thought that you wanted to read the medical record! Alas! "Medical case" and "medical record" sound the same in Chinese pronunciation. Chinese is really difficult.

Liu Chuanhua: Yes, it is. So you should try hard to learn Chinese better! Ok. Since you have brought the record of bed No. 2 here, we can review the patient's condition first.

Bairuidi: OK! (She reads the record.) Before hospitalized, the patient has had several relapses of acute respiratory tract infection. The day before admission, the patient started coughing and had massive hemoptysis...

Liu Chuanhua: This is a typical bronchiectasis case. Let me take you to see him.

Bairuidi: Alright.

2. Dialogue

He Tao: Hello! Doctor Liu!

Liu Chuanhua: Hello! This is student intern Bairuidi.

Bairuidi: Hello! Ah! How beautiful these flowers are! Wonderful sweet scent!

He Tao: They were brought by Su Jun's colleagues a moment ago.

Liu Chuanhua: Don't put flowers in the ward room. People of bronchial disease are easy to get allergic to the sweet scent of flowers.

He Tao: I see. I'll take them away.

Liu Chuanhua: Bairuidi, please have auscultation for bed No.2.

Bairuidi: Ok, Dr. Liu. I can't I hear the moist rales.

Liu Chuanhua (To He Tao): Did he remove phlegm with force?

He Tao: He coughed very badly, and spit a great deal of phlegm.

Liu Chuanhua (To Bairuidi): The moist rales would disappear temporarily after the patient remove phlegm with force. You can hear it after some time.

Bairuidi: Look, his fingers seem so big.

Liu Chuanhua: These are clubbed fingers. One third of the patients who have bronchiectasis for a long time have this symptom.

Bairuidi: I see.

3. Connected Speech (Bairuidi to He Tao)

Your husband had a bronchography examination, and bronchiectasis has been diagnosed. Bronchial patients are allergic to pollen, smoke, and fog. So please neither place flowers brought by friends in the ward room, nor permit your friends and relatives to smoke here. Make sure that the ward room has fresh air. If he perspires badly, please let him drink a lot of water. Also make sure to keep him warm. Please check his temperature often to see if there is a fever. Watch if he has hemoptysis. If any of these happens, you should tell us promptly. Foods such as egg, meat, fish, bean curd and fresh fruits and vegetables will do him good. But don't let him eat too much once. Eat just a small amount each time, but several times a day.

Lesson 4

Text

Persons

Intern supervisor—Zhou Daming

Intern—Shana

Inpatient of the Department of Digestive Internal Medicine—Li Gang (male, 44 years old, businessman)

1. Dialogue

Li Gang: Good morning! Doctor!

Shana: Hello, Mr. Li, were you just admitted for acute gastroenteritis? How are you feeling now?

Li Gang: My abdomen is still aching, and I feel decline in the whole body. I have had watery diarrhea for more than 10 times today.

Shana: (Looking at the medical record) Do you still vomit?

Li Gang: No.

Shana: Please lie down, and allow me to press your abdomen. Here. Is it painful?

Li Gang: Oh! It's very painful. The pain is killing me! Oh, No! I feel awful...

Shana: What's wrong?

Li Gang: I am sorry! I have to go to the toilet again!

(Li Gang came back from the toilet.)

Shana: You had watery diarrhea again? Is your abdomen still aching?

Li Gang: Emm, now it is not that aching, but still not at ease.

Shana: Please lie down, and I'll examine you again.

Li Gang: Ok. Oh, No! I feel awful...I have to go to the toilet again!

2. Dialogue (3 days later)

Shana: Mr. Li, I heard it from the doctor on duty that you had watery diarrhea for 7 to 8 times again last night.

Li Gang: Yes. The stool was like water. I became so weak afterwards that I almost couldn't stand up.

Shana: What happened? Weren't you much better yesterday?

Li Gang: My friends came to see me yesterday afternoon. When they heard that I had been better, they invited me out to have seafood.

Shana: What? You even had seafood?

Li Gang: (Blushing) I like seafood most, so I couldn't help eating some.

Shana: Good grief! You should have a routine stool test first, and then a blood test. I will make out the test forms for you.

Li Gang: Doctor, I am so sorry.

Shana: Mr. Li, you can't eat randomly any more, especially when you are sick.

Li Gang: Now I understand. I am so seriously ill this time that I will watch what I eat in future.

3. Connected Speech (Shana to Doctor Zhou)

Dr. Zhou, allow me to report the condition of bed No.8 to you. The patient was admitted 3 days ago because of acute gastroenteritis. His condition took a favorable turn after proper treatment. I had planed to discharge him from hospital tomorrow, but he ate seafood with his friends outside the hospital last night. He had a relapse of acute gastroenteritis. He vomited after feeling nausea. He also had severe diarrhea following pain in the stomach—He had 7 to 8 times of watery diarrhea last night. Abdomen examination shows obvious pain when pressed. A few minutes ago when I went for the ward rounds, I asked him to do a routine stool test and blood test, to see if there is any abnormality in them. I will report to you again when the result comes out.

Lesson 5

Text

Persons

Intern supervisor—Deng Jie

Intern—Shana, Li Li

Bed No.11 inpatient of the Department of Digestive Internal Medicine—
Zhu Zhiqi (male, 55 years old, manager)

1. Dialogue

Deng Jie: Hello. Shana. Would you please go over to get the results of CT and the blood serum examinations of the patient of bed No.11?

Shana: Yes. I have got the results. Here you are.

Deng Jie: Oh! The serum amylase is elevated and the CT reveals the pancreatic swelling, and the unclear edge of the pancreas.

Shana: Can we confirm the diagnosis of acute pancreatitis with all this?

Deng Jie: What are the physical signs of his abdomen?

Shana: The physical abdominal examination shows that there is tenderness in the left upper quadrant, and gray and purple spots on the waist skin.

Deng Jie: What is the complaint of the patient?

Shana: He went to a restaurant with his friend for dinner, and had a great deal of meat and sea food. He also drank much alcohol. After he went back home, there was suddenly a persistent abdominal pain. It was soon spread to the left back, and then followed by vomiting and a fever.

Deng Jie: According to the patient's complaint and lab examination results, I think we can make the diagnosis of acute pancreatitis.

2. Dialogue

Zhu Zhiqi: Doctor, what is my trouble?

Shana: It is acute pancreatitis.

Zhu Zhiqi: How have I got this disease?

Shana: It is caused by what you have eaten and drunk.

Zhu Zhiqi: Because they were unhealthy?

Shana: No, because you have eaten too much meat and seafood and also because you have drunk too much. Honestly, how much alcohol did you drink after all?

Zhu Zhiqi: About half kilogram of Maotai.

Shana: Oh! Half kilogram! That will kill you. Do you often drink in your every day life?

Zhu Zhiqi: Yes, I do.

Shana: You have the habit of drinking alcohol like that for quite some time. This time you also have drunk too much and had too much meat and seafood at the same time. That is why you have had acute pancreatitis.

Zhu Zhiqi: Oh! Eating and drinking too much is very dangerous!

Shana: Remember! You should not eat too much meat one time and you'd better stop drinking.

3. Connected Speech (Shana to Li Li)

Li Li, you know something? There is a patient at the Department of Digestive Internal Medicine. When he first came in, he had such a severe abdominal pain that his face turned terribly pale and he could hardly straiten up. He also vomited continuously. Anyway, he was very sick.

His chief complaint is that he had a persistent abdomen pain in the left quadrant, spreading to the waist and back. The abdominal examination showed that there was tenderness in the left quadrant, and gray and purple spots on the waist skin. Blood serum amylase was found to be elevated and the CT indicated the swelling of the pancreas. Dr. Deng told me that he was suffering from acute pancreatitis. The patient himself did not know how he got this disease. Nowadays the life has been improved and some people often go to restaurant to eat and drink. When they drink, they usually drink 500g to 1000g of alcohol at the risk of their lives. Meanwhile they eat too many things with high protein and fat. Today, there is an increasing number of patients with various diseases just because they eat and drink too much.

Lesson 6

Text

Persons

Intern supervisor—Wang Guanping

Intern—Kaqi

Bed No.15 inpatient of the Department of Digestive Internal Medicine—Chen Yan (male, 27 years old)

1. Dialogue

Kaqi: Bed No. 15, which part of your body is not feeling well now?

Chen Yan: My abdomen is aching.

Kaqi: Is it at the epigastrium?

Chen Yan: Yes.

Kaqi: How long has it been like this?

Chen Yan: It began from 10 pm the day before yesterday.

Kaqi: Can you indicate the aching place by point at it?

Chen Yan: The pain starts at the epigastrium, and then I feel the sharp pain at the right abdomen—here.

Kaqi: What kind of pain is it?

Chen Yan: It's a continuous pain. And it becomes sharper, like being cut by a knife. It's all the same whether I'm sitting up or lying down. Oh, it's killing me!

Kaqi: Is any other part of the body also affected?

Chen Yan: My right back aches, too. And the right lumbar region feels uncomfortable.

Kaqi: Do you feel a chill after the sharp pain? Do you have a fever?

Chen Yan: No chill, but I have a low fever.

Kaqi: What colour is your urine?

Chen Yan: Dark yellow.

Kaqi:	Do you remember what you had eaten the night before last?
Chen Yan:	Yes. That night, I ate a lot of beefsteak, chicken and fried eggs at our unit's dinner party. I felt uncomfortable and sick after getting home, and I even threw up.
Kaqi:	How many times have you vomited altogether?
Chen Yan:	About 4 or 5 times.
Kaqi:	What stuff have you thrown up? Is there any blood or green stuff?
Chen Yan:	No. No blood or green stuff. Mainly what I had drunk and eaten.
Kaqi:	Have you had such abdominal pain previously?
Chen Yan:	Yes. I have been attached by such aches for 8 years now, once or twice a year.
Kaqi:	Please try to recall. Were you attacked each time after eating too much greasy stuff?
Chen Yan:	Mostly so. It sometimes also happens as a result of tiredness after working too hard or having too much great time.

2. Connected Speech (Kaqi to Dr. Wang)

The patient of bed No.15 has right epigastrium pain for 8 years, and that usually happens after eating too much greasy stuff or being too tired. He was attacked again the night before last after eating a lot of beefsteak, chicken and fried eggs at his unit's dinner party. The pain started at the epigastrium, then the right abdomen felt sharp pain, and it is continuous. He didn't have chill but has a low fever. He had previously been diagnosed allbladder calculus and a cholecystit after B-mode ultrasonic and CT examination of the abdomen. He was treated with infusion, antibiotics and spasmolytic. I just made an examination for him: the patient's main symptoms include aching at the epigastrium, gallbladder swelling and positive of Murphy's Sign. My preliminary diagnosis is gallbladder calculus and cholecystitis and I will suggest that he have further examinations.

Lesson 7

Text

Persons

Intern supervisor—Wang Guangping

Interns—Bairuidi, Shana, Kaqi and Li Li

The patient in bed No. 9 of Department of Digestive Internal Medicine—

Li Qiang (male, 38 years old)

The family member of the patient—Wang Hua (Li's wife)

1. Dialogue

Wang Guangping: Today let's discuss the condition of the patient in bed No. 9. First please talk about the case history.

Kaqi: (Read the case record) Li Qiang, male, 38 yeas old. In the past he had gastric ulcer with bleeding.

Bairuidi: Twenty days ago occult blood in his stool was positive.

Shana: Recently he was very busy and often went out on official business. Three days ago he was caught in a rain and got a cold. After he had drunk a glass of alcohol , he suddenly vomited blood continuously.

Li Li: His wife quickly sent him to our hospital. After examination in the clinic, gastric hemorrhage was diagnosed. He was transferred to the inpatient department immediately.

Bairudi: After two day's treatment in the hospital, his hematemesis has not been relieved.

Wang Guangping: In this case it is possible to cause gastric perforation.

Kaqi: Should we transfer him to surgery for operation?

Wang Guangping: We must transfer him at once. If it's too late, we shall lose the opportunity for operation. First, you talk with his family about the condition.

Bairuidi, Kaqi, Shana and Li Li: All right ! We do that at once..

2. Dialogue

Kaqi: Are you the family of the bed No. 9?

Wang Hua: Yes ! I am his wife. He vomited blood again just now.

Li Qiang: Doctor, I have a serious abdominal pain.

Li Li: That is gastric hemorrhage caused by ulcer.

Wang Hua: Is his condition severe?

Shana: Dr. Wang said you must be transferred to the surgery department for operation.

Wang Hua: Operation? Is it very dangerous? Can he be cured without operation?

Bairuidi: We have applied internal medical treatment to Mr. Li for two days in our hospital, but without any effect. His conditions have not been improved. Now he'd better be sent to the surgery for operation .

Kaqi: If you did not have the operation as soon as possible, it would be very dangerous. We hope you will accept our suggestion.

Wang Hua: Oh! Since the doctor has said so, I agree, I agree to that!

Bairuidi: Well, now I will take you to go through the procedures for a transfer to the department of surgery.

Kaqi: Please tell the nurse to make preparations to send him to the surgery department.

3. Connected Speech (Kaqi to Dr. Wang)

Dr. Wang, according to your instruction, we went to see the patient in bed No. 9. His family said that he had vomited blood again. The patient himself said that he had severe abdominal pain. We found his face very pale. His limbs were cold with cold sweat. The family was very nervous. We said that Li's hemorrhage was very severe and may cause gastric perforation. It was necessary to transfer him to the surgery department for operation right now. At first the family had worried about the danger of operation, and didn't want him to have the operation. After our explanation she agreed to our suggestion. Now Bairuidi has taken his family over there to go through the transferring procedures. We have noticed that the nurse and his family are now making the preparations. Is there any thing else we can do?

Lesson 8

Text

> **Persons**
>
> Intern supervisor—Xie Xiaoping
>
> Intern—Kaqi
>
> Nurse—Guo Lan
>
> Bed No.20 inpatient of the Department of Cardiovascular—Qian Dongming (male, 65 years old)
>
> The family member of the patient—Qian Yongxing (son of Qian Dongming)

1. Dialogue

Qian Yongxing:	Dad! Good news! You won the lottery, first prize! That's 5 million Yuan!
Qian Dongming:	First prize? 5 million Yuan? Really? Oh! I have hit the Jackpot! I, I, Oh... no...
Qian Yongxing:	Dad! Dad! What's the matter with you? Nurse! Doctor! Somebody, please! Hurry up!
Kaqi:	Grandpa Qian, are you having pain here? (Qian Dongming nods) Nurse, quickly give him Nitroglycerol to be kept under the tongue!
Guo Lan:	Ok. (To Qian Dongming) Now, keep it under your tongue quickly. (Dr. Xie runs into the ward)
Kaqi:	Dr. Xie, bed No.20 was attacked again by pain in the pericardial region, and has just been given Nitroglycerol.
Xie Xiaoping:	Good. (To Qian Dongming) Grandpa Qian, do you feel better now?
Qian Dongming:	Much better now. My son told me that I won the lottery and I was so excited that I was attacked by chest pain again.
Xie Xiaoping:	I see. You need to be careful from now on not to become too excited.

Qian Dongming: Alas! I'm old now. My health is deteriorating. I can't even be excited.

2. Dialogue

Xie Xiaoping: Grandpa Qian, do you still have pain here?
Qian Dongming: No. No more pain.
Xie Xiaoping: How long did it last?
Kaqi: About 10 minutes. He has had that 3 or 4 times a day since he was hospitalized 3 days ago.
Xie Xiaoping: Have you had similar conditions previously?
Qian Dongming: It happened 2 years ago. It wasn't as painful. It lasted for about 3 or 4 minutes each time, and 2 or 3 times a week only.
Xie Xiaoping: Under what circumstances did this happen?
Qian Dongming: Usually when I became tired or excited. It stopped after good rest.
Xie Xiaoping: You must watch your mood and be careful not to be too excited. Please lie down and let me have lung and heart auscultation.
Kaqi: Dr. Xie, what kind of disease does he have?
Xie Xiaoping: Follow me to the office. We'll analyze his condition.

3. Connected Speech (Dr. Xie to Kaqi)

The patient of bed No.20 has a history of hypertension for 3 years. His father had coronary artery disease. I had heart auscultation for him. His cardiac sound is powerful, and has no murmur. Laboratory tests show that his cholesterol and triglyceride level are both high, but the X-ray of chest doesn't show abnormal condition in the heart and lung. The electrocardiogram indicates sinus rhythm and myocardial ischemia when the pain appears in the pericardial region. When Nitroglycerin is kept under the tongue in time, the pain disappears in several minutes, and then the electrocardiogram returns to normal following the disappearance of the pain. Judging from his history, physical condition and results of different examinations, I think that he is coronary artery disease with angina.

Lesson 9

Text

> **Persons**
> Intern supervisor—Li Ying
> Interns—Bairuidi, Shana
> Bed No.6 inpatient of the Department of Cardiovascular—Wu Xin (female, 72 years old)
> The family member of the patient—Wu Xue (the patient's daughter)

1. Dialogue

Li Ying: Bairuidi. A new patient has been admitted to our ward. Have you had a chance to see her? How is she?

Bairuidi: I have been very busy and haven't seen her yet. I was told that she had been transferred from a county hospital. She had acute gastroenteritis.

Li Ying: We'd better not make a conclusion just yet. Let's go and see the patient first.

(They entered the ward.)

Wu Xue: Doctors. My mother just had abdominal pain again.

Li Ying: Did she vomit?

Wu Xue: Yes. And she still feels nausea.

Li Ying: (To Bairuidi) Have you taken her temperature, pulse, respiration and blood pressure?

Bairuidi: The nurse did. (Looking at the case record) The temperature is 36.5℃, P is 80/min, R is 24/min and BP is 120/90mmHg.

Li Ying: Bairudi. Please make auscultation for her heart and lungs.

Bairuidi: Yes. Auscultation of the lungs shows the breath is clear. The rhythm is regular. There are no pathological murmurs in all valve areas.

Li Ying: Please make palpation for her abdomen.

Bairuidi: Yes. Her abdomen is distended, but there is no muscle rigidity.

Wu Xin: I still feel some pain here.

Bairuidi: Abdominal tenderness and rebound pain are not obvious.

Li Ying: Was ECG performed in the county hospital?

Wu Xue: No.

Li Ying: (To Bairuidi) I suspect that it is not acute gastroenteritis. Please have ECG examination for her.

(Half an hour later)

Bairuidi: Dr. Li, ECG reveals myocardial infarction.

Li Ying: Hurry up and transfer the patient to the Cardiovascular Department.

Bairuidi: All right!

2. Connected Speech (Bairuidi to Shana)

Shana, today we transferred a patient to the Cardiovascular Department. She was transferred from a county hospital where she was diagnosed as having acute gastroenteritis. Judging from the patient's conditions, Dr. Li of our Department suspected myocardial infarction, and ECG result proved it. I asked Dr. Li how she knew the patient had been misdiagnosed. She told me that when making diagnosis the patient's age factor must also be considered. The patient is 72 years old, an age when myocardial infarction is likely to occur. The clinical manifestations of myocardial infarction in senior patients can be obviously different from that in middle-aged or young patients. The latter often suffers angina pectoris, while some senior patients have symptoms with the main manifestations such as pain in the epigastrium, nausea, vomiting, abdominal distention and so on, which is similar to acute gastroenteritis, so it is likely to be misdiagnosed. 30% of senior myocardial infarction patients belong to this type.

Lesson 10

Text

Persons

Intern supervisor—Shi Ping

Interns—Li Li, Shana

Bed No.9 inpatient of the Department of Neurology—Li Jiangning (female, 68 years old)

The family member of the patient—Wang Jianjun (Li Jiangning's son)

1. Dialogue

Shi Ping: Hello. Li Li, Shana. Please take a look at the summary of the medical record of the patient in bed No. 9.

Li Li: OK! So, she was hospitalized on February 15th. It has been almost one month.

Shi Ping: Yes. Recently her condition has been rather stable.

Shana: May she be discharged?

Shi Ping: You will understand her condition first, and then go with me to see her. If examination shows everything is alright, we can arrange her to be discharged tomorrow.

Shana: Okay, Li Li. Let's read this together.

Li Li: Good. I'll read first and you listen: Li Jiangning, female, 68 years old. She has had hypertension for 10 years. On the 15th of February, after drinking alcohol, she felt headache and nausea. She vomited, and could not move her left limbs.

Shana: Does "left limbs couldn't move" mean that the left hand and left leg could not move.

Li Li: Yes, your Chinese is pretty good.

Shana: When the patient was hospitalized, her blood pressure was 220/120 mmHg, and her heart rate was 108/min.

Li Li: Let me read the following. She was in deep coma and she had urine incontinence. Cerebral hemorrhage was confirmed by CT examination. The haematoma of 20 ml was in the brain cortex.

Shana: Dr. Shi, now we have a preliminary understanding of the patient's condition.

Shi Ping: OK. Now let's go and see her.

2. Connected Speech (Shana to the family)

Your mother can be discharged tomorrow. After leaving the hospital, she must watch her diet. No alcohol, fewer high protein, high fat, and high calorie foods, but more beans, fruits, and vegetables. Make sure to keep warm in winter. Remember to take hypotensor. Don't stop taking the drugs even if her blood pressure becomes normal. In addition, the patient must remain calm, and should not become too excited. If her blood pressure becomes very high, or if she feels sudden severe headache, dizziness, nausea and vomiting, that is the sign for apoplexy. The patient should keep quiet and lie down to rest. Try not to remove her body at all; and shaking of the head is strictly forbidden. If the patient feels worse, you should call 120 for ambulance; or hold her head, keep her in the supine position, and send her to the hospital for treatment.

Lesson 11

Text

Persons

Intern supervisor—Jiang Haitao

Intern—Kaqi

Bed No.19 inpatient of the Department of Hematology—Chen Limin (female, 15 years old)

The family member of the patient—Zhang Min (the mother of Chen Limin)

1. Dialogue

Kaqi: Hi, Mrs. Zhang, I am Kaqi, an intern. Was your daughter admitted yesterday? Did she see any doctor before the admission?

Zhang Min: Yes. She saw a doctor at a district hospital and the diagnosis was upper respiratory tract inflammation.

Kaqi: What symptoms did she have at that time?

Zhang Min: Her face looked pale and she felt adynamic all over with occasional dizziness a month ago.

Kaqi: Does she have any fever?

Zhang Min: No. However, She began to have fever half a month ago, the lowest temperature has been 37.5℃ and the highest 39℃. She had cough but didn't have any sputum.

Kaqi: What medicine has she taken?

Zhang Min: Ampicillin and ribavirin. She stopped coughing after taking the medicine but a slight fever kept recurring with the temperature of 38℃.

Kaqi: Is she latest menstrual condition similar to the previous ones?

Zhang Min: No. It lasted 8 days while 5 days for previous periods, and the bleeding was much heavier.

Kaqi: Thank you. I will go to see if her examination results come out or not.

2. Dialogue

Kaqi: Dr. Jiang, the examination results of the patient in bed No. 19 patient have come out.

Jiang Haitao: What is the blood routine test result?

Kaqi: Leucocyte is 8.4×10^9/ L, erythrocyte is 1.74×10^{12}/ L, hemoglobin is 57 g/L , blood platelet is 29×10^9/ L.

Jiang Haitao: This is anaemia. How about the bone marrow smear result?

Kaqi: It is an ANLL-M_2 type bone marrow symptom.

Jiang Haitao: Our primary diagnose is acute leukemia when the patient has just been hospitalized. And the examination result confirmed it.

Kaqi: Dr. Jiang, what is ANLL called in Chinese?

Jiang Haitao: 急性非淋巴细胞白血病 , one type of acute leukemia.

Kaqi: What are the main symptoms of leukemia?

Jiang Haitao: Dizziness, adynamia, anaemia, fever, bleeding and so on. And it is also common for female patients to have increased menstrual bleeding volume.

3. Connected Speech (Kaqi speaks to Zhang Min)

Mrs. Zhang, your daughter's examination result has come out. She is diagnosed with acute leukemia rather than upper respiratory tract inflammation. Acute leukemia is one type of diseases that can become dangerous. Dr. Jiang has said that your daughter needs to be treated with chemotherapy. Please consider Dr. Jiang's suggestion. If you agree, the first course of treatment needs to be in hospital and the subsequent courses can be done at home. Your daughter will feel extremely uncomfortable and bad during chemotherapy and she will lose her hair too. Therefore you should look after her. The treatment course for this disease can be quite lengthy, generally several years are necessary. Your daughter is still young and her chance of recovery is high. So, you need to have confidence. If the chemotherapy effect is not satisfactory, we'll consider taking bone marrow transplant as our next step.

Lesson 12

Text

Persons

Intern supervisor—Zhang Li

Intern—Bairuidi

Bed No.1 inpatient of the department of Urology—Deng Mei (female, 28 years old)

The family member of the patient—Mr. Li (Deng Mei's husband)

1. Dialogue

Bairuidi: Dr. Zhang, I have asked the patient in bed No. 1 to have her urine and blood samples tested according to your instruction.

Zhang Li: Please tell me her physical signs, ok?

Bairuidi: I think that she is abnormally fat.

Zhang Li: She is not fat, she has dropsy with her. I saw she had dropsy all over the body when she was admitted into our hospital yesterday.

Bairuidi: I see. There is severe dropsy on her face, especially around the eyelids. She almost cannot open her eyes.

Zhang Li: How does she look?

Bairuidi: I think she doesn't look lively. She said she felt tired, had hypodynamia, and sore waist.

Zhang Li: How is her urinary excretion?

Bairuidi: She said that the quantity of urine was obviously smaller than usual, and the color was deep yellow, without frequent micturition, urgent micturition and pain in urination.

Zhang Li: How is her appetite?

Bairuidi: She felt nausea, and began vomiting 2 days ago, and felt abdominal distension. She has no appetite.

2. Dialogue

Bairuidi: Miss Deng, your test results have come out.

Deng Mei: What disease do I have?

Bairuidi: According to the urine and blood routine test results, and others exams you took when you came to hospitalization, Dr. Zhang diagnosed you with chronic glomerulonephritis and renal insufficiency.

Deng Mei: Is this disease easy to treat?

Bairuidi: It takes quite a long time to treat this kind of disease.

Deng Mei: Can it be cured then?

Bairuidi: Don't be so worried. After a period of time for hospital treatment, its conditions can be stabilized.

Deng Mei: How long should I stay in the hospital?

Bairuidi: About 1 month. Then you can go home for treatment to consolidate the effects, and come back to the hospital for regular examination.

Deng Mei: I am not afraid now after you told me this, thank you. I'll definitely cooperate with doctors in the treatment process.

3. Connected Speech (Bairuidi to Mr. Li)

Mr. Li, when you were admitted to the hospital the day before yesterday, you said that your wife began to have a fever 12 days ago and her urine volume decreased obviously 5 days later, dropsy started from the eyelids, then spread to the whole body. In these days, she felt sore in waist, felt tired, dizzy, had abdominal distension, nausea and bad appetite. Two days before admission, she began vomiting, 2—3 times a day. She gained about 8 kilograms in weight. She had symptoms of oliguria, and dropsy all over the body when she was 16 years old. She was diagnosed with nephritis in that time. We had her urine and blood tested yesterday. Based on the symptoms and test results of your wife, Doctor Zhang diagnosed chronic glomerulonephritis and chronic renal insufficiency. The treatment will take quite a long time, and may not result in full recovery. But if the patient cooperates actively with doctors in the treatment process, her condition can be controlled. We expect you to show more concern to your wife and encourage her to cooperate actively with the doctors.

Lesson 13

Text

Persons

Intern supervisor—Chen Xiaoting

Interns—Li Li, Shana, Kaqi, Bairuidi

Inpatient of Division of Nephrology, Department of Internal Medicine—Wu Liwei (male, 38 years old)

1. Dialogue

Chen Xiaoting: This patient has just been transferred from the outpatient department. You can start to ask about his medical history.

Kaqi: Mr. Wu, when did you begin feeling unwell?

Wu Liwei: I began to feel short of breath and had a fever after overworking myself a week ago. The temperature was between 37.5℃ and 38.5℃; the highest reached 39℃.

Shana: Have you had any cough?

Wu Liwei: Yes, but without any sputum.

Shana: It's obvious that you've got swollen eyelids. Let us take a look at your legs.

Bairuidi: Dropsy in legs is also very obvious. Do you have normal urine volume?

Wu Liwei: Much smaller than usual, roughly 600-800ml one day and it's more foamy.

Kaqi: Did you have similar symptoms before?

Wu Liwei: Yes, I had similar symptoms 2 years ago, but without a fever.

Shana: Did you go to see a doctor?

Wu Liwei: Yes, I did and had a urine test at a local hospital. The diagnosis was nephritic syndrome.

Bairuidi:	Let me look at your medical record—proteinuria "+ + +", the medicine prescribed is prednisone.
Shana:	What was the effect after taking the medicine?
Wu Liwei:	Swelling disappeared after a week and the urine volume increased, but proteinuria was still "+ + +". I kept taking the medicine for one and a half years. Proteinuria maintains a level of "+".
Kaqi:	How long have you stopped taking the medicine?
Wu Liwei:	Half a year. This is the urine test which I took at the outpatient department here which shows that proteinuria is "+ + + +".
Shana:	Dr. Chen, is this nephritic syndrome?
Chen Xiaoting:	Yes, but he may have other diseases as well.
Kaqi:	What shall we do now?
Chen Xiaoting:	Let's start by giving him routine blood and urine tests, biochemical tests, a liver function test and a 24-hour quantitative testing of urinary protein.

2. Connected Speech (Kaqi to Li Li)

Li Li, our division had a new patient the day before yesterday. He had symptoms of a low-grade fever of 37.8 ℃, obvious pitting edema in eyelids and legs, and tiredness when he came. He told us that he began to feel short of breath, started coughing, his urine volume started to fall much below the normal level and had bad appetite after overworking himself a week ago. He was found to have swollen abdomen and purple striae in legs and abdomen in our visual examination. We also found that his breathing sound was rough and had fine moist rales in the right lower lung without dry rales. We gave him routine blood, routine urine tests, biochemical testing, liver function test and 24-hour of quantitative examination of urinary protein. Based on his symptoms and examination results, Dr. Chen diagnosed him with nephritic syndrome, acute renal failure, metabolic acidosis, hypokalemia, hyponatremia and pneumonia in the right lower lung. I'd like to observe how Dr. Chen treats a patient with these symptoms.

Lesson 14

Text

Persons

Intern supervisor—Huang Ming

Intern—Bairuidi

Bed No.3 inpatient of the Department of Endocrinology—Zhou Heting (female, 28 years old)

1. Dialogue

Bairuidi: Hello Miss Zhou. I am Bairuidi, an intern here. Dr. Huang asked me to talk to you to get a detailed account of your medical history.

Zhou Heting: Ok. 5 years ago, I was diagnosed with hyperthyroidism because of heat intolerance, excessive sweating, increased appetite and weight loss.

Bairuidi: What medicine did you take then?

Zhou Heting: Tapazole, propranolol, vitamin C and so on.

Bairuidi: Did you have your thyroid gland function monitored regularly?

Zhou Heting: No. After taking the medicine for about 3 years, I felt relieved of the symptoms, so I stopped taking the medicine.

Bairuidi: How are you feeling recently?

Zhou Heting: 2 months ago, my weight began to drop, and I lost almost 10 kilograms by now despite an increased appetite.

Bairuidi: Any other symptoms?

Zhou Heting: Excessive sweating, heart-throb, decreased menstrual bleeding volume, increased bowel movements, more than 3 times a day, with yellow watery stools.

2. Dialogue

Huang Ming: Bairuidi, come over and look at the result of bed No.3 patient's thyroid function examination.

Bairuidi:	Can the outcome lead to a diagnosis of hyperthyroidism?
Huang Ming:	Yes. She got hyperthyroidism 5 years ago, and it recurred with more severity this time. She needs hospitalized for treatment.
Bairuidi:	Dr. Huang, what are the typical symptoms of hyperthyroidism patients?
Huang Ming:	Heart-throb, chest tightness, heat intolerance, excessive sweating, hands trembling, insomnia, increased appetite with weight loss, fatigue, diarrhea, goiter with vascular murmur, trembling, and eyeball protruding.
Bairuidi:	Oh! As I saw bed No.3 patient's grossly protruding eyeballs, I thought they looked the same way as they used to.
Huang Ming:	Some patients don't show signs of gross eyeball protrusion or no sign of it at all.
Bairuidi:	Are tapazole and carbimazole the common medicine to treat this disease?
Huang Ming:	Yes. But medication should be adjusted according to specific conditions of patients such as the factor of whether they have any other diseases.

3. Connected Speech (Bairuidi to Zhou Heting)

Miss Zhou, according to the outcome from each item of your physical and thyroid gland function test after admission, you are diagnosed hyperthyroidism, or recurrence of hyperthyroidism. Your conditions are severe, and need to be treated in the hospital. You'll be discharged when your conditions improve and then continue your medication treatment. Patients with hyperthyroidism should increase nutrition intake, and eat foods high in calorie and protein, and rich in vitamins. So in the course of your treatment you should eat more beef, pork, mutton, fresh water fish and fruits and vegetables rich in vitamins. Patients young as you should eat more foods rich in fats. Don't be afraid of getting fat, and try your best to gain weight. But try to avoid hot pepper, and those foods rich in iodine. Avoid marine products. Drink strong tea and coffee as little as possible. No smoking. No alcohol drinking. And you should rest more, and keep a happy mind.

Lesson 15

Text

Persons

Intern supervisor—Xie Wenlong

Interns—Kaqi, Shana

Bed No.30 inpatient of the Department of Endocrinology—Deng Xin (male, 56 years old)

The family member of the patient—Wang Shuixian

1. Dialogue

(In the doctor's office)

Kaqi: Shana, the patient of bed No.30 is the one who insisted on going home at noon, isn't he? Why did he come back?

Shana: Coma of hypoglycemia again! He is being treated with intravenous injection of glucose.

Kaqi: I heard he has type 2-diabetes mellitus.

Shana: Right. He saw a doctor at the outpatient department 3 days ago. The doctor told him to adjust his diet and take more exercises rather than taking any medicine. But he took the largest dose of Glibenclamide following his friend's suggestion.

Kaqi: This should be hypoglycemia reaction resulted from taking blood glucose lowering drugs.

(Entering the ward)

Shana: Look, bed No.30 patient awoke. Let's call Dr. Xie to come here.

Xie Wenlong: Mr. Deng, are you feeling much better now?

Deng Xin: Yes, I'm. Doctor, you said that my coma resulted from taking Glibenclamide, but I didn't take it after I went home at noon. Why did it still happen?

Xie Wenlong:	Did you have any lunch after you got home?
Wang Shuixian:	As soon as he got home, he said he was tired and wanted to sleep and then he slept without eating anything. We couldn't wake him up after more than 3 hours no matter how hard we tried so we had to send him back to the hospital.
Xie Wenlong:	So, all that was because he skipped the lunch.
Deng Xin:	Why?
Xie Wenlong:	Although you had glucose injection in the morning and didn't take Glibenclamide afterwards, its effect can last up to more than 24 hours. You didn't take in carbohydrates in time at midday; therefore hypoglycemia reaction appeared once more.
Kaqi:	Will hypoglycemia coma occur to all the patients who take Glibenclamide?
Xie Wenlong:	No. Each person's situation is different, therefore the treatment of diabetes requires patience, and medication must be taken under doctor's instruction and patients shouldn't take others' advice blindly.

2. Connected Speech (Shana to Deng Xin and Wang Shuixian)

Hi, I am really happy that Mr. Deng can be discharged from hospital today. Mr. Deng has but only a mild type of diabetes. Dr. Xie says that you don't need to take medicine for the time being, and then come back to reexamine blood sugar one month later. Mr. Deng, you are quite obese so you must control your diet. You should mainly eat grains and vegetables; eat less the foods high in protein, fat and sugar. You should take proper exercises every day and go for a walk after meals. You'd better bring some food with you when you go out so that when you feel hungry and rapid heartbeat or develop some other symptoms of hypoglycemia reaction, eat them in time to avoid hypoglycemia coma. So long as you can follow the advice above, your diabetes can be kept well under control. Aunt Wang, you should take care to watch for signs of physical changes in Mr. Deng. If he develops polyuria, polydipsia, polyphagia and loss of weight which are the typical "三多一少" symptoms of diabetes, you must send him to the hospital immediately for examinations.

Lesson 16

Text

Persons

Intern supersisor—Zhou Mei

Intern—Kaqi

Bed No.21 inpatient of the Department of General Surgery—Zhang Ping (female, 45 years old)

1. Dialogue

    Kaqi: Hello! What's the matter?

    Zhang Ping: Doctor, I have a severe abdominal pain.

    Kaqi: In the upper or lower part?

    Zhang Ping: In the upper right side.

    Kaqi: What was the pain like? Colic or dull pain?

    Zhang Ping: At first the pain was dull, later it became worse and worse, and turned into colicky pain. And especially after meals I felt nausea and vomited.

    Kaqi: Does the pain become more severe after eating fatty food?

    Zhang Ping: Oh, yes.

    Kaqi: Do you have other discomfort?

    Zhang Ping: I have ache in my right shoulder, back and waist, too.

    Kaqi: How long have you had these symptoms?

    Zhang Ping: About one week. Do you think I may get stomach trouble?

    Kaqi: Not quite likely. Lie down on your back. Let me palpate your gallbladder.

2. Dialogue

    Kaqi: Dr. Zhou, I think the patient of bed No.21 suffers from gallstone.

    Zhou Mei: What symptoms has she got?

Kaqi:	She complains of colicky pain in the right upper quadrant and radiating pain in the shoulder and back accompanied by nausea and vomiting.
Zhou Mei:	Have you palpated her gallbladder?
Kaqi:	Yes, I have. An enlarged gallbladder was felt and there was tenderness and palpability.
Zhou Mei:	Gallbladder tenderness indicates that the patient may develop gallstone with cholecystitis.
Kaqi:	Here's the patient's type B ultrasound examination result. Please take a look at it.
Zhou Mei:	Well, you see. There is a stone in her gallbladder about 3 to 4 cm in diameter. Now our initial diagnosis can be confirmed.
Kaqi:	Is it necessary to perform operation on her?
Zhou Mei:	The patient's symptoms are very apparent and the stone is rather big. I think she should be operated as early as possible. Please talk to her about it.

3. Connected Speech (Kaqi to Zhang Ping)

Mrs. Zhang, based on your clinical symptoms and the result of type B ultrasound examination, we diagnose you with gallstone. But don't worry about it too much as it is a common disease. We suggest you have cholecystectomy operation as soon as possible. It is the best treatment for gallstone. Don't worry. We have a new method that enables us to use laparoscopy to do this operation. You'll hardly suffer any pain. To prepare for the operation you should get relaxed these two days. Besides, after the operation, you should take Pravastatin Sodium in time to improve cholesterol metabolism. Usually, you should eat more green vegetables and fruits high in vitamins and eat as little as possible the foods with high fat and cholesterol such as viscera, egg yolk, and fatty meat. You should keep a happy mood and exercise regularly. Don't sit for a long time. In doing so, you can effectively prevent gallstone relapse.

Lesson 17

Text

Persons

Intern supervisor—Wang Yao

Intern—Shana, Lili

Bed No.13 inpatient of the Department of General Surgery—Qi Hui (male, 25 years old)

1. Dialogue

Wang Yao: Shana, please go to see the patient in bed 13 and ask him about the history of his illness and the symptoms.

Shana: Ok.

Qi Hui: Doctor, I'm feeling terribly unwell with my abdomen.

Shana: Don't worry, I'll examine you right now. Please tell me the position of your discomfort in detail.

Qi Hui: At first I had a pain in the upper part of the abdomen, later it shifted to the navel.

Shana: When did the pain shift to the navel?

Qi Hui: About 7 to 8 hours later.

Shana: Is the pain serious?

Qi Hui: Mostly it is dull pain but sometimes it is very serious. Besides, I feel nausea and have no appetite for anything.

Shana: Have you had your temperature taken?

Qi Hui: Yes, it is 39°C.

Shana: I suspect you have acute appendicitis.

Qi Hui: Appendicitis? Was it caused by my playing basketball after lunch the day before yesterday?

Shana: The exercise after meals won't lead directly to appendicitis. At present we cannot make a definite diagnosis. We'll arrange other examinations for you.

2. Dialogue

Wang Yao: How is the condition of the bed No.13 patient?

Shana: He has a typical shifting abdominal pain, a high fever and symptoms of the gastrointestinal tract. I suspect that he has acute appendicitis.

Wang Yao: Does he have any other signs?

Shana: I gave him a percussion test. There was tenderness in the Mcburney's point. Is that an important feature of acute appendicitis?

Wang Yao: Yes, it is. Does he have any sign of peritoneal irritation?

Shana: Yes. The patient has not only tenderness but also rebound tenderness.

Wang Yao: These indicate the inflammation of appendicitis has spread to the peritoneum.

Shana: No wonder the patient has abdominal muscle rigidity and decreased bowel sound.

Wang Yao: Have you got the result of blood routine examination?

Shana: Yes, He has leukocytosis with white blood cell count of 15×10^9 /L. So inflammation is apparent.

Wang Yao: Now we can confirm our diagnosis for appendicitis. In order to avoid more severe complications, we must perform appendectomy on the patient as quickly as possible.

3. Connected Speech (Shana to Lili)

Lili, today we have admitted a patient with abdominal pain. Dr. Wang asked me to inquire about the patient's condition. The patient told me that he had shifting abdominal pain. After a physical examination for him, I found that he had tenderness in Mcburney's point. The blood routine test revealed highly increased WBC. I diagnosed him with acute appendicitis. Dr. Wang agreed with my diagnosis and suggested the patient have appendectomy operation immediately. Do you know at first the patient thought that his appendicitis was caused by playing basketball just after the meal several days ago? Before I began to study medicine, I had the same worry that physical exercise after meals could force the food to drop into the cecum and thus cause appendicitis. Now I know it is not necessary to have fear like that. Tomorrow I shall remind the patient that though exercise after meals doesn't lead to appendicitis, we shouldn't do strenuous exercises after meals because they can have negative effect on the gastrointestinal movement and absorption, and do harm to our health.

附录四　课外练习部分参考答案

第一课

3.（1）诊断　（2）症状　（3）继续　（4）呼吸　（5）量
（6）湿啰音　炎症　（7）感觉　（8）干咳　（9）拍　（10）胸口

5.（1）怎么样　咳嗽　厉害　痰
（2）体温　烧　X光片　小片状模糊阴影　肺炎

第二课

3. 拍—X光片　冒—冷汗　量—体温　打—针　听—肺　写—病历　吃—药

5.（1）发作　洗澡　着凉　症状　急促　冷汗　发绀　平卧　哮鸣音
　　　值班　肺部听诊
（2）怎么样　好多了　可厉害了　肺部听诊　哮鸣音　怎么样　恢复
　　　躺着/平卧　注意　着凉

第三课

3.（1）病例　（2）病历　（3）感染　（4）反复　（5）咯血
（6）患　（7）确诊　（8）过敏　（9）排　暂时　（10）杵状指

5.（1）怎么样　反复发作的呼吸道感染　大量咯血　支气管扩张的病例
　　　哪些症状　杵状指　杵状指　特别大特别肥/又肥又大
（2）怎么样　咳嗽得很厉害　什么病　支气管造影　可以抽烟吗
　　　身体没好处　过敏　哪些问题　喝水　着凉　发高烧或咯血
　　　鸡蛋、肉、鱼、豆腐和新鲜的水果、蔬菜　谢谢您　不客气

附录四　课外练习部分参考答案

第四课

3. 开—化验单　吃—海鲜　做—常规检查　验—血　出现—腹泻
   上—洗手间　拉—肚子

4.（1）肠胃炎　（2）腹泻/呕吐　（3）腹泻/呕吐　（4）严重
   （5）大便　（6）无力　（7）全身　（8）拉　（9）常规　（10）好转

6.（1）急性肠胃炎　肚子　无力　呕吐　躺下　疼不疼　疼死
   （2）又拉了七八次　大便　没力气　怎么回事　叫我一起出去吃海鲜
       忍不住　大便常规检查　化验单　不好意思

第五课

3.（1）主诉　（2）持续　（3）引起　（4）检查　（5）淀粉酶　肿大
   （6）急性　（7）长期　（8）放射　（9）高蛋白　（10）暴饮暴食

5.（1）血清　淀粉酶　急性胰腺炎　有没有肿大　急性胰腺炎　腹部
       体征　左上腹
   （2）急性胰腺炎　这个病　吃出来　喝酒　急性胰腺炎

第六课

3.（1）一直　（2）抗生素　（3）油腻　胆囊炎　（4）侧　（5）再次
   （6）B超　（7）肿大　呈　（8）初步

5. 胆结石　胆囊炎　油腻　这样的情况吗/这样的症状吗/这样的腹痛吗
   右上腹　抗生素　解痉药　小便　体格　胆囊　墨菲　阳

第七课

3. 做—手术　止—血　办—手续　失去—机会　吩咐—家属
   看—门诊　患—胃溃疡　接受—治疗

4.（1）止　（2）门诊　（3）手术　（4）失去　（5）四肢

295

（6）吩咐　（7）办　（8）接受　（9）潜血　（10）危险

6. 吩咐　吐血　面色苍白　发冷的情况好转了吗　胃穿孔　手术　转科手续

第八课

3.（1）心电图　（2）冠心病　（3）心血管　（4）硝酸甘油片
　（5）杂音　（6）胆固醇　甘油三酯　（7）心肌
　（8）心绞痛　（9）心前区　（10）劳累

5. 血常规　甘油三酯　窦性　缺血　心音　杂音　冠心病

第九课

3. 测—脉搏　考虑—病人的年龄　下—结论　腹—胀　反跳痛—明显
　腹肌—紧张　病理性—杂音　临床—表现

4.（1）胀　（2）触诊　（3）结论　（4）病理性　（5）脉搏
　（6）心肌梗死　（7）考虑　（8）测　（9）清晰　（10）反跳痛

6.（1）心肌梗死　心血管内科　转科手续
　（2）6床/新来的　脉搏　血压　测过　体温　呼吸　mmHg
　　　心肺　心律　病理性杂音　腹肌　反跳痛　心电图

第十课

3.（1）脑出血　（2）先兆　（3）肢体　（4）神经内科
　（5）失禁　（6）昏迷　（7）心率　血压　（8）大脑额叶
　（9）降压药　（10）病情　稳定

5.（1）病情　220/120mmHg　108次/分　深昏迷　失禁　肢体　脑出血
　　　血肿　大脑额叶
　（2）左侧肢体　血压　心率　血肿　脑出血

第十一课

3.（1）贫血　（2）白细胞　红细胞　（3）急性白血病　化疗　（4）疗程　（5）骨髓涂片　（6）骨髓移植

5. 白细胞 8.4×10^9/L，红细胞 1.74×10^{12}/L，血红蛋白 57g/L，血小板 29×10^9/L　骨髓　ANLL-M_2型骨髓象　急性白血病　病名　急性非淋巴细胞白血病　急性白血病　头晕　无力　贫血　比以前多也很常见

第十二课

3.（1）睁—眼　排—尿　各—项　腰—酸　尿—频（尿—尿，尿—酸）
　（2）眼睑—浮肿　积极—配合　巩固—治疗　定期—检查　控制—病情
　　　（答案不唯一）

4.（1）食欲　（2）鼓励　（3）控制　（4）定期　（5）巩固
　（6）睁　（7）浮肿　（8）配合　（9）减少　（10）积极

6.（1）检查结果　得的是什么病　血常规检查　慢性肾小球肾炎
　　　慢性肾功能不全　完全治好　鼓励　积极配合治疗
　（2）发热　尿量明显减少　颜色　酸　乏　晕　腹　食欲　呕吐
　　　吐几次　体重　症状　浮肿　诊断

第十三课

3.（1）患者　（2）粗　（3）疲倦　（4）视诊　（5）消退
　（6）维持　（7）服　（8）肝功能　（9）凹陷　（10）定量

5.（1）体温怎么样　咳嗽厉害　浮肿　尿常规
　（2）情况怎么样　发低烧　视诊的情况怎么样　双肺呼吸音比较粗
　　　细小的水泡音　尿常规　肝功能　尿蛋白定量

6.（1）×　（2）√　（3）×　（4）√　（5）√　（6）×

第十四课

3.（1）调整　（2）下降　旺盛　（3）复发　（4）监测　（5）眼球
（6）失眠　（7）甲亢　（8）他巴唑　甲亢平　（9）抖

5.（1）他巴唑　维生素C　甲状腺功能　监测　持续下降　旺盛　心悸　像水一样
（2）病史　甲状腺功能　甲亢　复发　典型症状　胸闷　手抖　失眠　旺盛　甲状腺　震颤　眼球

6.（1）×　（2）√　（3）×　（4）×　（5）√

第十五课

3. 服—降糖药　补充—碳水化合物/食物　患有—糖尿病　控制—饮食　输—液　出现—反应　听信—别人的话　携带—食物

4.（1）反应　引起　（2）以免　（3）昏迷　（4）饮食
（5）剂量　（6）葡萄糖　（7）补充　（8）携带　（9）适当

6. 感觉　还会昏迷　吃午饭了吗　低血糖反应　低血糖昏迷　糖尿病　用药　听信

7.（1）√　（2）×　（3）×　（4）×　（5）√

第十六课

3.（1）隐痛　（2）胆结石　伴有　（3）直径　（4）肩部
（5）尽快　（6）加强　（7）含量　（8）预防　（9）疗法

5. 右上腹绞痛　放射痛　胆囊触诊　肿大　实性感　胆结石　胆囊炎　直径　胆石症

6.（1）×　（2）√　（3）√　（4）×　（5）√　（6）×

第十七课

3. （1）减弱　（2）判断　（3）剧烈　（4）转移　（5）阑尾炎
　　（6）叩诊　（7）诱发　（8）避免　（9）直接　（10）难怪

5. （1）肚子疼　上腹部　转移　肚脐　隐痛　很厉害
　　（2）转移性　高热　叩诊　压痛　征象　反跳痛　波及　非常紧张
　　　　肠鸣音　白细胞　明显　确诊　阑尾切除手术

附录五 生词总表

A

哎哟	āiyō	叹	ouch	4
安排	ānpái	动	to arrange	10
氨苄西林	ānbiànxīlín	名	ampicillin	11
按	àn	动	to press	4
凹陷	āoxiàn	动	to depress	13

B

B 超	B chāo	名	B-mode ultrasonic	6
白细胞	báixìbāo	名	white blood cell (leukocyte)	11
白血病	báixuèbìng	名	leukemia	11
斑	bān	名	spot, macula	5
办	bàn	动	to do, to transact	7
伴	bàn	动	to be accompanied by	16
瓣膜	bànmó	名	valve	9
保暖	bǎo nuǎn		to keep warm	10
暴饮暴食	bàoyǐn-bàoshí		to eat and drink too much	5
避免	bìmiǎn	动	to avoid	17
边缘	biānyuán	名	edge, margin	5
表现	biǎoxiàn	动	to manifest	9

并	bìng	连	and, also	7
并发症	bìngfāzhèng	名	complication	17
病毒唑	bìngdúzuò	名	ribavirin	11
病理性	bìnglǐxìng	形	pathological	9
病历	bìnglì	名	case history	1
病例	bìnglì	名	case	3
病情	bìngqíng	名	state of an illness	10
病史	bìngshǐ	名	medical history, case history	3
波及	bōjí	动	to spread to	17
补充	bǔchōng	动	to supplement	15

C

彩票	cǎipiào	名	lottery	8
苍白	cāngbái	形	pale	7
侧	cè	名	side	6
测	cè	动	to take	9
肠鸣音	chángmíngyīn	名	bowel sound	17
肠胃炎	chángwèiyán	名	enterogastritis	4
常规	chángguī	名	routine	4
呈	chéng	动	to be, to assume	6
持续	chíxù	动	to last, to continue	5
初步	chūbù	形	primary	6
杵状指	chǔzhuàngzhǐ	名	clubbed finger	3

触诊	chùzhěn	动	to palpate	9
床位	chuángwèi	名	bed	1
唇	chún	名	lip	2
刺激	cìjī	动	to stimulate	17
粗	cū	形	harsh	13

D

大便	dàbiàn	名	stool, feces, excrement	4
大量	dàliàng	形	mass, a great deal of	3
大脑	dànǎo	名	brain	10
代谢性酸中毒	dàixièxìng suān zhòng dú		metabolic acidosis	13
胆固醇	dǎngùchún	名	cholesterol	8
胆囊	dǎnnáng	名	gallbladder, cholecyst	6
胆石症	dǎnshízhèng	名	gallstone, cholelithiasis	16
淡水	dànshuǐ	名	fresh water	14
蛋白	dànbái	名	protein	5
低钾血症	dījiǎxuèzhèng	名	hypokalemia	13
低钠血症	dīnàxuèzhèng	名	hyponatremia	13
低血糖	dīxuètáng	名	hypoglycemia	15
典型	diǎnxíng	形	representative, typical	3
碘	diǎn	名	iodine	14
淀粉酶	diànfěnméi	名	amylase	5
定量	dìngliàng	名	quantification	13

定期	dìngqī	形	regular	12
抖	dǒu	动	to shiver, to shake	14
窦性心律	dòuxìng xīnlǜ		sinus rhythm	8
肚脐	dùqí	名	umbilicus	17

E

额部	ébù	名	forehead	2
额叶	éyè	名	frontal lobe	10
恶心	ěxin	形	feel like vomiting, sick	4
2型糖尿病	èrxíng tángniàobìng		2-diabetes mellitus	15

F

发病	fā bìng		(of a disease) occur, (of a person) fall ill	6
发绀	fāgàn	动	cyanosis	2
发冷	fā lěng		to be algid, to feel chilly	6
发作	fāzuò	动	to be attacked with, to attack	2
乏力	fálì	形	hypodynamic	12
反复	fǎnfù	副	repeatedly, again and again	3
反跳痛	fǎntiàotòng	名	rebound tenderness	9
反应	fǎnyìng	名	reaction	15
放射	fàngshè	动	to radiate	5
放射痛	fàngshètòng	形	radiating pain	16

非淋巴细胞	fēilínbā xìbāo		nonlymphocyte	11
肺	fèi	名	lung	1
肺炎	fèiyán	名	pneumonia	1
吩咐	fēnfù	动	to give instructions	7
服	fú	动	to take (medicines)	13
浮肿	fúzhǒng	动	dropsy	12
负责	fùzé	动	to be responsible for	1
复发	fùfā	动	to relapse	14
腹部	fùbù	名	belly, abdomen	4
腹肌	fùjī	名	abdominal muscle	9
腹膜	fùmó	名	peritoneum	17
腹腔镜	fùqiāngjìng	名	laparoscope	16
腹泻	fùxiè	动	to diarrhea	4

G

甘油三酯	gānyóusānzhǐ	名	triglyceride	8
肝功能	gāngōngnéng	名	liver function	13
赶紧	gǎnjǐn	副	without delay	9
感觉	gǎnjué	动	to feel	1
感染	gǎnrǎn	动	to infect	3
干咳	gānké	动	to have a dry cough	1
干啰音	gānluóyīn	名	dry rales	13
高血压	gāoxuèyā	名	hypertension	8

咯血	kǎ xiě		hemoptysis	3
割	gē	动	to cut or slice (with a knife)	6
巩固	gǒnggù	动	to consolidate	12
谷物	gǔwù	名	cereal	15
骨髓	gǔsuǐ	名	bone marrow	11
鼓励	gǔlì	动	to encourage	12
冠心病	guānxīnbìng	名	coronary artery disease	8
过敏	guòmǐn	动	to be allergic to	3

H

含	hán	动	to keep in mouth	8
含量	hánliàng	名	content	16
毫米汞柱	háomǐ-gǒngzhù		mmHg	9
好转	hǎozhuǎn	动	to make a turn for the better	4
红细胞	hóngxìbāo	名	red blood cell (erythrocyte)	11
呼气	hū qì		to breath out, to exhale	2
呼吸	hūxī	动	to respire, to breathe	1
呼吸道	hūxīdào	名	windpipe	3
化疗	huàliáo	动	to chemotherapy	11
化验单	huàyàndān	名	test form	4
怀疑	huáiyí	动	to suspect	9
患	huàn	动	to contract (an illness), to suffer from	3
患者	huànzhě	名	patient	13

恢复	huīfù	动	to recover	2
汇报	huìbào	动	to report, to give an account of	4
昏迷	hūnmí	动	to be in a coma	10
（化）验	(huà) yàn	动	to examine; to check	4

J

饥饿	jī'è	形	hungry	15
积极	jījí	形	active	12
及时	jíshí	形	in time, timely	2
急促	jícù	形	rapid (breathing)	2
急性	jíxìng	形	acute	3
疾病	jíbìng	名	disease, sickness, illness	5
计数	jìshù	动	to count	17
记录	jìlù	动	to record, to write down	3
剂量	jìliàng	名	dosage	15
既然	jìrán	连	so long as, since	7
继续	jìxù	动	to continue	1
加强	jiāqiáng	动	to promote	16
家属	jiāshǔ	名	family members	3
甲亢 / 甲状腺功能亢进症	jiǎkàng / jiǎzhuàngxiàn gōngnéng kàngjìnzhèng	名	hyperthyroidism	14
甲亢平	jiǎkàngpíng	名	carbimazole	14

肩部	jiānbù	名	shoulder	16
监测	jiāncè	动	to monitor	14
减轻	jiǎnqīng	动	to relieve	14
减弱	jiǎnruò	动	to weaken, to attenuate	17
减少	jiǎnshǎo	动	to decrease	12
建议	jiànyì	动	to suggest	6
降糖药	jiàngtángyào	名	blood glucose lowering drug	15
降压药	jiàngyāyào	名	antihypertensive drugs	10
绞痛	jiǎotòng	形	angina, colicky pain	16
接受	jiēshòu	动	to accept, to receive	7
结论	jiélùn	名	conclusion	9
结石	jiéshí	名	calculus, lithiasis	6
解痉药	jiějìngyào	名	spasmolytic	6
尽快	jǐnkuài	副	as soon as possible	16
尽早	jǐnzǎo	副	as early as possible	16
进一步	jìnyíbù	副	more, further	6
精神	jīngshen	名	vitality	12
静脉	jìngmài	名	vein	15
剧烈	jùliè	形	intense	17
剧痛	jùtòng	名	megalgia, sharp pain	6

K

抗生素	kàngshēngsù	名	antibiotic	6

考虑	kǎolǜ	动	to think over, to consider	9
控制	kòngzhì	动	to control	12
叩诊	kòuzhěn	动	percussion	17
扩张	kuòzhāng	动	to dilate	3

L

拉	lā	动	to empty the bowels	4
阑尾炎	lánwěiyán	名	appendicitis	17
劳累	láolèi	形	tired, overworked	8
类	lèi	名	kind	11
类似	lèisì	动	to be similar to	8
冷汗	lěnghàn	名	cold sweat	2
厘米	límǐ	名	centimeter	16
厉害	lìhai	形	serious	1
量	liàng	名	quantity	12
疗程	liáochéng	名	therapy of treatment	11
疗法	liáofǎ	名	therapy	16
临床	línchuáng	动	to be at the sicked providing medical services	9

M

| 麦氏点 | màishìdiǎn | 名 | McBurney's point | 17 |
| 脉搏 | màibó | 名 | pulse | 9 |

慢性	mànxìng	形	chronic	12
盲肠	mángcháng	名	cecum	17
茅台	Máotái	名	the name of a famous white spirit of China	5
冒（汗）	mào (hàn)		to perspire, to sweat	2
门诊	ménzhěn	名	clinic	7
面色	miànsè	名	complexion, colour (of the facial skin)	7
明显	míngxiǎn	形	evident, obvious, distinct	9
命	mìng	名	life	5
模糊	móhu	形	dim, unclear	1
墨菲征	mòfēizhēng	名	Murphy's Sign	6

N

难怪	nánguài	副	no wonder	17
难受	nánshòu	形	uncomfortable	2
脑出血	nǎochūxuè	名	cerebral hemorrhage	10
脑中风	nǎozhòngfēng	名	apoplexy	10
内分泌	nèifēnmì	名	incretion	14
内脏	nèizàng	名	internal organ, viscus	16
尿	niào	名	urine	10
尿急	niàojí	形	urgent micturition	12
尿频	niàopín	形	frequent micturition	12
尿痛	niàotòng	形	odynuria	12

O

呕吐	ǒutù	动	to vomit	4

P

拍	pāi	动	to have (an x-ray film)	1
排	pái	动	to exclude, to eject, to discharge	3
判断	pànduàn	动	to decide	17
泡沫	pàomò	名	foam	13
配合	pèihé	动	to cooperate	12
皮肤	pífū	名	skin, cutis	5
疲倦	píjuàn	形	tired	13
片状	piànzhuàng	名	patch	1
贫血	pínxuè	名	anaemia	11
平常	píngcháng	名	usually	16
平卧	píngwò	动	to be supine	2
泼尼松	pōnísōng	名	prednisone（又名"强的松"）	13
葡萄糖	pútaotáng	名	glucose	15
普伐他汀钠	pǔfátātīngnà	名	pravastatin sodium	16

Q

气促	qì cù		shortness of breath	13
潜血	qiánxuè	名	occult blood	7
切除术	qiēchúshù	名	resection	16

轻度	qīngdù	形	mild	15
清晰	qīngxī	形	clear	9
情绪	qíngxù	名	mood	8
全身	quánshēn	名	the whole body, all over (the body)	4
确诊	quèzhěn	动	to diagnose	3

R

热量	rèliàng	名	heat	10

S

神经	shénjīng	名	nerve	10
肾	shèn	名	kidney	12
肾病综合征	shènbìng zōnghézhēng		nephritic syndrome	13
肾功能不全	shèngōngnéng bù quán		renal insufficiency	12
肾小球肾炎	shènxiǎoqiú shènyán		glomerulonephritis	12
生化	shēnghuà	名	biochemistry	13
失禁	shī jìn		to suffer from incontinence	10
失眠	shī mián		to have insomnia	14
失去	shīqù	动	to lose	7
湿啰音	shīluóyīn	名	moist rale	1
实性感	shíxìnggǎn	名	palpability	16

食欲	shíyù	名	appetite	12
视诊	shìzhěn	动	to inspect	13
适当	shìdàng	形	proper	15
手术	shǒushù	名	surgery, operation	7
手续	shǒuxù	名	formality, procedure	7
输	shū	动	to transfuse	15
输液	shū yè		to transfuse	4
水泡音	shuǐpàoyīn	名	bubble sound	13
水样便	shuǐyàngbiàn	名	watery diarrhea	4
四肢	sìzhī	名	(four) limbs	7
酸	suān	形	sour, acid	12
随身	suíshēn	形	(take) with one	15

T

他巴唑	tābāzuò	名	tapazole	14
痰	tán	名	sputum	1
碳水化合物	tànshuǐ-huàhéwù		carbohydrate	15
体格	tǐgé	名	physique	6
体征	tǐzhēng	名	physical sign	5
调整	tiáozhěng	动	to modify, to rectify	14
听信	tīngxìn	动	to believe what one hears	15
听诊	tīngzhěn	动	to auscultate	2
头晕	tóu yūn		to feel dizzy	10

突出	tūchū	动	to protrude	14
涂片	túpiàn	名	smear slide (biopsy)	11

W

旺盛	wàngshèng	形	rich, abundant	14
危险	wēixiǎn	形	dangerous, risky	7
为	wéi	动	to be	5
维持	wéichí	动	to maintain	13
维生素	wéishēngsù	名	vitamin	14
胃出血	wèichūxiě	名	gastric hemorrhage	7
胃穿孔	wèichuānkǒng	名	gastric perforation	7
胃溃疡	wèikuìyáng	名	gastric ulcer	7
纹	wén	名	vein, line	13
稳定	wěndìng	形	stable	10
无力	wúlì	动	to feel weak	4
误诊	wùzhěn	动	to misdiagnose	9

X

X光片	X-guāngpiàn	名	X-ray film	1
吸气	xī qì		to inhale air, to draw in breath	2
吸收	xīshōu	动	to absorb	17
下	xià	动	to draw, to deduce	9
下降	xiàjiàng	动	to decrease, to fall	14

先兆	xiānzhào	名	sign, omen	10
项	xiàng	量	item	8
象	xiàng	名	symptom, syndrome	11
消化	xiāohuà	动	to digest	4
消失	xiāoshī	动	to disappear	3
消退	xiāotuì	动	to vanish	13
硝酸甘油	xiāosuāngānyóu	名	nitroglycerin	8
小便	xiǎobiàn	名	urine	6
哮喘	xiàochuǎn	名	asthma	2
哮鸣音	xiàomíngyīn	名	wheezing, stridor	2
效果	xiàoguǒ	名	effect	11
携带	xiédài	动	to carry, to take along	15
心得安	xīndé'ān	名	propranolol	14
心电图	xīndiàntú	名	electrocardiogram	8
心慌	xīn huāng		(of the heart) beating rapidly	15
心肌	xīnjī	名	cardiac muscle	8
心肌梗死	xīnjī gěngsǐ		myocardial infarction	9
心悸	xīnjì	动	to heart-throb	14
心绞痛	xīnjiǎotòng	名	angina	8
心率	xīnlǜ	名	heart rate	10
心前区	xīnqiánqū	名	pericardial region	8
心音	xīnyīn	名	cardiac sound	8
型	xíng		style	11

胸口	xiōngkǒu	名	chest	1
胸闷	xiōngmèn	动	to have chest tightness	14
胸片	xiōngpiàn	名	X-ray film	8
血管	xuèguǎn	名	blood vessel	8
血红蛋白	xuèhóngdànbái	名	hemoglobin	11
血清	xuèqīng	名	blood serum	5
血小板	xuèxiǎobǎn	名	blood platelet (thrombocyte)	11
血液病	xuèyèbìng	名	blood disorder	11
血肿	xuèzhǒng	名	hematoma	10

Y

压痛	yātòng	名	tenderness	4
严重	yánzhòng	形	serious, grave, critical	4
炎症	yánzhèng	名	inflammation	1
眼睑	yǎnjiǎn	名	eyelid	12
眼球	yǎnqiú	名	eyeball	14
阳性	yángxìng	名	positive	6
一阵子	yízhènzi	数量	a period of time	17
一直	yìzhí	副	all the time	6
胰腺	yíxiàn	名	pancreas	5
移植	yízhí	动	to transplant	11
以免	yǐmiǎn	连	in order to avoid, so as not to	15
异样	yìyàng	形	different, unusual	4

阴影	yīnyǐng	名	shadow, opacity	1
引起	yǐnqǐ	动	to give rise to, to lead to, to cause	5
隐痛	yǐntòng	名	dull heavy ache	16
优降糖	yōujiàngtáng	名	glibenclamide	15
油腻	yóunì	形	pinguid, greasy, oily	6
有效	yǒuxiào	动	to have effects	16
诱发	yòufā	动	to induce	17
预防	yùfáng	动	to prevent	16
遇	yù	动	to meet, to be caught	7
月经	yuèjīng	名	menstrual cycle	11

Z

杂音	záyīn	名	murmur	8
再次	zàicì	副	once again	6
在……之间	zài……zhījiān		between	13
暂时	zànshí	形	temporary	3
造影	zàoyǐng	动	to visualize	3
摘要	zhāiyào	名	summary, abstract	10
长期	chángqī	名	a long period of time	5
胀	zhàng	动	to distend	9
照顾	zhàogù	动	to look after	11
着凉	zháo liáng		to have a cold	2
诊断	zhěnduàn	动	to diagnose	1

震颤	zhènchàn	动	to shiver, to tremble	14
征象	zhēngxiàng	名	sign	17
睁	zhēng	动	to open	12
正常	zhèngcháng	形	normal	2
症状	zhèngzhuàng	名	symptom	1
支气管	zhīqìguǎn	名	bronchus, bronchial tube	3
肢体	zhītǐ	名	limb	10
脂肪	zhīfáng	名	fat	5
直接	zhíjiē	形	direct	17
直径	zhíjìng	名	diameter	16
值班	zhí bān		to be on duty	2
止	zhǐ	动	to stop, to halt	7
指	zhǐ	名	finger	2
指头	zhǐtou	名	finger	3
治疗	zhìliáo	动	to cure, to treat	2
中奖	zhòng jiǎng		to win a prize in a lottery	8
肿大	zhǒngdà	形	swelling, swollen	5
主诉	zhǔsù	动	chief complaint	5
注射液	zhùshèyè	名	injection	15
转科	zhuǎn kē		to transfer to another department	7
转移	zhuǎnyí	动	to shift	17

节奏汉语演唱者名单

课数	学生	Passport Name	国　籍	年　级
1	阿比	Abinash Panda	印度	南方医科大学 2019 级 MBBS 留学生
	康夫	Cliff Syndor	印度	南方医科大学 2012 级 MBBS 留学生
2	查理	Wajahat Ali Raza	印度	南方医科大学 2014 级 MBBS 留学生
3	拉瓦力	Dan Jouma Amadou Maman Lawali Niger	尼日尔	南方医科大学 2019 级 汉补进修研究生
4	查理	Wajahat Ali Raza	印度	南方医科大学 2014 级 MBBS 留学生
5	宋佳	Sonjoy Sutradhar Monilal	孟加拉国	南方医科大学 2016 级 MBBS 留学生
6	宋佳	Sonjoy Sutradhar Monilal	孟加拉国	南方医科大学 2016 级 MBBS 留学生
7	何郎	Pherbak Kharmawphlang Nohwir	印度	南方医科大学 2016 级 MBBS 留学生
8	何郎	Pherbak Kharmawphlang Nohwir	印度	南方医科大学 2016 级 MBBS 留学生
9	阿比	Abinash Panda	印度	南方医科大学 2019 级 MBBS 留学生
10	奥迪	Kiruba Gideon	印度	南方医科大学 2014 级 MBBS 留学生
11	何郎	Pherbak Kharmawphlang Nohwir	印度	南方医科大学 2016 级 MBBS 留学生
12	爱文	Evan Noel Dympep	印度	南方医科大学 2019 级 MBBS 留学生
13	何郎	Pherbak Kharmawphlang Nohwir	印度	南方医科大学 2016 级 MBBS 留学生
14	奥迪	Kiruba Gideon	印度	南方医科大学 2014 级 MBBS 留学生
15	波波	Virginio Bibang Ndong	赤道几内亚	南方医科大学 2016 级 MBBS 留学生
16	波波	Virginio Bibang Ndong	赤道几内亚	南方医科大学 2016 级 MBBS 留学生
17	爱文	Evan Noel Dympep	印度	南方医科大学 2019 级 MBBS 留学生